GROWING PAINS:
AN AUTOBIOGRAPHY

EMILY CARR

GROWING PAINS: AN AUTOBIOGRAPHY

with a foreword by Ira Dilworth

Irwin Publishing
Toronto, Canada

Copyright © 1946 Irwin Publishing Inc.

Canadian Cataloguing in Publication Data

Carr, Emily, 1871-1945
Growing pains: an autobiography

Originally published: Toronto: Clarke Irwin, 1971.
ISBN 0-7725-1614-6

1. Carr, Emily, 1871-1945. 2. Painters – Canada – Biography. I. Title.

ND249.C3A2 1986a   759.11   C86-093172-2

Cover painting: *Sunshine and Tumult* (c. 1938-1939)
by Emily Carr, oil on paper, 87.0 X 57.7 cm.
Collection: Art Gallery of Hamilton,
bequest of H.S. Southam, Esq., C.M.G., LL.D., 1966.

Printed in Canada by Webcom Limited

Published by Irwin Publishing Inc.

*We acknowledge for their financial support of our
publishing program the Canada Council, the Ontario Arts Council,
and the Government of Canada through the Book Publishing Industry
Development Program (BPIDP).*

To LAWREN HARRIS

CONTENTS

Foreword   ix

PART I

Baptism   3
Mother   4
Drawing and Insubordination   11
Graduation   15
Reasons   20
The Outdoor Sketch Class   26
Nellie and the Lily Field   27
Difference Between Nude and Naked   29
Beany   32
Evil   35
The Roarats   40
Gladness   44
Colour-Sense   46
Sisters Coming—Sisters Going   48
Last Chance   50
Mrs. Tucket   55
Telegraph Hill   59
The Mansion   62
Back to Canada   65

PART II

Home Again   73
Love and Poetry   80
The Voyage and Aunt Amelia   83
Aunt Amelia's PG House   87

St. Paul's   90
Letters of Introduction   93
Westminster Abbey—Architectural Museum   96
Life Class   99
Mrs. Radcliffe   102
Mrs. Simpson's   109
Leaving Miss Green's—Vincent Square   112
Pain and Mrs. Radcliffe—The Vicarage   118
Kicking The Regent Street Shoe-Man   123
Are You Saved?   125
Queen Victoria   131
English Spring   136
My Sister's Visit   139
Martyn   140
The Radcliffes' Art and District Visiting   146
London Tasted   153
The Other Side of Life   157
St. Ives   165
Bushey   176
Birds   182
Bitter Goodbye   189

PART III

Cariboo Gold   197
Vancouver   205
France   215
Rejected   227
New York   241
Lawren Harris   252
Green   261
Alternative   263
Seventieth Birthday and A Kiss For Canada   270
The Book of Small   276
Wild Geese   279

Foreword

Dear Emily:

You have asked me to write a foreword to your auto-biography—this summing up of a number of things that have mattered in your life. It is a hard task but one for which I thank you.

What can I say? Certainly nothing that can possibly matter much. I know how courageous your life has been, how dauntless your purpose, how unshaken and unshake-able your faith that this is not all, that we go on. I know too how intensely you have felt the influence of nature—its loveliness, its deep solemnity, its mystic, overwhelming power to strike awe and sometimes terror in our hearts. You have told us of your reactions to those forces in your painting and your writing. Canadians will remember as they open this book and will be grateful.

You will understand when I say that I should like a poem to stand as preface to your book, a poem which we have both admired so much, Thomas Hardy's *Afterwards*. I know and you know that Hardy did not think it a sad poem—just a comment and a summing up. So, Emily, I shirk my task and set as foreword to your autobiography these lines:

When the present has latched its postern behind my tremulous
        stay
        And the May month flaps its glad green leaves like wings,
Delicate-filmed as new-spun silk, will the neighbours say,
        "He was a man who used to notice such things"?

Growing Pains

If it be in the dusk when, like an eyelid's soundless blink,
  The dew-fall hawk comes crossing the shades to alight
Upon the wind-warped upland thorn, a gazer may think,
  "To him this must have been a familiar sight."

If I pass during some nocturnal blackness, mothy and warm,
  When the hedgehog travels furtively over the lawn,
One may say, "He strove that such innocent creatures should
      come to no harm,
  But he could do little for them; and now he is gone."

If, when hearing that I have been stilled at last, they stand at
      the door,
  Watching the full-starred heavens that winter sees,
Will this thought rise on those who will meet my face no more,
  "He was one who had an eye for such mysteries"?

And will any say when my bell of quittance is heard in the
      gloom,
  And a crossing breeze cuts a pause in its outrollings,
Till they rise again, as they were a new bell's boom,
  "He hears it not now, but used to notice such things"?

There is a change somewhere in the east. In my western garden this evening grosbeaks are paying their annual visit, a brief pause in our elm trees during their migration; and high in the Canadian sky wild geese, great flocks of them, are shouting their mysterious cry. They are all going on as you and I must, Emily. Life will not stand still.

So, fare forward, dear soul.

IRA DILWORTH

GROWING PAINS
THE AUTOBIOGRAPHY OF EMILY CARR

PART ONE

Baptism

MY BAPTISM is an unpleasant memory. I was a little over four years of age. My brother was an infant. We were done together, and in our own home. Dr. Reid, a Presbyterian parson, baptized us. He was dining at our house.

We were playing in the sitting room. Brother Dick was in his cradle. Mother came into the room with water in her best china bowl. While she lighted the lamp my big sister caught me, dragged me to the kitchen pump and scrubbed my face to smarting. I was then given to Dr. Reid who presented me kicking furiously to God.

I would have been quite content to sit on Dr. Reid's knee, but his tipping me flat like a baby infuriated me. I tried to bolt. Dr. Reid hung on to a curl and a button long enough to splash water on my hair ribbon and tell God I was Emily; then the button burst off and I wrenched the curl from his hand and ran to Mother. Dr. Reid and Mother exchanged button for baby. Dick gurgled sweetly when the water splashed him.

Father sat at the table with the fat family Bible open at the page on which the names of his seven other children were written. He added ours, Richard and Emily, which as well as being ours were his own name and Mother's. The covers of the Bible banged, shutting us all in. The Bible says that I was born on the thirteenth day of December, 1871.

Mother

TO SHOW Mother I must picture Father, because Mother was Father's reflection—smooth, liquid reflecting of definite, steel-cold reality.

Our childhood was ruled by Father's unbendable iron will, the obeying of which would have been intolerable but for Mother's patient polishing of its dull metal so that it shone and reflected the beauty of orderliness that was in all Father's ways, a beauty you had to admire, for, in spite of Father's severity and his overbearing omnipotence, you had to admit the justice even in his dictatorial bluster. But somehow Mother's reflecting was stronger than Father's reality, for, after her death, it lived on in our memories and strengthened, while Father's tyrannical reality shrivelled up and was submerged under our own development.

Father looked taller than he really was because he was so straight. Mother was small-made and frail. Our oldest sister was like Father; she helped Mother raise us and finished our upbringing when Mother died.

I was twelve when Mother died—the raw, green Victoria age, twelve years old.

The routine of our childhood home ran with mechanical precision. Father was ultra-English, a straight, stern autocrat. No one ever dreamt of crossing his will. Mother loved him and obeyed because it was her loyal pleasure to do so. We children *had* to obey from both fear and reverence.

Nurse Randal has told me of my first birthday. I was born during a mid-December snow storm; the north wind

howled and bit. Contrary from the start, I kept the family
in suspense all day. A row of sparrows, puffed with cold,
sat on the rail of the balcony outside Mother's window,
bracing themselves against the danger of being blown into
the drifted snow piled against the window. Icicles hung,
wind moaned, I dallied. At three in the morning I sent
Father plowing on foot through knee-deep snow to fetch
Nurse Randal.

I never did feel that it was necessary to apologize to my
father for being late. It made variety for him, seeing that
he always got his way in everything—when Father com-
manded everybody ran.

Every evening at a quarter to six Mother would say,
"Children, is every gate properly shut and fastened? Are
no toys littering the garden, no dolls sitting on humans'
chairs? Wash your faces, then, and put on clean pinafores;
your father will soon be home."

If visiting children happened to be playing with us in
our garden, or a neighbour calling on Mother, they scurried
for the gate as fast as they could. Father would not have
said anything if he had found them in his house—that
was just it, he would not have said anything to them at
all. He would have stalked in our front door, rushed
through the house and out of the side door frowning terribly, hurrying to tend Isabella, the great, purple-fruited
grapevine that crawled half over our house and entirely
over Father's heart. Her grapes were most beautifully fog-
ged with dusky bloom, behind which she pretended her
fruit was luscious; but they were really tough-skinned,
sour old grapes.

Father was burstingly proud of miserable old Isabella.
He glassed her top so that her upstairs grapes ripened a
whole month earlier than her downstairs ones. He tacked
Isabella up, he pinched her back, petted, trained her, gave
her everything a vine could possibly want, endured far more
waywardness from her than all of us together would dare
to show.

After Father had fussed over Isabella and eaten a good

dinner, he went upstairs to see Mother who was far more often in bed ill than up. He was good to Mother in his own way, gave her every possible comfort, good help, good doctoring, best food, but I resented that he went to Isabella first and Mother after. He was grumpy too when he did go. He sat beside her bed for half an hour in almost complete silence, then he went downstairs to read his paper till bedtime.

I heard a lady say to Mother, "Isn't it difficult, Mrs. Carr, to discipline our babies when their fathers spoil them so?"

Mother replied, "My husband takes no notice of mine till they are old enough to run round after him. He then recognizes them as human beings and as his children, accepts their adoration. You know how little tots worship big, strong men!"

The other mother nodded and my mother continued, "Each of my children in turn my husband makes his special favourite when they come to this man-adoring age. When this child shows signs of having a will of its own he returns it to the nursery and raises the next youngest to favour. This one," she put her hand on me, "has overdrawn her share of favouritism because there was no little sister to step into her shoes. Our small son is much younger and very delicate. His father accuses me of coddling him, but he is the only boy I have left—I lost three."

Father kept sturdy me as his pet for a long time.

"Ah," he would say, "this one should have been the boy."

The very frailness of her little son made Mother love him harder. She did not mind the anxiety and trouble if only he lived.

Father insisted that I be at his heels every moment that he was at home. I helped him in the garden, popping the bulbs into holes that he dug, holding the strips of cloth and the tacks while he trained Isabella. I walked nearly all the way to town with him every morning. He let me snuggle under his arm and sleep during the long Presbyterian sermons. I held his hand during the walk to and from church. This all seemed to me fine until I began to think for myself—then I saw that I was being used as a soother for Father's tantrums; like a bone to a dog, I was being flung to quiet Father's temper. When he was extra cranky I was taken into town by my big sister and left at Father's wholesale warehouse to walk home with him because my chatter soothed him. I resented this and began to question why Father should act as if he was God. Why should people dance after him and let him think he was? I decided disciplining would be good for Father and I made up my mind to cross his will sometimes. At first he laughed, trying to coax the waywardness out of me, but when he saw I was serious his fury rose against me. He turned and was harder on me than on any of the others. His soul was so bitter that he was even sometimes cruel to me.

"Mother," I begged, "need I be sent to town any more to walk home with Father?"

Mother looked at me hard. "Child," she cried, "what ails you? You have always loved to be with your father. He adores you. What is the matter?"

"He is cross, he thinks he is as important as God."

Mother was supremely shocked; she had brought her family up under the English tradition that the men of a woman's family were created to be worshipped. My insurrection pained her. She was as troubled as a hen that has hatched a duck. She wanted to question me but her loyalty to Father forbade.

She said to me, "Shall you and I have a picnic?"—She knew that above all things I loved a picnic.

"All to ourselves?" I asked.

"Just you and I."

It was the most wonderful thing she could have suggested. I was so proud. Mother, who always shared herself equally among us, was giving to me a whole afternoon of herself!

It was wild lily time. We went through our garden, our cow-yard and pasture, and came to our wild lily field. Here we stood a little, quietly looking. Millions upon mil-

7

lions of white lilies were spangled over the green field. Every lily's brown eye looked down into the earth but her petals rolled back over her head and pointed at the pine-tree tops and the sky. No one could make words to tell how fresh and sweet they smelled. The perfume was delicate yet had such power its memory clung through the rest of your life and could carry you back any time to the old lily field, even after the field had become city and there were no more lilies in it—just houses and houses. Yes, even then your nose could ride on the smell and come galloping back to the lily field.

Between our lily field and Beacon Hill Park there was nothing but a black, tarred fence. From the bag that carried Mother's sewing and our picnic, she took a big key and fitted it into the padlock. The binding-chain fell away from the pickets. I stepped with Mother beyond the confines of our very fenced childhood. Pickets and snake fences had always separated us from the tremendous world. Beacon Hill Park was just as it had always been from the beginning of time, not cleared, not trimmed. Mother and I squeezed through a crack in its greenery; bushes whacked against our push. Soon we came to a tiny, grassy opening, filled with sunshine and we sat down under a mock-orange bush, white with blossom and deliciously sweet.

I made a daisy chain and Mother sewed. All round the opening crowded spiraea bushes loaded with droops of creamy blossom having a hot, fluffy smell. In these, bees droned and butterflies fluttered, but our mock-orange bush was whiter and smelled stronger and sweeter. We talked very little as we sat there.

Mother was always a quiet woman—a little shy of her own children. I am glad she was not chatty, glad she did not perpetually "dear" us as so many English mothers that we knew did with their children. If she had been noisier or quieter, more demonstrative or less loving, she would not have been just right. She was a small, grey-eyed, dark-haired woman, had pink cheeks and struggled breathing. I do not remember to have ever heard her laugh out loud, yet she was always happy and contented. I was surprised once to hear her tell the Bishop, "My heart is always singing." How did hearts sing? I had never heard Mother's, I had just heard her difficult, gasping little breaths. Mother's moving was slow and weak, yet I always think of her as having Jenny-Wren-bird's quickness. I felt instinctively that was her nature. I became aware of this along with many other things about my mother, things that unfolded to me in my own development.

Our picnic that day was perfect. I was for once Mother's oldest, youngest, her companion-child. While her small, neat hands hurried the little stitches down the long, white seams of her sewing, and my daisy chains grew and grew, while the flowers of the bushes smelled and smelled and sunshine and silence were spread all round, it almost seemed rude to crunch the sweet biscuit which was our picnic—ordinary munching of biscuits did not seem right for such a splendid time.

When I had three daisy chains round my neck, when all Mother's seams were stitched, and when the glint of sunshine had gone quiet, then we went again through our gate, locked the world out, and went back to the others.

It was only a short while after our picnic that Mother died. Her death broke Father; we saw then how he had loved her, how alone he was without her—none of us could make up to him for her loss. He retired from business. His office desk and chair were brought home and put into the room below Mother's bedroom. Here Father sat, staring over his garden. His stare was as empty as a pulpit without a preacher and with no congregation in front of it. We saw him there when we came from school and went stupidly wandering over the house from room to room instead of rushing straight up to Mother's bedroom. By-and-by, when we couldn't bear it any longer, we'd creep up the stairs, turn the door handle, go into emptiness, get caught there and scolded for having red eyes and no bravery.

I was often troublesome in those miserable days after Mother died. I provoked my big sister and, when her patience was at an end, she would say, trying to shame me, "Poor Mother worried about leaving you. She was happy about her other children, knowing she could trust them to behave—good reasonable children—you are different!"

This cut me to the quick. For years I had spells of crying about it. Then by-and-by I had a sweetheart. He wanted me to love him and I couldn't, but one day I almost did— he found me crying and coaxed.

"Tell me."

I told him what my big sister had said. He came close and whispered in my ear, "Don't cry, little girl. If you were the naughtiest, you can bet your mother loved you a tiny bit the best—that's the way mothers are."

Drawing and Insubordination

I WANTED to draw a dog. I sat beside Carlow's kennel and stared at him for a long time. Then I took a charred stick from the grate, split open a large brown-paper sack and drew a dog on the sack.

My married sister who had taken drawing lessons looked at my dog and said, "Not bad." Father spread the drawing on top of his newspaper, put on his spectacles, looked, said, "Um!" Mother said, "You are blacked with charred wood, wash!" The paper sack was found years later among Father's papers. He had written on it, "By Emily, aged eight".

I was allowed to take drawing lessons at the little private school which I attended. Miss Emily Woods came every Monday with a portfolio of copies under her arm. I got the prize for copying a boy with a rabbit. Bessie Nuthall nearly won because her drawing was neat and clean, but my rabbit and boy were better drawn.

Father pruned the cherry tree under our bedroom window. The cherry sticks were twisty but I took three of the straightest, tied them at one end and straddled them at the other and put two big nails in the wood to hold a drawing-board. With this easel under the dormer window of our bedroom I felt completely an artist. My sister Alice who shared the room complained when she swept round the legs of the easel.

When I went to the big public school with my sisters we were allowed on Fridays after school to go to Miss Withrow's house for drawing lessons. I got sick for fear

I'd be kept in and miss any of the lesson, so Mother wrote a note to the teacher asking that I be let out on time. My sisters Lizzie and Alice painted flowers, I drew heads.

Miss Withrow sewed small photographs into little squares with white cotton thread, then she ruled a big sheet of paper with big squares and I drew as much in a big square as there was in a little one. In this way I swelled Father and Mother and my sister's baby. Father put Mother and himself in gilt frames and gave me five gold dollars. My sister thought my drawn baby was not good enough to be her child.

The Victoria tombstone-maker got some plaster casts of noses, hands, lips and eyes, to help him model angels for his tombstones. I heard that to draw from casts was the way they learned at Art schools, so I saved my pocket money and bought some of these over-size human features and drew them over and over.

My mother died when I was twelve years old and my father died two years later. When Father died I was still at school getting into a great deal of trouble for drawing faces on my fingernails and pinafores and textbooks. My sisters and brother were good students. When I moved up a grade the new teacher said, "Ah, another good Carr!" but was disappointed.

After Father and Mother died my big sister ruled; she was stern like Father. She was twenty years older than the youngest of us. Our family had a wide gap near the top where three brothers had died, so there was Mother's big family of two grown-up girls and her little family of three small girls and a boy. The second of the big sisters married. The biggest sister owned everything and us too when Father died.

Lizzie and Alice were easy children and good. Lizzie was very religious. Alice was patient and took the way of least resistance always. Dick too was good enough, but I was rebellious. Little Dick and I got the riding whip every day. It was a swishy whip and cut and curled around our black stockinged legs very hurtfully.

The most particular sin for which we were whipped was called insubordination. Most always it arose from the same cause—remittance men, or remittance men's wives. Canada was infested at that time by Old Country younger sons and ne'er-do-wells, people who had been shipped to Canada on a one-way ticket. These people lived on small remittances received from home. They were too lazy and too incompetent to work, stuck up, indolent, considering it beneath their dignity to earn but not beneath their dignity to take all a Canadian was willing to hand out.

My two elder sisters were born in England. The one who ruled us felt very much "first born" in the English way, feeling herself better than the rest of us because she was oldest. She was proud of being top. She listened to all the hard-luck stories of the remittance people and said, "I too was born in England." She sympathized with their homesickness and filled our home with these people.

Dick and I hated the intruders. Lizzie and Alice resented them too, but quietly. My sister tried to compel my brother and me by means of the riding whip.

A couple called Piddington sat on us for six months. The wife was a hypochondriac and exploited ill-health. The man was an idle loafer and a cruel bully. Anger at his impertinence and sponging kept the riding whip actively busy on our young legs. Things came to a climax when we rented a sea-side cottage in the holidays. The man took a party of boys and girls out in the boat. The sea was rough. I asked to be put ashore. Seeing my green face the man shipped his oars and cried delightedly, "We'll make the kid seasick." He rocked the boat back and forth till he succeeded. I was shamed before all the boys and girls. He knew, too, how it infuriated me to be called "kid" by him.

"You are not a gentleman anyway!" I cried. "You are a sponger and a bully!"

Purple with rage the man pulled ashore and rushed to his wife saying, "The kid has insulted me!"

For insulting a guest in her house my sister thrashed

me till I fainted; but I refused to apologize, and the bully and I went round glowering at each other. I said to my sister, "I am almost sixteen now and the next time you thrash me I shall strike back." That was my last whipping.

Dick went East to school. The whip dangled idle on the hall peg, except after school and on Saturdays when I took it out as an ornament and went galloping over the country on old Johnny.

Johnny had been a circus pony. He knew a lot. When he had galloped me beyond the town and over the highway till all houses and fences were passed, he would saunter, stopping now and then to sniff the roadside bushes as if considering. Suddenly he would nose into the greenery finding a trail no one else could see, pressing forward so hard that the bushes parted, caressing him and me as we passed, and closing behind us shutting us from every "towny" thing. Johnny pressed and pressed till we were hidden from seeing, noise and people. When we came to some mossy little clearing where soft shade-growing grass grew Johnny stopped with a satisfied sigh. I let down his bridle and we nibbled, he on the grass, I at the deep sacred beauty of Canada's still woods. Maybe after all I owe a "thank you" to the remittance ones and to the riding whip for driving me out into the woods. Certainly I do to old Johnny for finding the deep lovely places that were the very foundation on which my work as a painter was to be built.

Graduation

THOUGH I had graduated from whippings life at home was neither easy nor peaceful. Outsiders saw our life all smoothed on top by a good deal of mid-Victorian kissing and a palaver of family devotion; the hypocrisy galled me. I was the disturbing element of the family. The others were prim, orthodox, religious. My sister's rule was dictatorial, hard. Though her whip beat me no more her head shook harder and her tongue lashed. Not content with fighting my own battles, I must decide to battle for the family rights of all us younger children. I would not sham, pretending that we were a nest of doves, knowing well that in our home bitterness and resentment writhed. We younger ones had no rights in the home at all. Our house had been left by my father as a home for us all but everything was in big sister's name. We younger ones did not exist.

I marched to the dignified, musty office of the old Scotch gentleman whom my father had appointed as our guardian. He knew nothing of our inner home life. His kind, surprised eyes looked at me over the top of his glasses. No other ward of his—he had others beside us—had ever sought him personally in his den.

"What can I do for you, Emily?"

"Please, I want to go away from home. There is an Art School in San Francisco—may I go there?"

My guardian frowned. He said, "San Francisco is a big and wicked city for a little girl to be alone in."

"I am sixteen, almost."

"You do not look it."

"Nobody is allowed to grow up in our house."

My guardian grew stern.

"Your sister," he said, "is an excellent woman and has been a mother to you younger children. Is this Art idea just naughtiness, a passing whim?"

"No, it is very real—it has been growing for a long time."

He looked at me steadily.

"It can be arranged."

When he smiled at me I was glad I had come.

My sister, when she heard what I had done without her advice, blackened. The breaking storm was checked by her chuckle, "So you want to run away from authority? All right, I shall place you under the supervision of the Piddingtons!"

I had forgotten that the hated Piddingtons were now living in San Francisco. I was so glad for them to have moved that I had not cared where they went; but neither the Piddingtons nor the wickedness of San Francisco could crack my joy. Without my sister watching I could defy the Piddingtons. I'd be busy studying Art. I had always been fond of drawing and of beautiful places, particularly woods, which stirred me deeper than anything. Now I would learn how to put the two together. The wickedness of San Francisco caused me no anxiety. Big naughtiness like immorality, drunkenness, vice I knew nothing of. Lies, destructiveness, impertinence were the worst forms of evil of which I was aware.

The wickedness of San Francisco did not show in the least when our boat pushed through sea-fog and entered the Golden Gate. Telegraph Hill sticking up on our right was very naughty the Captain said but it looked beautiful to me perched on the bluff as I stood on the bridge beside the Captain. The sordid shabbiness of Telegraph Hill was wreathed in mist. Our ship eased slowly up to a dirty wharf. Here, smart and trim, stood Mrs. Piddington, an eye full of "ogle" ready for the Captain to whose care I had been entrusted. I was feeling like a tissue-wrapped valuable when he handed me over, but as Mrs. Piddington took me I changed into a common brown paper bundle. She scowled at my luggage—a straw suitcase and a battered birdcage containing a canary in full moult. I felt like a stray pup following elegant Mrs. Piddington from the wharf.

The Piddingtons lived in a large private hotel on Geary Street. They occupied a corner suite on the first floor. A little room was found for me at the top of the house. Until I looked out of its window I had not known there were so many chimney-pots in the world. I hung old Dick in the window and he began to sing at once, and then the strangeness of everything faded and my eyes were full of curiosity.

The San Francisco people swallowed Mrs. Piddington. She tasted nice to them because her tongue made glib use of titles and her voice was extra English. Americans did not notice the missing "aitches"; they liked the cut of her clothes. She was not at all proud of me and was careful to explain that I was no relation, just a Canadian girl put under her care come to San Francisco to study Art.

She hustled me down to the school as soon as possible. The San Francisco School of Art was up over the old Pine Street Public Market, a squalid district, mostly wholesale. From the dismal street you climbed a dirty stair. In a dark, stuffy office at the top sat a lean, long-bearded Curator tugging and tugging at his whiskers as if they operated his brain and he had to think a great deal. Mrs. Piddington did not consider him worth ogling. She told him I was Canadian, but as Canada had no Art Schools and England was too far there was nothing to be done but send me here. She intimated that personally she thought very little of America. However, being handy to Canada,—could I enroll?

The Curator pulled his beard and asked, "What d'you know, girl?"

"Nothing," I replied.

"Oh," said Mrs. Piddington, "she draws very prettily!"

I could have killed her when I saw her hold out a little roll of my drawings that she had got from my sister.

17

The Curator pushed them aside and said to me, *not* Mrs. Piddington, "You come along." There was nothing for her to do but go and for me to do but follow.

We passed through a big room hung with oriental rugs and dust. It was not part of the Art School. The Art School lay beyond, but this was the only way in. The School had been a great hall once. The centre was lit by a big skylight, there were high windows all down the north side. Under those windows the hall was cut into long alcoves by grey screens. One corner was boarded closed,—on the door was printed "Life Class, Keep Out". The whole place smelt of rats. Decaying vegetables lay on tables—still-life studies.

Long rows of students sat with lap-boards which had straddled hind legs that rested on the floor. Other students stood at easels drawing. In the centre of the room under a skylight were great plaster images on pedestals. More students were drawing from these images. I was given a lap-board in the first alcove, and a chunk of bread. A very dirty janitor was hacking up a huge crusty loaf; all the students were scrambling for pieces. The floor was littered with old charcoal-blackened crusts. Charcoal scrapings were everywhere. There were men students as well as women. All wore smocks or very dirty painting pinafores. I went back to the office with the Curator to buy charcoal and paper, then I took my place in the long row. On one side of me was a fair, sharp-featured, sweet-faced girl with long, square-toed shoes like a pair of glove boxes. She wore a black dress and a small black apron of silk with a pocket from which she kept pulling a little lace-bordered handkerchief to flip the crumbs and charcoal from her lap. On the other side of me sat a dirty old man with a tobacco-stained beard. Art School was not exactly what I had expected but this was a beginning and I was eager to attack the big plaster foot they set before me to draw.

"My name is Adda," said the little girl in black with the flipping handkerchief. "What is yours?"

"Emily."

"I was new last week. I come from Los Angeles. Where is your home?"

"Canada!"

"Oh how terrible for you! I mean coming from a foreign country so far away! How long were you on the sea coming?"

"Three days."

"It took me less than one whole day. I'd die if I was farther than one day away from Momma and Poppa. I have a little sister too and a brother. I am dreadfully homesick. The School is very dirty, isn't it? Just wait till you see the next alcove and smell it, dead birds and fish, and rotting vegetables, still life you know. Shoo, shoo!" Her voice rose to a shrill squeal and the lace bordered handkerchief flipped furiously. A rat was boldly marching a crust to his hole under the pedestal of a near image. "Momma said I must be prepared to face things when I went out into the world, but Momma never dreamt there would be rats!"

Adda seemed much older than I but, after a while, I discovered that she was younger. She knew more about the world. Her mother had prepared her to meet any emergency, had told her how to elude evil and, if she could not dodge, then how to face it. Adda said, "Momma says San Francisco is very, very wicked!"

"That is what my guardian said too. It doesn't look bad to me, does it to you?"

"Momma would never say it was bad if it wasn't. She came all the way up from Los Angeles to find a safe home for me to live in. How did your mother manage to see you were safe fixed? You live so far away."

"My mother is dead."

"Oh!" Adda said no more but from that moment she took care of me, sharing with me Momma's warnings, advice, extracts from Momma's letters.

Reasons

BEYOND the last alcove in the great hall was a little dressing room which contained a cracked mirror, a leaky washbasin, a row of coat pegs, and a twisty little stair leading to an attic. I was searching for still-life material. Being quite new to the school I did not know its queer corners. One of the High Society students, Miss Hatter, was powdering her nose, trying to make the crack in the looking glass divide her face exactly so that she could balance the rouge and powder on both cheeks. She spat out a mouthful of swansdown puff to say, "Lots of junk for studies up there," and pointed to the attic.

That was the way in this old San Francisco School of Art, even a top-swell student was ready to help little new nobodies.

I climbed the stair and squeezed gingerly through a small door which the wind caught and banged behind me. The attic was low-roofed and dim. My sleeve brushed something that vibrated—a dry crackly rattle, some shadowy thing that moved. I put out my hand to feel for the door knob —the attic was nearly dark. I found myself clutching the rib of a skeleton whose eyesockets poured ghastly stares over me, vacant, dumbing stares. The dreadful thing grinned and dangled its arms and legs. The skeleton hung rotating from a hook on the low roof. It was angry with my sleeve for disturbing the stillness. I saw the white knob of the door-handle and, wrenching the door open, tumbled down the stairs screeching!

"Heavens, child, look what you've done to me!" Miss

Hatter was dimmed by a blizzard of powder. "One would think you had seen a ghost up there!"

"Oh, worse—more dead—horrible!"

"Why, that's only old Bonesy. He lives up there! One of these days you will be drawing him, learning what is underneath human skin and fat."

"I couldn't sit up in that spooky attic being stared at by a skeleton!"

"Of course not, Bonesy will come down to you. He loves little holidays and if he can make people's teeth chatter so much the better. It is the only way he can converse with fellow bones. People are too cluttered with flesh for Bonesy to feel companionable with."

I saw that we were not alone in the dressing room. A pair of sad, listening eyes was peeping from behind the row of jackets on the rack. The eyes belonged to Nellie McCormick, a student. She came out when Miss Hatter left the room.

"Say, d'you believe in spooks? Up in the attic there is a table that raps. Let's Therese, Lal, you and me go up at lunch-time—ask the spooks things. Lal has only one arm, so it makes seven hands for the table. Spooks like the number seven."

"Couldn't a two-handed person put just one hand on the table?"

"Wouldn't be the same—got to be wholehearted with spooks or they won't work."

Bolting our lunches we hurried to the attic.

The rapping-table was close beside Bonesy. His stare enveloped us. Finger to finger, thumb to thumb, our hands spread themselves upon the table. We trembled a little in the tense silence—rats scuttled—an enormous spider lowered himself from the roof, swayed above the circle of hands, deciding which, dropped on Lal's one hand. Lal screamed. Nellie scowled, rats squeaked, the table tipped a little, tipped harder, rapped, moved sideways, moved forward, became violent! We moved with it, scuffling our feet over the uneven floor, pushing Bonesy crooked.

All his joints rattled, his legs kicked, his hands slapped, his head was fast to the hook on the rafter but his body circled, circled. A city clock struck one. We waited until the cackle of voices in the dressing-room subsided. Then four nerve-flushed girls crept down the attic stairs.

Nellie McCormick's strangeness drew me as apparently I drew her. She had few friends; you found her crouched beside the pedestal of this or that great image, the Venus de Milo, the Dancing Faun, the Greek Slave. Nellie was always thinking—her eyes were such a clear blue there seemed only the merest film between her thoughts and you. Had she thought in words you could have read them.

We talked little when we were together, Nellie and I. One day turning to me sharply she asked, "Is your mother decent?"

"My mother is dead."

"Lucky for you. My mother is a beast!"

There were many different nationalities represented in the Art School. Every type of American; there were Jews, Chinese, Japs, poor and wealthy students, old and young students, society women, cripples, deformed, hunchbacked, squint-eyed. There was a deaf-mute girl with one arm, and there was a halfwit. Most of them had come to study seriously, a few came for refuge from some home misery. There was one English girl (Stevie), fresh from the Old Country, homesick. I was not English but I was nearer English than any of the others. I had English ways, English speech, from my English parents though I was born and bred Canadian.

Stevie took comfort in me. Every morning she brought a tiny posy of mignonette and white sweetpeas and laid it on my easel-board. I smelled it the moment I rounded the screen. Its white sweetness seemed rather "in memoriam" to me. I felt as though I ought to be dead; but it was just Stevie's way of paying tribute to England's memory. She felt me British or, at least, I was not American.

Students never thought of having their overall work-aprons washed. We were a grubby looking lot. A few of the swell girls wore embroidered smocks. The very swellest wore no protection for their fine clothes, intimating that paint spots were of no moment, they had plenty more clothes at home.

A shy girl with a very red pigtail and a very strong squint came to the School. She was strange. Everyone said, "Someone ought to do something to make her feel better." Her shyness made us bashful. It was agreed that the first one who could catch her eye should speak but the shy girl's eyes were so busy looking at each other behind her nose that nobody could catch one. There was more hope of capturing one of her looks under the red pigtail than there was of catching one in her face.

A big circus parade came to San Francisco. We all climbed out of the attic window onto the flat roof to watch the procession. Poor "Squinty" slipped on a skylight and her leg, knitted into a red worsted stocking, plunged through the skylight to the market below, plunged right to the knee. Everyone held their breath while "Squinty" pulled her leg out with both hands. When we were sure the red worsted stocking was not blood, when we saw that "Squinty" herself laughed, everyone roared, thinking how funny it must have looked below in the market to see a scarlet leg dangling from the roof. Laughing broke "Squinty's" shyness; she brought her little parcel of lunch and joined us round the school stove after that. We always gathered about the Art School stove to eat our lunches.

Anne said, "Confound Jimmy Swinnerton!" and screwed her lunch paper hard and flung it into the stove. It flared and jammy trickles hissed out.

"Jimmy's frightfully clever, isn't he?" asked "Squinty".

"Clever? Baa! Look at our morning's work!" The floor of the big room was strewn with easels sprawled on their backs; smudged, smeared, paled, charcoal studies, face down or face up.

To roam in and out among the easels, a ball of twine unrolling as he went, was one of Jimmy's little "jokes"; its point was to go behind the screen and pull the string.

With a clatter every easel fell. Every study was ruined, every student infuriated.

Mrs. Major, a stout, motherly student known as "The Drum" sighed, "Poor orphan, he's being ruined by the scandalous prices the newspapers pay for his cartoons, enough to send any lad to the devil, poor motherless lamb!"

"Mothers are just as likely to drive one to the devil as to pull them back," said Nellie McCormick, bitterly adding, "I come to Art School to get away from mine."

Adda's lips tightened to pale threads.

"I suppose half of us don't really come here to study Art," said Sophie Nye.

"What do they come for then?" snapped Adda.

"To have fun and escape housework."

"If my parents like to think they have produced a genius and stick me in Art School let 'em—passes the time between school and marriage."

The speaker was so unattractive one wondered how long the interval between school and marriage might be for her.

"In my family there is a tradition," said a colourless girl who produced studies as anaemic and flavourless as herself, "that once in every generation a painter is born into our tribe. Aunt Fan, our last genius, painted a picture and when it was hung in an exhibition she was so astonished she died! Someone had to carry on—rest of clan busy —I was thrown to art." She shrugged.

The little hunchback was crouched by the pedestal of the Venus de Milo. She rose to her full mean height, wound long spidery arms about the feet of Venus. "I adore beauty," she cried, "beauty means more to me than anything else in the world. I'm going to be a great artist!"

We all drew long sorry breaths. Poor little hunchback, never had she won any other "crit" from the drawing master than, "Turn, make a fresh start." Her work was hopeless.

Suddenly a crash of irrelevant chatter, kind, hiding chatter. A few had kept out of the discussed reasons for "our Art". There was a general move to pick up the Jimmy-spoiled studies, set easels on their legs. Adda and I alone were left sitting beside the stove.

"Adda, were you pushed into Art or did you come because you wanted to?"

"I wanted to, and you, Dummy?"

I nodded. I was always "Dummy" in the San Francisco Art School. I don't know who gave me the name or why, but "Dummy" I was from the day I joined to the day I left.

The Outdoor Sketch Class

OF ALL the classes and all the masters the outdoor sketching class and Mr. Latimer were my favourites.

Every Wednesday morning those students who wished met the master at the ferry boat. There were students who preferred to remain in the Art School and work rather than be exposed to insects, staring eyes, and sun freckles. We sketchers crossed the Bay to some quiet spot and I must say people *did* stare. Thirty or forty men and women of all ages and descriptions done up in smocks, pinafores and sunbonnets, sitting on campstools before easels down in cow pastures or in vacant lots drawing chicken houses, or trees, or a bit of fence and a bush, the little Professor hopping from student to student advising and encouraging.

Outdoor study was as different from studio study as eating is from drinking. Indoors we munched and chewed our subjects. Fingertips roamed objects, feeling for bumps and depressions. We tested textures, observed contours. Sketching outdoors was a fluid process, half looking, half dreaming, awaiting invitation from the spirit of the subject to "come, meet me half way". Outdoor sketching was as much longing as labour. Atmosphere, space cannot be touched, bullied like the vegetables of still life or like the plaster casts. These space things asked to be felt not with fingertips but with one's whole self.

Nellie and the Lily Field

ONE SULTRY Public Holiday the Art School was empty but not shut. Having nothing particular to do I followed my heels and they took me the daily way. I climbed the dirty Art School stair and found the big, drab room solemn with emptiness. Even the rats were not squeaking and scuttling; there were no breadcrusts to be scrimmaged for. Half-drawn, half-erased studies on the drawing-boards looked particularly like nothing. Everything had stopped in the middle of going-to-be. The parched stare of a big red tommy-cod and a half dozen dried-to-a-curve, smelly smelts sprawled on one of the still-life tables. On another table was a vase of chrysanthemums prematurely dead, limp petals folded over their starved hearts. Even the doings of the plaster images seemed to have halted before completing their objectives. The Dancing Faun had stopped in the middle of his dance. The Greek Slave's serving was suspended, Venus was arrested at the peak of her beauty.

A moment's quiver of homesickness for Canada strangled the Art longing in me. To ease it I began to hum, humming turned into singing, singing into that special favourite of mine, *Consider the Lilies*. Whenever I let that song sing itself in me, it jumped me back to our wild lily field at home. I could see the lilies, smell, touch, love them. I could see the old meandering snake fence round the field's edge, the pine trees overtop, the red substantial cow, knee-deep and chewing among the lilies.

Still singing, I looked up—there over the top of my

drawing-board were Nellie McCormick's clear blue eyes staring straight into mine. I knew that Nellie was seeing our lily field too. I knew the clearness of her eyes was visioning the reflection from my own. Perhaps she did not see the actual lilies—I do not know, but she was feeling their loveliness, their glow, their stillness.

I finished the song. Except for the scrape of my charcoal against the paper there was silence in the room.

"Sing it again."

Again I sang the lily song. Then a long quiet brooded over the big, empty room—only the charcoal's scrape and a sigh that was half sob from Nellie. "You rest me," she said, and was gone.

It was not me, it was the lilies that rested Nellie. I knew our wild lilies. They rested me too, often.

When no one was about Nellie would say to me, "Sing it," and Nellie and I together went into the lovely home lily field.

Difference Between Nude and Naked

ADDA WAS of Puritan stock. I was Early Victorian. We were a couple of prim prudes by education. Neither her family nor mine had ever produced an artist or even known one—tales of artists' life in Paris were not among the type of literature that was read by our people. If they had ever heard of studying Art from the nude, I am sure they only connected it with loose life in wicked Paris, not with Art. The modesty of our families was so great it almost amounted to wearing a bathing suit when you took a bath in a dark room. Their idea of beauty was the clothes that draped you, not the live body underneath. So because of our upbringing Adda and I supposed our art should be draped. Neither of our families nor we ourselves dreamed that Art Schools in new clean countries like Canada and the United States would have any other kind. It was a shock to us to see that close walled corner in the school with the notice "Life Class—Keep Out". Mrs. Piddington nosed curiously and asked me questions; balked by the "keep out" notice on the Life Class door, satisfied that my ignorance and indifference were not put on, she gave up bothering.

One morning a student of the Life Class, a woman of mature years and of great ability, offered to give me a criticism. Everyone acknowledged that "a crit" from a life-class student was worthwhile. They did not know how to draw. The woman gave my work keen attention.

"You should now go into the Life Class, your work is ready," she said.

"I will never draw from the nude."

"Oh? Then you will never be a true artist, never acquire the subtlety in your work which only drawing from the nude teaches both hand and eye, tenderness of flowing line, spiritual quality, life gleaming through living flesh."

"Why should Art show best through live bareness? Aren't statues naked enough?"

"Child, you've got things wrong, surface vision is not Art. Beauty lies deep, deep; it has power to draw, to absorb, make you part of itself. It is so lovely it actually makes you ache all the time that it is raising you right up out of yourself, to make you part of itself." Her eyes strayed across the room to the Venus, beautiful but cold standing there on her pedestal. "One misses warmth of blood, flutter or breath in that."

A girl model slipped through the outer door and darted behind the curtain that hung before the entrance to the Life Class. Priggishly stubborn, I persisted, "*I* shall go on studying from the cast. Look how the creature scuttles behind the curtain hiding herself while she turns the door knob."

The woman's voice softened. "Poor little shrinking thing ashamed of her lovely body, never trained to have a model's pride."

"Is there anything to learn in being a model? Could a model be proud of being a model?"

"Indeed, there is much to learn and professional models are very proud of their job; most of them too are deeply interested in Art. San Francisco is too new yet, there are not enough professional artists for nude models to earn a livelihood at posing. The school picks up any unfortunate who, at his wit's end to make an honest living, takes what he can get."

"Modelling an honest living!"

"Assuredly, that little girl supports her aged parents, hiding from everyone how she does it, burning with shame, in constant agony that someone will find out. A trained model would exult in her profession, be proud of her

lovely body, of the poses she has taught it to hold by long
hours of patient practice, proud that artists should rejoice
in her beauty and reproduce it on their canvas, proud of
the delight and tenderness that flow through the artist's
hand as he directs the paint or the charcoal, proud that it
was her lovely life that provoked his inspiration, made her
come alive on the canvas, will keep her there even after her
flesh-self has gone. Child, don't let false ideas cramp your
Art. Statues are beautiful but they do not throb with life."

Her talk showed me the difference between the words
nude and naked. So convinced was I of the rightness of
nude and the wrongness of naked in Art that I said nothing
to Adda. Momma was always hovering in Adda's background. Momma's eye was a microscope under which her
every action was placed. Had it not been for Momma I
could have made Adda understand. Momma never would.
I did not discuss naked and nude with Adda.

Beany

MISS BEANER the little hunchback did not feel herself insignificant. She did not come up to any of our shoulders as she stood at her easel.

She always picked the biggest images to draw from, preferably Venus. There she stood, her square little chin thrust out, her large feet firmly planted, claw-fingers clutching her charcoal, long arms swinging, and such pitifully poor results! She stood so close under the great images she drew that they were violently foreshortened and became twice as difficult to draw. With her pathetic eyes rolled upwards devouringly and her misshapen body Beany looked foreshortened herself as if a heavy weight had crushed her head down into her hips forcing what was between into a cruel humped ridge.

Beany's art efforts were entirely ineffectual. The drawing-master obviously disliked going near the deformed creature. Noted always for his terse criticism, all Beany ever got from him was, "Turn over and begin again." Beany turned and turned, her eyes filled with tears. She never got beyond beginnings.

As soon as the master left the room one or another student would go to Beany and say, "He gave everyone a rotten lesson today." That made Beany feel better. Then the student would find something encouraging to say about the poor lines and smudges on her paper and Beany's long spidery arms would flurry around the helper's neck, her head burrow into their waist-line. Beany hugged with a horrible tightness when grateful.

Coming from school one day I found a kitten trapped behind the heavy street door at the foot of the outer stair. It was ravenous for food and for petting. It begged so hard to be hugged that I thought of Beany. Maybe the kitten would satisfy her hug-longing. I took it home that night and offered it to Beany next day. She was delighted. As it was a half holiday, I said I would take it to her house that afternoon.

Beany lived in one of the older and shabbier parts of San Francisco. The front door of the house opened right into the parlour, a drab room full of vases filled with artificial flowers. There was, too, a stuffed canary under glass and some sea shells. The room was a sepulchre. The mantelpiece was draped with the stars and stripes. On the stone hearth (fireless because it was summer) sat a plate of fish cleaned and ready to cook. The kitten made a dart towards the fish. Beany raised them to the mantelpiece, remarking as she fanned her hot face with a small brass fire shovel, "Our parlour hearth is the coolest place in the house." She was delighted with her kitten and hugged and hugged, first the kitten, then me. Poor Beany, she had so little and could have done with so much. I felt furious all over again with the drawing master's cruel "crits", his not bothering to hide how he loathed her person and despised her work.

The Frenchman who taught us painting was different from the drawing-master. His "crits" were severe, but his heart was soft—too soft almost. He championed any poor, weak thing. One day he found the little halfwit Jew-boy with his head down on a table of still-life stuff crying into the heap of carrots, onions and beets.

"What is it, Benny?" The master's hand on the boy's head covered it like a hat.

Benny lifted a wet, swollen cheek.

"Dis' mornin' I woked an' de' look-glass tell, 'You got de' toot'-ache, Benny.' Boys dey say, 'Why you so fat one side, Benny?' I say, 'De look-glass say I got toot'-ache.' Boys make tease of me!"

33

Growing Pains

A group of grinning students were peeping from behind the screen.

"Make off there! None of that!" roared the professor.

After that he always kept an eye on Benny. That was the spirit of the old Art School. It seemed that here there was always a champion for the Beanys and the Bennys

Evil

I WAS TOO busy at the Art School to pay much heed to Lyndhurst and Piddington affairs. Mrs. Piddington was watching me closely. Because she was English she called me "my dear" which did not in the least mean that I was dear to her nor she to me. I kept out of Frank's way. Mrs. Piddington had a good many friends (those people in the Lyndhurst hotel whom she thought worthwhile). Among them was a widow with two daughters about my own age. I had nothing in common with these girls.

Mrs. Piddington said, "Marie is having a birthday party. She is not asking you because she says she knows no friends of hers who would get on with you."

"Thank goodness she is not asking me. I hate her stuck-up companions."

"It is a pity you are not more friendly. You are very much alone."

"I have lots of friends, thank you, and I have my work."

"That Art School outfit!" sniffed Mrs. Piddington.

One day Mrs. Piddington said, "How did you get through the square today? I went out just after you and found it impossible because of the dense throng attending that large funeral in the Anglican church."

"I managed. I found a quiet, lovely little street, so quaint, not one soul in it. The house doors opened so quaintly right onto the pavement. All the windows had close green shutters, nearly every shutter had a lady peeping through. There was a red lantern hanging over each door. It was all romantic, like old songs and old books! I wonder if the

ladies flutter little lace handkerchiefs and throw red roses
to gentlemen playing mandolins under their windows at
night?"

"Stop it! Little donkey!" shouted Mrs. Piddington.
"Don't tell me you went through Grant Street?"

"Yes, that was the name."

"You went into Grant Street? Haven't you seen the
headlines in the newspaper for the last week? Grant Street
a scandal in the heart of San Francisco's shopping area!"

"I have not time to read the paper. Why is Grant Street
a scandal?"

"It is a red light district."

"What is a red light district?"

"A place of prostitutes."

"What are prostitutes?"

Mrs. Piddington gave an impatient tongue click.

"If I ever hear of your going into Grant or any other
such place again, home I send you packing! Straight to
school, straight home again! Main thoroughfares, no short
cuts, d'you hear?"

Frank came into the room. There was an evil grin on
his face. He had heard her snapping tones, saw our red
faces.

"In hot water, eh kid?"

I hurried from the room.

We had just come up from dinner. Mrs. Piddington
was commenting on the family who sat opposite to us at
table.

"The man seems very decent to that child."

"Why shouldn't he be decent to his own son?" I asked.

"The child is not his."

"Was the woman married twice? The child calls him
father."

"No, she was not married twice, the boy is not the man's
son."

"He *must* be!"

She noted my frown of puzzle.

Frank was out. "Sit there, little fool, your sister has no

36

right to send you out into the world as green as a cabbage!"
She drew a chair close to mine, facing me. "Now, it is
time you learned that it takes more than a wedding ring
to produce children. Listen!"

Half an hour later I crept up to my own room at the top
of the house afraid of every shadowed corner, afraid of
my own tread smugged into the carpet's soft pile. Horrors
hid in corners, terrors were behind doors. I had thought
the Lyndhurst provided safety as well as board and lodging. Boarding houses I had supposed were temporary
homes in which one was all right. No matter if San Francisco was wicked, I thought the great heavy door of the
Lyndhurst and my board money could shut it all out. Mrs.
Piddington told me that evil lurked everywhere. She said
even under the sidewalks in certain districts of San Francisco were dens that had trap doors that dropped girls into
terrible places when they were just walking along the street.
The girls were never heard of again. They were taken into
what was called "white slavery", hidden away in those
dreadful underground dens, never found, never heard of.

Mrs. Piddington spared me nothing. Opium dens in
Chinatown, drug addicts, kidnappings, murder, prostitu-
tion she poured into my burning, frightened ears, determined to terrify the greenness out of me.

I was glad when the carpet of the hallways and stairs
came to an end, glad when I heard my own heels tap, tap
on the bare top-stair treads and landing. I looked around
my room fearfully before I closed and locked my door.
Then I went over to the window. I wanted to see if San
Francisco looked any different now that I knew what she
was really like. No, she did not! My hand was on old
Dick's cage as I looked over the chimneys and roofs. Old
Dick nibbled at my finger. It gave me such a curious feeling of protection and reality.

"Dick, I don't believe it, not all. If it was as wicked as
she said the black would come up the chimneys and smudge
the sky; wicked ones can shut their doors and windows
but not their chimneys. There is direct communication

always between the inside of the houses and the sky. There is no smudge on the sky above the chimneys. San Francisco's sky is clear and high and blue. She even said, Dick, that she was not sure of that dirty old Art School of mine— it was in a squalid district and that I was never, never to go off the main thoroughfares. I was never to speak to anyone and I was never to answer if anyone spoke to me. All right, Dick, I'll do that but all the rest I am going to forget!"

The most close-up ugliness I saw during my stay in San Francisco was right in the Lyndhurst, in Mrs. Piddington's own private sitting room.

It was Christmas Eve. The Piddingtons had gone to the theatre and left me sitting there by their fire writing letters home. There was a big cake on the table beside me just come from home along with parcels that were not to be opened till Christmas morning.

A tap on the door. A friend of Frank Piddington's was there with a great bunch of roses to Christmas Mrs. Piddington.

"She is not in," I said.

"'Sno matter, I'll wait."

"They will be very late."

"Thas-all-right."

He pushed past me into the sitting room, steadying himself by laying his hands one on either of my shoulders. He was very unsteady. I thought he was going to fall.

"Don' feel s'good," he said, and flung himself into an arm chair and the roses onto the table.

I went to get water for the flowers and when I came back he was already heavily asleep. His flushed face had rolled over and was pillowed on my home cake.

I stood looking in dismay. He must be very ill. He had seemed hardly able to walk at all. He had gone to sleep with a lighted cigar between his fingers, its live end was almost touching the upholstery of the chair. I dare not take it from his hand, I dare not go to my room and leave it burning. The evening was early. I sat and watched and watched. The cigar smouldered to its very end. The ash did not fall but kept its shape. Would the cigar burn him when it reached his skin and wake him? No, just before it reached the end it went out.

Creak, slam! creak, slam! went the heavy old door of the Lyndhurst, surely it must have swallowed all its inmates by now; but the Piddingtons did not come. I could not go now because Mrs. Piddington enjoyed fainting at shocks. If she came in after midnight and saw a man asleep in her sitting-room she was sure to faint. Half after midnight I heard her hand on the door-knob and sprang!

"Don't be frightened, he's asleep and very ill!"

"Who's asleep? Who's ill?"

"Mr. Piddington's friend."

Mrs. Piddington circled the sleeping man sniffing.

"Frank, take that drunk home!"

Frank burst into guffaws of coarse laughter.

"Our innocent!—entertaining drunks after midnight on Christmas Eve! Ha, ha!"

The Roarats

MRS. PIDDINGTON twiddled the envelope. Her eyes upon my face warned me, "Don't forget I am your boss!"

"You are to call on the Roarats at once," she said, and shook my sister's letter in my face.

"I don't intend to call upon the Roarats, I hate them."

"Your hating is neither here nor there. They were old friends of your parents in the days of the California gold rush. Your sister insists."

"And if I won't go?"

"In place of your monthly check you will receive a boat ticket for home. You have the Roarats' address? Very well, next Saturday afternoon, then."

Mrs. Piddington approved the Roarats' address.

"Um, moneyed district."

"They are disgustingly rich, miserably horrible!"

The following perfectly good Saturday afternoon I wasted on the Roarats. The household consisted of Mr., Mrs., Aunt Rodgers, a slatternly Irish servant and an ill-tempered parrot called Laura.

Mr. Roarat was an evil old man with a hateful leer, a bad temper, and cancer of the tongue. Mrs. Roarat was diminutive in every way but she had thickened up and coarsened from long association with Mr. Roarat. She loathed him but stuck to him with a syrupy stick because of his money. Aunt Rodgers had the shapeless up-and-downness of a sere cob of corn, old and still in its sheath of wrinkled yellow, parched right through and extremely disagreeable. Ellen the Irish maid had a violent temper

40

and a fearful tongue. No other family than one specializing in bad temper would have put up with her. The parrot was spiteful and bit to the bone. Her eyes contracted and dilated as she reeled off great oaths taught her by Mr. Roarat. Then with a slithering movement she sidled along her perch, calling, "Honey, honey" in the hypocritical softness of Mrs. Roarat's voice.

The Roarats said they were glad to see me. It was not me they welcomed, anything was a diversion. When I left I was disgusted to discover that I had committed myself to further visits and had, besides, accepted an invitation to eat Thanksgiving dinner at their house.

The turkey was overcooked for Mr. Roarat's taste, the cranberry too tart for Mrs. Roarat's. Aunt Rodgers found everything wrong. Ellen's temper and that of the parrot were at their worst.

Laura, the parrot, had a special dinner-table perch. She sat beside Mr. Roarat and ate disgustingly. If the parrot's plate was not changed with the others she flapped, screamed and hurled it on the floor. Thoroughout the meal everyone snarled disagreeable comments. Aunt Rodgers' acidity furred one's teeth. The old man swore, and Mrs. Roarat syruped and called us all "Honey".

"Pop goes the weasel!" yelled Laura, squawking, flapping and sending her plate spinning across the floor.

"There, there, Laura, honey!" soothed Mrs. Roarat and rang for Ellen who came in heavy-footed and scowling with brush and dustpan. When she stooped to gather up the food and broken plate Laura bit her ear. Ellen smacked back, there was a few moments' pandemonium, Mr. R., Aunt R., Ellen and Laura all cursing in quartette. Then Mrs. Roarat lifted Laura, perch and all, and we followed into the parlour. For my entertainment a great basket of snapshots was produced. The snaps were all of Mrs. Roarat's relatives.

"Why do they always pose doing silly things?" I asked.

"You see, Honey, this household being what it is, my folks naturally want to cheer me."

Aunt Rodgers gave a snort, Mr. Roarat a malevolent belch. The parrot in a sweet, tender voice (Mrs. Roarat's syrupiest) sang, "Glory be to God on high!"

"Yes, Laura, honey," quavered Mrs. Roarat, and to her husband, "Time you and Laura were in bed."

Mr. Roarat would not budge, he sat glowering and belching. Aunt Rodgers put the parrot in her cage and covered it with a cloth but Laura snatched the cloth off and shrieked fearfully. Aunt Rodgers beat the cage with a volume of poems by Frances Ridley Havergal. It broke a wire of the cage and the book did not silence the bird who screamed and tore till her cover was in shreds.

Mrs. Roarat came back to her relatives in the snapshot basket for comfort.

"Here is a really funny one," she said, selecting a snap of a bearded man in a baby's bonnet kissing a doll.

Mr. Roarat was now sagging with sleep and permitted his wife and Aunt Rodgers to boost one on either side till they got him upstairs. It took a long time. During one of their halts Ellen came from the back in a terrible feathered hat.

"Goin' out," she announced and flung the front door wide. In rushed a great slice of thick fog. Mrs. Roarat looked back and called to me, "It's dense out, Honey, you will have to stay the night." I drew back the window curtain; fog thick as cotton wool pressed against the window.

The Roarats had a spare room. Mr. and Mrs. Piddington would get home very late and would suppose I was up in my bed. Mrs. Roarat's "honey" and Aunt Rodgers' vinegar had so neutralized me that I did not care what I did if I could only get away from that basket of snapshots.

The door of the spare room yawned black. We passed it and out rushed new paint smells. "Redecorating," said Mrs. Roarat. "You will sleep with Aunt Rodgers!"

"Oh!"

"It's all right, Honey, Aunt Rodgers won't mind much."

Aunt Rodger's room had no air space, it was all furniture. She rushed ahead to turn on the light.

"Look out!" she just saved me a plunge into a large bath tub of water set in the middle of the floor.

"Fleas—San Francisco's sand this time of year! Each night I shake everything over water, especially if I have been out on the street."

Immediately she began to take off and to flutter every garment over the tub. When she was down to her "next-the-skins", I hurried a gasping, "Please, what do I sleep in?"

Too late, the "skin-nexts" had dropped!

Aunt Rodgers said, "Of course child!" and quite unembarrassed but holding a stocking in front of her she crossed the room and took the hottest gown I ever slept in out of a drawer. I jumped it over my head intending to stay under it till Aunt Rodgers was all shaken and reclothed. I stewed like a teapot under its cosy. At last I *had* to poke my head out of the neck to breathe; then I dived my face down into the counterpane to say my prayers.

After a long time the bed creaked so I got up. On Aunt Rodgers' pillow was a pink shininess, on the bed post hung a cluster of brown frizz, there was a lipless grin drowning in a glass of water. Without spectacles Aunt Rodgers' eyes looked like half-cooked gooseberries. Her two cheeks sank down into her throat like a couple of heavy muffins. A Laura's claw reached for the light pull. I kept as far to my own side of the bed as possible.

Dark—Aunt Rodgers' sleeping out loud! It had never occurred to me that I *could* ever be homesick for my tiny room on top of the old Lyndhurst but I was.

Gladness

IN GEARY Street Square, close to the Lyndhurst, was a Church of England with so high a ritual that our Evangelical Bishop would have called it Popish.

On Easter morning I went into the Geary Street Square. The church-bell was calling and I entered the church and sat down in a middle pew. The congregation poured in. Soon the body of the church was a solid pack of new Easter hats. From the roof the congregation must have looked like an enormous bouquet spread upon the floor of the church. But the decoration of the ladies' heads was nothing compared to the decoration of the church, for her flowers were real, banks of Arum and St. Joseph's lilies, flowers of every colour, smell and texture. Every corner of the church was piled with blossoms, such as we would have had to coax in greenhouses in Canada; but here, in California, there was no cold to frighten flowers, nothing had to be persuaded to grow. Stained-glass windows dyed some of the white flowers vivid. White flowers in shadowy corners glowed whiter because of the shine of lighted candles. Incense and flower-perfume mixed and strayed up to the roof. Hush melted and tendered everything. The hush and holiness were so strong that they made you terribly happy. You wanted to cry or sing or something.

Suddenly high up under the roof, where incense and the fragrance of flowers had met, sounded a loveliness that caught your breath. For a moment you thought a bird had stolen into the church, then you found there were words as well as sound.

"Jesus Christ is risen today, Hallelujah!"

Quickly following the words, a violin exquisitely wailed the same thought, and, bursting hurriedly as if they could hardly wait for the voice and the violin to finish, the booming organ and the choir shouted, "Hallelujah! Hallelujah!"

It was a tremendous gladness to be shut up in a building; it was the gladness of all outdoors.

Either the church or I was trembling. The person on either side of me quivered too, even the artificial hat-flowers shook.

A clergyman climbed up into the pulpit and lifted arms puffy in Bishop's sleeves.

The church hushed to even greater stillness, a stillness like that of the live flowers which, like us, seemed to be waiting for the Bishop's words.

Colour-Sense

I HAD advanced from the drawing of casts and was now painting "still life" under the ogling eye of the French Professor. I was afraid of him, not of his harsh criticisms but of his ogle-eyes, jet black pupils rolling in huge whites, like shoe buttons touring round soup-plates.

He said to me, "You have good colour-sense. Let me see your eyes, their colour."

The way he ogled down into my eyes made me squirm; nor did it seem to me necessary that he should require to look so often into my "colour-sense".

He was powerful and enormous, one dare not refuse. His criticism most often was, "Scrape, re-paint".

Three times that morning he had stood behind my easel and roared, "Scrape!" When he came the fourth time and said it again, my face went red.

"I have, and I have, and I have!" I shouted.

"Then scrape again!"

I dashed my palette knife down the canvas and wiped the grey ooze on my paint rag.

In great gobbing paint splashes I hurled the study of tawny ragged chrysanthemums onto the canvas again. Why must he stand at my elbow watching—grinning?

The moment he was gone I slammed shut my paint-box, gathered up my dirty brushes, rushed from the room.

"Finished?" asked my neighbour.

"Finished with scraping for that old beast." She saw my angry tears.

46

The Professor came back and found my place empty. "Where is the little Canadian?"

"Gone home mad!"

"Poor youngster, too bad, too bad! But look there!" He pointed to my study—"Capital! Spirit! Colour! It has to be tormented out of the girl, though. Make her mad, and she can paint."

The hard-faced woman student, the one who ordered birds for her still-life studies to be smothered so that blood should not soil their plumage, the student we called "Wooden-heart", spoke from her easel in the corner.

"Professor, you are very hard on that young Canadian girl!"

"Hard?" The Professor shrugged, spread his palms. "Art—the girl has 'makings'. It takes red-hot fury to dig 'em up. If I'm harsh it's for her own good. More often than not worthwhile things hurt. Art's worthwhile."

Again he shrugged.

Sisters Coming—Sisters Going

HAVING once gone to my guardian for advice, I continued to do so. The ice was broken—I wrote him acknowledging my check each month and telling him my little news, dull nothings, but he troubled to comment on them. He was a busy man to be bothered writing the formal little interested notes in answer to my letters. I respected my guardian very much and had a suspicion that my going to him direct for advice had pleased him. He was Scotch, wise, handled our money with great care but had no comprehension of Art whatsoever. The camera satisfied him. He sent my board and school fees. I don't suppose it ever occurred to him I needed clothes and painting material. I had to scrape along as best I could in these matters.

My guardian thought very highly of my big sister. I have no doubt that his consenting to let me go to San Francisco was as much for her peace as for my art education. I was not given to good works and religious exercises like the rest of my family. I was not biddable or orthodox. I did not stick to old ways because the family had always done this or that. My guardian thought it was good for me to go away, be tamed and taught to appreciate my home. Art was as good an excuse as any.

Undoubtedly things did run smoother at home without me but, after I had been away one year, the family decided to follow me. My sister rented the old home and the three of them came to San Francisco for a year. My big sister still had a deep infatuation for Mrs. Piddington. It was really Mrs. Piddington that she wanted to see, not me.

48

Mrs. Piddington took a flat and we boarded with her but domestic arrangements did not run too smoothly. My sister liked bossing better than boarding, and, in a final clash, dashed off home leaving my other two sisters to follow. Almost simultaneously Frank Piddington got a better job in another city and they too left San Francisco. Then I was all alone among San Francisco's wickedness. Mrs. Piddington handed me over to a friend of a friend of a friend, without investigating the suitability or comfort of my new quarters. The woman I was donated to was an artist. She lived in Oakland. I had to commute. I plunged wholeheartedly into my studies.

The year that my family spent in San Francisco my work had practically been at a standstill. I did attend the Art School but joined in all the family doings, excursions, picnics, explorings. No one took my work seriously. I began to get careless about myself.

Mrs. Tuckett, the friend of the friend was a widow with two children, no income and a fancy for art. She resented that she could not give her whole time to it, was envious that I should be able to. The living arrangements of her cottage were most uncomfortable. Still, I enjoyed my independence and worked very hard. Perhaps after all the "ogle-eyed" French professor and my big sister were right, maybe I needed the whip, needed goading and discomfort to get the best out of me. Easy, soft living might have induced laziness. The harder I worked the happier I was, and I made progress.

We were a happy bunch of students. I do not remember that we discussed Art much; as yet we had not accumulated knowledge enough to discuss. We just worked steadily, earnestly, laying our foundations. San Francisco did not have much to offer in the way of art study other than the school itself, no galleries, no picture exhibitions. Art was just beginning out west. The school was new. Students came here to make a start. Their goal was always to press further afield. San Francisco did not see the finish, only the beginning of their art.

Last Chance

DURING my sisters' visit I said to Alice, "Can it be possible that the entire wicked awfulness of the world is stuffed into San Francisco?"

"Why do you think that?"

"Mrs. Piddington said. . . ." But I did not tell Alice what Mrs. Piddington said. She was a contented person, did not nose round into odd corners. This and that did not interest Alice, only the things right in the beaten path. The things she had always been accustomed to—those she clung to.

Before leaving Victoria various friends had asked of her, "Look up my cousin, look up my aunt." Alice good naturedly always said, "Certainly," and accepted a long list of miscellaneous look-ups. People could just as well have sent a letter to ask how their friends did, or if they liked the New World. They all seemed to have come from the Old. When I said so, Alice replied that I was selfish and that people liked hearing from the mouth of an eye-witness how their relatives are. Alice was rather shy and made me go along though I was not amiable about these visits.

First we went to see the cousin of a friend. She was eighty and had an epileptic son of sixty. He had stopped development at the age of seven or eight; mind and body were dwarfed. He had an immense head, a nondescript body, foolish little-boy legs that dangled from the chair edge as he sat in the parlour opposite to us, nursing his straw hat as if he were the visitor.

His mother said, "Shake hands with the ladies, Jumble."

(Jumble was the name he had given himself and it was very appropriate.)

Jumble leapt from his chair as if he were leaping from a house-top, skipped to the far side of the room and laid his hat down on the floor. He came running back and held out two wide short-fingered paws. We each took one and he gave us each a separate little hop which was supposed to be a bow.

"The ladies come from Canada, Jumble."

He clapped his hands. "I like Canada. She sends pretty stamps on her letter; Jumble has a stamp book! Jumble likes stamps, he likes plum cake too! Jumble wants his tea, quick! quick!" He pattered in to the adjoining room where tea was laid, climbed into his chair and began to beat on his plate with a spoon.

"He is all I have," sighed the woman and motioned us to follow, whispering, "I hope, my dears, you are not nervous? Jumble may have a fit during tea."

We had never seen anything but a cat in a fit but we lied and said we were not nervous.

Jumble consumed vast wedges of plum cake but he did not have a fit.

After tea they saw us to our tram—eight-year hobble and trot, trot of a halfwit, escorting us. Once aboard, I groaned, "Who next?"

Alice produced her list.

"Mable's Aunt; now don't be mean, Millie. People naturally want to hear from an eye-witness."

"Pleasanter for them than seeing for themselves."

Mable's Aunt was gaunt. She lived in a drab district. She kissed us before ever we got the chance to say why we had come, but, when we said we came from Mable she fell on us again and kissed and kissed. She had never seen Mable but she had known Mable's mother years before Mable was born. Every time we mentioned Mable's name she jumped up and kissed us again. Needless to say she was English. In time we learned to avoid mention of Mable. That restricted conversation to the weather and Mable's

Aunt's cat, a fine tabby. While we were grappling for fresh talk material, the Aunt said:

"Oh my dears, such a drive! Such lovely, lovely flowers!"

"Where? When?" We were ager at the turn the conversation had taken,—flowers seemed a safe pleasant topic.

"My son took me this morning. It is a long way. There were marvellous carpets of flowers, every colour, every kind. Oh my dears, such flowers!"

"My son is a doctor, visiting doctor for the 'Last Chance'. He takes me with him for the drive. Flowers all the way! I don't mind waiting while he is inside. I look at the flowers."

"What is the 'Last Chance'?" I asked.

"Terrible, terrible, oh my dears! Thank God that you are normal, usual." She sprang to kiss us again because we were complete, ordinary girls.

Again I asked, "What is the 'Last Chance'?"

"A place behind bars where they put monstrosities, abnormalities while doctors decide if anything can be done for them." She began describing cases. "Of course I've only seen a little through the bars."

The little she had seen was enough to send Alice and me greenish white. We tried to lead her back to the flowers. It was no use, we took our leave.

We walked along in silence for some time. "Let's forget it," I said. "All the people on your list seem to have some queerness, be the same type. Suppose we lose the list!"

Alice said, "For shame, Millie. People at home want to hear about their relatives. It is selfish of you to grouse over their peculiarities!"

"Relatives' peculiarities would do just as well in letters and only cost three cents. I'd willingly pay the stamp. They are not even relatives of our own friends. For them we might endure but for these nearly strangers why should we?"

Again Alice's, "For shame, selfish girl!"

It happened that Mrs. Piddington had arranged a flower-picking picnic for the very next Saturday. Someone had told her of a marvellous place. You walked through Golden

Gate Park and then on and on. There were fields and fields of flowers, all wild and to be had for the picking.

At last we got there only to be confronted by a great strong gate on which hung a notice "Keep Out"! The flowers were beautiful all right. Just outside the gate was a power-house and a reservoir. We asked permission at the office and were told we might go through the gate and gather.

"What is the big building just inside the enclosure?" asked Mrs. Piddington but just then the man was summoned back into the office.

"Last Chance," he called over his shoulder. Alice and I looked at each other. We felt sick. "Know-it-all" old Piddington explained. "Windows all barred! Um, doubtless it is a reformatory of some sort."

We scuttled under the barred windows, Alice and I trying to draw our party over toward a little hill away from the building. The hill was lightly wooded and a sunny little path ran through the wood. Flowers were everywhere —also snakes! They lay in the path sunning themselves and slowly wriggled out of our way quivering the grass at the path side. You had to watch your feet for fear of treading on one. Alice and I could not help throwing scared glances behind at the brick, bar-windowed building. Shadowy forms moved on the other side of the bars. We clothed them in Mable's Aunt's describings.

There were not many big trees in the wood. It was all low scrub bush. You could see over the top of it. I was leading on the path. I had been giving one of my backward, fearful glances at "Last Chance" and turned front suddenly. I was at the brink of a great hole several yards around. My foot hung over the hole. With a fearful scream I backed onto the rest of the party. They scolded and were furious with me.

"Look for yourselves, then!"

They did and screamed as hard as I.

The hole was several feet deep. It was filled with a slithering moil of snakes, coiling and uncoiling. Had my lifted foot taken one more step, I should have plunged headlong among the snakes and I should have gone mad! Mrs. Piddington was too horrified even to faint. She yelled out, "I've been told there are 'rattlers' this side of the park too!" Turning aside, we broke into mad running, helter skelter through the thicket heading for the open. Snakes writhed over and under the scrub to get out of our way. The flowers of our gathering were thrown far and wide. Horrible, horrible! Our nerves prickled and we sobbed with hurrying. We passed the "Last Chance" with scarcely one glance and rushed through the gate, coming back empty-handed. We did not even see the flowers along the way, our minds were too full of snakes.

"Girls," I cried, "I want to go back to Canada. California can have her flowers, her sunshine and her snakes. I don't like San Francisco. I want to go home."

But when my sisters did go back to Victoria I was not with them. I was stuck to the Art School.

Mrs. Tucket

THE WOMAN who was supposed to have assumed Mrs. Piddington's custody of me bodily and morally ignored everything connected with me except the board money I paid. I was her income. I had to be made to stretch over herself, her two children and myself. The capacity of my check was so severely taxed by all our wants that towards the end of the month it wore gossamer and ceased altogether. Then we lived for the last few days of each month on scraps fried on my spirit lamp to economize kitchen fuel.

The woman's children (a girl of six and a boy of four) any Mother might have been proud of, but she referred to them as "my encumbrances" because they prevented her from devoting her entire time to Art. Mrs. Tucket was jealous of my youngness, jealous of my freedom. An Art dealer had once praised a sketch done by her and from that time she knew no peace from the longing which possessed her to give her life, all of it, to Art.

The boy Kirkby, aged four, and I were great chums. He was at my heels every moment I was in the house—a loving little fellow who had two deep terrors—blood and music. The sight of blood would turn the child dead white, one note of music would send him running outdoors away anywhere from the sound, his hands to his ears. He angrily resented my guitar; pushing it out of my lap he would climb in himself and, reaching his hand to my forehead, would say, "I feel a story in there, tell it." It was a surprise to his Mother and to me, after a few months, instead of pushing away the guitar he would sidle up, pat the instrument, and say, "I like her a little now, sing!"

Mrs. Tucket had health notions, all based on economy. Uninterrupted passage of air through the cottage was one. She said it nourished as much as food. All the inner doors of the house were removed, there was no privacy whatever. No hangings were at the windows, no cushions on chairs or couch. The beds were hard and had coverings inadequate for such cyclonic surges of wind as swept in and out of the rooms. No comfort was in that cottage.

Mrs. Tucket had, too, absolute faith in a greasy pack of fortune-telling cards. She foretold every event (after it had happened). *After* Kirkby had cut his head open she knew he was going to be cut. *After* Anna got the measles she knew the child had been exposed. When I missed the ferry-boat she said the cards had foretold it (but so had the clock). After the dealer had praised her sketch she vowed that she had been prepared because the cards indicated someone would. She was angry because I laughed and would not have my cards read. I got so sick of being haunted by the ace of spades and the queen of hearts that I suggested we read a book aloud after the children were in bed at night. Mrs. Tucket read well but chose depressing books, delighting in deathbed scenes and broken love affairs. She would lay the book down on the table and sob into her handkerchief. It embarrassed me so much that I said, "S'pose we find a good merry funeral story to cheer us up!" Then she was offended and said I was without romance or sentiment.

One day as I came in from school Mrs. Tucket beckoned to me from the doorway of her bedroom. The wind was busy in there, tearing the covers off the bed, whirling the pincushion and clanking the window blind.

"Listen!" In the middle of the turmoil a cruel, tearing breathing.

"Kirkby's!"

I bent over the bed. The child did not know me.

"Get a doctor quick!"

"But doctors are so expensive," she complained.

"Quick." I stamped my foot.

She got a homeopathist, not that she believed in homeopathy but this doctor-woman was a friend of hers and would not charge. We moved a cot into the unfurnished front of the cottage and took turn and turn about sitting on an apple box beside it watching.

Little Kirkby battled with death in this grim setting. The crisis came one night just as I had turned in for my four hours of rest.

"Come!"

The cottage was full of moonlight. She had switched out all the lights so that Kirkby should not see the blood. There was hemorrhage. We worked in and out between shadows and moonlight, doing what we could. The exhausted child dropped back on the pillow like a wilted snowdrop. The woman yawned.

"I'll take forty winks now, your bed I think, handier should you need me."

As she passed through the living room she switched on a light and stood, wrapped in admiration of the sketch the dealer had praised. It was framed and hung on the wall. I heard a deep, deep sigh, then blackness, the sounds of sleep. Moonlight flooded the bare room. The life of the child flickered. Kirkby in the bed was scarcely more tangible than the moonlight. I sat the night out on the apple box. "Art I hate you, I hate you! You steal from babies!" I cried and would not go to school next morning. I did not go back for a whole week. I told stories and sang to Kirkby feeling very tender towards the child and bitter towards Art and the woman.

Summer vacation came. I did not like summer vacation. I was compelled to spend it at Auntie's in San Jose. Auntie undertook to discipline me for two years each vacation, the year that was past and the year to come. Between Aunt and me there was no love.

Mrs. Tucket was giving up the cottage. She was joining a friend in Chicago. They were to run a boarding house.

She was full of plans. Kirkby and I watched her packing, Kirkby, a mere shadow child, clinging to his chair to keep the wind from blowing him away. Mrs. Tucket held up his little patched pants. The wind filled them; their empty legs were vigorous with kickings. Kirkby laughed.

"My pants are fatter than me."

The woman pressed the wind out of the pants and tumbled them into the trunk.

"I am not going to Chicago!"

She banged down the trunk lid.

"What has happened?" I asked. "All your arrangements are made."

"The cards say I shall not go!"

When I returned from San Jose the cottage was for rent. I never heard of Mrs. Tucket, her Art or little Kirkby again.

Telegraph Hill

EXIT MRS. Piddington, and vice and terror faded from my consciousness. Free, unfearful I roamed San Francisco interested in everything, most particularly interested in my art studies. Suddenly I was brought face to face with Piddington horrors again.

I was taking guitar lessons from an old German professor. The frets on my guitar needed resetting, the professor said.

"Take to de' musics-man he sharge you big moneys. My fren' dat make fiddle he do sheep for you!"

He wrote an address on a card and off I started, my guitar in a green cloth bag. I called in at Adda's on the way. It was Saturday afternoon. We often spent the half holiday together.

"Where are you going?"

"To get my guitar fixed."

"I'll come for the walk."

"Hurry then, Adda, it dusks early."

On and on we tramped. It seemed a very long way but we asked direction now and again from people we met. Yes, we were going in the right direction but—they looked at us queerly as if they wondered.

By and by the smells of the sea and tarry wharf smells met our noses. Ah, here was the name on our card. We turned into a wide, quiet street. It had an abandoned, strange look. In front of us was a great building with a sign, "Telegraph Hill Foundry and Storage". Telegraph

Hill! "Why, Adda, this is the awful, wicked place Captain pointed out as we came through the Golden Gate, the place I was never to go near."

"It does look very queer," said Adda. "Shall we turn back?"

"No, this is number 213. Ours will be two blocks further on. It is best to show our business but it is almost too dark to see the numbers over the doors."

We walked the two blocks in silence except that I said, "Adda, let's walk in the middle of the street."

Suddenly a burst of light from street lamps and simultaneously over every door came a little red twinkling light. There were big shop windows dazzlingly bright on either side of the way. In them were displayed, not goods but women, scantily clad women, swaying in rocking chairs and showing a great deal of leg. Some toyed with fancy work, some simpered, some stared with blank, unseeing eyes, all rocked restlessly.

"Momma, Momma!" gasped Adda again. "Shall we turn back?" she asked of me.

My head shook. I shook all over because of Mrs. Piddington's horrible tales.

"Here's the great mock fiddle. I'll go in and show why I came. Oh, Adda!"

I was quaking. "Hold the door wide, Adda, don't let them shut me in! Don't, don't!"

Adda braced, spread her members like a starfish, clinging octopus-wise to the floor and to all sides of the door's frame.

The little shop was full of men and smoke. There was only one dim light in the place. An old man pushed forward to take the green bag from my arms. He took the guitar out, touched her strings lovingly.

"She is sweet-toned," he smiled down at me, "but these frets, ach, they tear the little fingers! She is ready Monday."

He laid the instrument upon his work shelf.

Adda released the door posts and grabbed me as if I had just come back from the dead. Momma herself could not have been more protecting towards me, more belligerent towards my danger than was dear, staunch Adda.

We hurried into the middle of the street with firm stepping, determined not to break into a tell-tale run. We nearly burst ourselves for wanting to draw deep breaths and not daring to do so for hurry and worry. We turned the corner and met a policeman. I never knew a policeman could look so beautiful, so safe.

"Momma, Momma, if you knew!" whispered Adda, to me, "Of course you won't go back for the guitar, Dummy?"

"I must, Adda. It belongs to my big sister. You see if I went home without it I would have to explain—and then . . . !"

"I'll go with you, but I won't tell Momma till afterwards. Of course I couldn't deceive Momma. I must tell sometime, but after will be best."

The Mansion

ONE MORNING I climbed the old grubby stair of the Art School to find everything in excitement and confusion. Clumps of students congested the Oriental Rug Room, groups of students were in the hall, the office was full. The old Curator was tugging at his beard harder than ever, shaking his head, nodding answers or ignoring questions as excitement permitted.

Supposing it to be some American anniversary, I strode through the hubbub into the work hall. Here I found professors, model and janitor in close confabulation around the stove. Obviously some common interest had levelled rank and profession. The only unmoved person I could see was the wooden-faced, stone-hearted painter of still life, the woman who ordered her birds smothered so that their plumage should not be soiled by blood for her studies, the woman who painted tables full of fish with eyes that ogled even when dead and whose stiffened bodies curled and smelled in spite of the fact that she kept trying to revive one last glitter by slopping water over them periodically. On a still-life table stood a forsaken vase of red roses, sagging, prematurely dead, no water. Stevie dashed in to stick her daily posy of mignonette and sweet peas on my easel board—dashed out again. What! Stevie too? Then this was no American do, this excitement. Stevie would not be so unpatriotic as to recognize an American occasion! In bustled Adda tying the strings of her little black silk apron.

"Aren't you excited, Dummy?"

"Excited? What about?"

"The move, of course!"

"What move?"

"Dummy, you *are* dumb! The School move, of course."

"Is the School moving?"

"This very day. Look!" She pointed out the window, where men were tearing down our chimneys, ripping at our roof.

"Time this dilapidated dreadfulness disappeared," scorned Adda. "A mansion! A perfectly clean mansion fallen from the sky! Oh, won't Momma be pleased!"

"Adda, do tell me what it is all about!"

"Well, our lease was up and the market and Art School building is condemned. Haven't you seen how the poor old Curator has torn at his beard the last week? I wonder he did not pull it out! No place for his School to go! Then this mansion falls straight from heaven! Mrs. Hopkins could not take it with her, could she? So she dropped it from heaven's gate. Down it tumbled stuffed with her best wishes for Science and Art!"

Adda's sharp little teeth bit on her lip.

"Oh, Momma, I'm so sorry, you would not, I know, like me to mix heaven and Art. But Dummy, no more smells, no more rats! Lovely, lovely!"

I frowned.

"I'm sorry. I love this old place and don't want to move."

"Oh Dummy, imagine anybody loving this old School."

Adda's lace-bordered hanky swished, a rat scuttled.

I said, "It is the underneath of it that I love."

"Underneath! that disgusting market!"

"Not exactly, though the market with its honest old roots and chickens and cheese is all right, it is comfortable, commonsense. But I was not thinking of the market, Adda. It is the space and freedom we have here in this old School. We can splash and experiment all we like. Nobody grumbles at us. Our work is not hampered by bullying, 'Don't, don't.' We sharpen charcoal, toss bread crusts. Nobody calls us pigs even if they think we are. Art students are a little like

pigs, aren't they, Adda? They'd far rather root in earth
and mud than eat the daintiest chef-made swill out of
china bowls."

Adda shuddered.

"Dummy, you are...! What would Momma say?
Momma never eats pork, not even bacon, and she can't
bear the mention of a pig!"

The mantels, banisters and newel posts of the mansion
were all elaborately carved. There were all sorts of cun-
ningly devised secret places in the mansion, places in which
to hide money or jewels. (Mrs. Hopkins could not have
had much faith in banks.) In the dining room you pressed
a certain wooden grape in a carved bunch over the mantel
and out sprang a little drawer. In the library you squeezed
the eye of a carved lion and out shot a cabinet. A towel
rack in the bathroom pulled right out and behind it was
an iron safe. There were panels that slid and disclosed little
rooms between walls. We delighted in going round squeezing and poking to see what would happen next. Ali the
treasure places were empty. Mrs. Hopkins had cleared
them all out before she willed the mansion.

The public roamed from room to room and stared; of
course they did not know about all the strange corners
that we knew. Occasionally "a public" would stray up our
stairs and gaze at us as if we had been part of their fifty
cents' worth. They need not have thought us so extraordinary for in the mansion we were quite ordinary, quite
normal. If it had been the old school, well ... but no sightseers had ever thought of climbing those dirty stairs. Art
students were just part of the squalor that surrounded the
market. Nobody was interested in them! But now that we
were stupid and elegant and an institution people wanted
to see how we looked.

Back to Canada

SAN FRANCISCO boarding houses were always changing hands. Sometimes I stayed by the change, sometimes I moved.

All boarding houses seemed to specialize in derelict grandmothers and childless widows, nosey old ladies with nothing to do but sleep, eat, dress up, go out, come back to eat again. Being lonely and bored they swooped upon anything that they thought ought to be mothered. They concentrated on me. I was soon very overmothered. They had only been out in the New World a generation or two. My English upbringing reminded them of their own childhood. They liked my soap-shiny, unpowdered nose, liked my using the names Father and Mother instead of Momma and Poppa. Not for one moment would they exchange their smart, quick-in-the-uptake granddaughters for me but they did take grim satisfaction out of my dowdy, old-fashioned clothes and my shyness. Their young people were so sophisticated, so independent. They tried lending me little bits of finery, a bow or a bit of jewellery to smarten me, should I be invited out, which was not often. One old lady of sixty wanted me to wear a "pansy flat" (her best hat) when someone took me to see *Robin Hood*. It hurt them that I refused their finery, preferring to wear my own clothes which I felt were more suitable to age and comfort even though they were not smart. I had a birthday coming and three of them got together and made me a new dress. The result disheartened them—they had to admit that somehow I looked best, and was most me, in my own things.

The landlady's daughter and I were friends. We decided we would teach ourselves to sew and make our own clothes. We bought Butterick's patterns, spread them on the floor of the top landing where our little rooms were, and in which there was not much more than space to turn round.

One day I was cutting out on the hall floor. The landlady's daughter was basting. Spitting out six pins she said, "Seen Mother's new boarder?" and pointed to the door of a suite up on our floor.

I replied, "No, what flavour is she?"

"Loud! The old house tabbies are furious at Ma for taking her but we have to live, there is so much competition now."

"The house is big. Those who wish to be exclusive can keep out of each other's way."

"The new girl has her own sitting room—double suite if you please! I don't think I like her much and you won't but she's going to your Art School so you will see her quite a bit."

"If she is such a swell she won't bother about me."

Next morning I slammed the front door and ran down the steps. I had no sooner reached the pavement than the door re-opened and Ishbel Dane, the new boarder, came out.

"Can I come along? I rather hate beginning."

She had large bold eyes, a strong mouth. You would not have suspected her of being shy, but she was. She was very smartly dressed, fur coat, jewellery, fancy shoes. I took her into the school office and left her signing up. I went on up to the studios.

"Who?" I was asked and nudged by students.

"New boarder at my place."

Adda frowned, she had never approved of my boarding house—too big, too mixed. Adda was an only boarder and only sure about places that were "Momma-approved".

Suddenly she had a thought. Diving into her pocket she brought out a letter.

"Momma is coming!" she said. "Brother is taking a course at Berkeley University; Momma and sister are coming along; I will join them. We shall rent a house in Berkeley. I've given notice. Why not take my room? Shall I ask them to save it for you?"

"No, thanks, I am very well where I am."

Adda said no more. She watched Ishbel but refused to meet her.

In the evenings I practised on my guitar. There was a tap on my door and there was almost pleading in Ishbel Dane's voice as she said, "Come to my sitting room and have a cup of tea with me?"

I went wondering. We had not got to know each other very well. We were in different studios at School. My "grandmother guardians" in the boarding house advised of Ishbel Dane, "Not your sort my dear." Having found they could not direct my clothes they were extra dictatorial over my morals. I resented it a little, though I knew they meant well. They were very cool to Ishbel, confined conversation to the weather. All they had against the girl was her elegant clothes—she overdressed for their taste.

Ishbel had made her sitting room very attractive—flowers, books, cushions, a quaint silver tea service which she told me had been her mother's. She saw my eyes stray to a beautiful banjo lying on the sofa.

"Yes, I play. I belong to a banjo, mandolin and guitar club. Wouldn't you like to join? It helps one. I have learnt ever so much since I practised with others."

I said slowly, "I'll think." I knew the old grandmothers, the landlady's daughter and Adda would disapprove. When I left, Ishbel took my hand.

"Come again," she said. "It's lonely. My mother died when I was only a baby; Father brought me up. Father's friends are all men, old and dull. A few of them have looked me up for Father's sake. Father is in the South."

I joined the practice club. My friendship with Ishbel

warmed while the old ladies' affection chilled towards me. Adda was actively distressed. She moved to Berkeley. Her last shot as she started for her new home was, "My old room is still vacant."

Trouble was in her eyes, anxiety for me, but I liked Ishbel and I knew Ishbel and I knew my friendship meant a lot to her.

I had to go to the music studio for some music. The Club leader was giving a lesson. He shut his pupil into the studio with her tinkling mandolin, followed me out onto the landing. As I took the roll of music from him he caught me round the wrists.

"Little girl," he said, "be good to Ishbel, you are her *only* woman friend and she loves you. God bless you!" His door banged.

I a woman's friend! Suddenly I felt grown up. Mysteriously Ishbel—a woman—had been put into my care. Ishbel was my trust. I went down stairs slowly, each tread seemed to stretch me, as if my head had remained on the landing while my feet and legs elongated me. On reaching the pavement I was grown up, a woman with a trust. I did not quite know how or why Ishbel needed me. I only knew she did and was proud.

While I was out a letter had come. I opened it. My guardian thought I had "played at Art" long enough. I was to come home and start Life in earnest.

Ishbel clung to me. "Funny little mother-girl," she said, kissing me. "I am going to miss you!"

A man's head was just appearing over the banister rail. She poked something under my arm, pushed me gently towards my own room. A great lump was in my throat. Ishbel was the only one of them all who hadn't wanted to change some part of me—the only one who had. Under my arm she had pushed a portrait of herself.

I came home one week before Christmas. The house was decorated, there was some snow, fires crackled in every grate of every room, their warmth drew spicy delight from the boughs of pine and cedar decorating everywhere.

There were bunches of scarlet berries and holly. The pantry bulged with good things already cooked. In the yard was something for me, something I had wanted all my life, a dog!

They were glad to have me home. We were very merry. All day the postman was bringing cards and letters; flitter, flitter, they dropped through the slit near the front door and we all darted crying, "Whose? whose?"

I got my full share but there were two disappointments —no letter from Nellie McCormick, none from Ishbel Dane. New Year passed before I heard of either.

Adda wrote, "Nellie McCormick could endure home tyranny no longer, she shot herself."

From the boarding house one of the grandmothers absolutely sniffed in writing, "Ishbel Dane died in the 'Good Samaritan' hospital on Christmas Eve. Under the circumstances, my dear, perhaps it was best."

Nellie my friend! Ishbel my trust!

I carried my crying into the snowy woods. The weather was bitter, my tears were too.

Part II

Home Again

THE TYPE of work which I brought home from San Francisco was humdrum and unemotional—objects honestly portrayed, nothing more. As yet I had not considered what was underneath surfaces, nor had I considered the inside of myself. I was like a child printing alphabet letters. I had not begun to make words with the letters.

No one was teaching drawing in Victoria: mothers asked me to start a children's class. I did not want to teach. I was afraid of pupils, but I did teach and soon I got fond of the children and liked the work. I taught my class in our dining room. The light was bad; the room got messed up; there was trouble after every class.

We had two large barns: one housed our cow, the other our horse. Clambering over the cow, I explored her loft. Low roof, only one tiny window, no door other than a small trap-door over the cow's head and a great double door that opened into space and had a gibbet over the top for the hauling up of bales of hay. The boards of the floor and walls were knotholed, the wood buckled, the roof leaked. But it was a large loft, high in the middle, low at the side walls.

My eldest sister was tyrannical, an autocrat like Father. She claimed every inch of the old home, though really it belonged to us all. Independence had taught me courage.

"Can I have the loft of the old cow barn for a studio?"

"Certainly not. It's the cow's."

"Couldn't the cow share with the horse?"

"Have you come home to unsettle the family and worry the cow?"

My sister knew the cow's barn was very much out of repair. When I offered to mend it she reluctantly consented to my using the loft. I called in a carpenter.

"It's the floor," I said.

"No, the roof," my sister corrected.

"It's the walls!" declared the carpenter with a determined tongue-click and a head-shake.

I said, "As long as everything relates in being bad, let's patch all over and let it go at that. But, carpenter, there *must* be an outside stair up to the big door and another window for light."

So the carpenter let in a wide dormer, hung a little stair onto the outer wall, patched leaks, straightened boards and we were snug. But it was still too dark for work and all my money was spent. The old garden Chinaman and I mounted the roof with saws and cut a great hole. This we fitted with two old window sashes, making a skylight. Now we had lots of light and lots of leak too. I put a tin gutter all round the skylight and drained the leaks into a flower box, shoved a stovepipe into the wash-house chimney which ran through the loft, blocked up pigeon holes, burlapped walls. There we were cosy as anything, with little more than an eggshell's thickness of wood full of splits, knotholes and cracks and perched right out in the middle of the elements—rain drumming, wind whistling, sun warming, and everybody happy—pupils, me, even the cow and chickens below.

Under my loft the barn contained a wash-house, an apple-storing room, a tool shed, three cow stalls, a chicken house and an immense wood-shed, big enough to accomodate twelve cords of wood (half oak, half fir, for the household's winter burning).

"Please, the cow smells like a cow, may she move to the other barn?" I asked my sister.

"She may not."

I did not really mind sharing with the cow—I was really not keen on her smell but she cosied things.

When I worked at night under a big coal-oil lamp suspended from the rafter under an immense reflector, made by myself out of split coal-oil cans, it was nice to hear the cow's contented chew, chew, chew below. I loved to stick my head through the trap-door above her stall into the warm dark and say, "Hello, old cow." She answered with great hay-fragrant sniff-puffs that filled the barn. Any sudden noise sent the hens on their roosts below hiccoughing in their sleep. On moonlight nights the rooster crowed. Rats and mice saw no reason to change their way of living because we had come—after I brought home a half-drowned kitten from the beach it was different. A peacock came down from Beacon Hill Park and made his daytime quarters on the studio roof, strutting before the doubled-back dormer, using it as a mirror. Most splendid of all was my very own big dog. No studio has ever been so dear to me as that old loft, smelling of hay and apples, new sawed wood, Monday washings, earthy garden tools.—The cow's great sighs! Such delicious content!

In dusk's half-light the dog and I left the studio and raced over Beacon Hill and the beach. Specially permitted friends held trysts in the studio with their sweethearts, sitting on the model throne looking down into the pure delight of a blossoming cherry tree below, or toasting their toes, along with the cat, in front of the open-fronted stove.

I was rebellious about religion. In our home it was forced upon you in large, furious helps. The miserableness of continually sprawling across doubled-over ladies, with their noses on the seats of our chairs, and their praying knees down on our carpets, annoyed me. You never knew in which room nor at what hour.

The Y.W.C.A. was just beginning in Victoria; my sisters were among its founders, and enthusiastic over the concern. As the society had, as yet, no headquarters, they used to come to our house to pray. I was always bursting in on them. The knocked-over-ones glowered, and, over their horizontal backs, my sister's eyes shot fire at me. She hung on to her prayer voice till afterwards—and then—!

Then too there was the missionary blight. My second sister wanted to be a Missionary and filled our house with long-faced samples. Missionaries roosted on us during migration, others hopped in to meals while waiting for boats. Missionary steamers had no particular dates or hours of sailing, because they went to outlandish places and waited for cargoes. There was the Sunday School blight too. That was very bad. All there was left of home on Sunday afternoon was the wood pile or you could go off to the lily field. Every room in the house accommodated a Sunday School class. My sister wanted me to conduct one for small boys in the kitchen and called me stubborn and ungodly because I refused.

Artists from the Old World said our West was crude, unpaintable. Its bigness angered, its vastness and wild spaces terrified them. Browsing cows, hooves well sunk in the grass (hooves were hard to draw!), placid streams with an artistic wriggle meandering through pastoral landscape—that was the Old World idea of a picture. Should they feel violent, the artists made blood-red sunsets, disciplined by a smear of haze. They would as soon have thought of making pictures of their own insides as of the depths of our forests.

I was tremendously awed when a real French artist with an English artist-wife came to Victoria. I expected to see something wonderful, but they painted a few faraway mountains floating in something hazy that was not Canadian air, a Chinaman's shack on which they put a curved roof like an Eastern temple, then they banged down the lids of their paintboxes, packed up, went back to the Old World. Canada had no scenery, they said. They said also that the only places you could learn to paint in were London or Paris. I was disappointed at hearing that, but immediately began to save. I slung an old pair of shoes across the studio rafters. When pupils paid me I shoved the money away in my shoes.

"I am going abroad to study!" I told my astonished family.

A Missionary took a liking to me. She had a very long face but a good heart. She was negotiating for my sister to accompany her back to her lonely mission up the West Coast of Vancouver Island, so that she might try out the loneliness and Indians. When the Missionary saw how interested I was in her description of these wild places, she said to me, "Wouldn't you like to come to Ucluelet to sketch in the summer holidays?"

"I would like to frightfully," I replied.

The Willapa was a small coast steamer. I was the only woman on board, indeed the only passenger. We nosed into dark little coves to dump goods at canneries. We stood off rocky bluffs, hooting until a tiny speck would separate itself from the dark of the shoreline. It grew and presently sprouted legs that crawled it across the water. The black nob in its middle was a man. We threw him a rope and he held on, his eyes chewing the parcel in the purser's hands, his face alight.

"Money?" shouted the purser. The man's face unlit. He made a pretence of searching through his ragged clothes and shook his head. The purser threw the parcel back on our deck and tossed a letter into the man's boat. The man ripped the envelope, tore out his remittance and waved it, the parcel thudded into the boat! We tooted and were away. The tiny boat got smaller and smaller, a mere speck on the grey spread of water. Then it was gone. Vastness had swallowed boat and man.

Life in the Mission House was stark, almost awesome, but you could not awe our Missionary, she had no nerves. She was of cement hardened into a mould. She was not inhuman, there was earth underneath. It was just her crust that was hard and smooth. The slow, heavy Indians had not decided whether or not to accept religion. They accepted missionary "magic" in the shape of castor oil and Epsom salts. But religion? They were pondering. The Missionaries were obliged to restrain their physic-giving. If you gave an Indian a bottle of medicine he drank it all down at once and died or not according to his constitution.

He had to be given only one dose at a time. But the Missionaries expected to give the Indians the whole of religion at one go. The Indians held back. If physic was given in prolonged doses, why not religion?

"Toxis", as the Indians called the Mission House, squatted back to forest face to sea just above the frill of foam that said, "No further," to the sea and, "So far," to the land. The Indian village was a mile distant on one side of the Mission House, the cannery store a mile on the other. At high tide we went to them by canoe, at low tide we walked in and out among the drift logs lying stranded on the beach.

No part of living was normal. We lived on fish and fresh air. We sat on things not meant for sitting on, ate out of vessels not meant to hold food, slept on hardness that bruised us; but the lovely, wild vastness did something to it all. I loved every bit of it—no boundaries, no beginning, no end, one continual shove of growing—edge of land meeting edge of water, with just a ribbon of sand between. Sometimes the ribbon was smooth, sometimes fussed with foam. Trouble was only on the edges; both sea and forests in their depths were calm and still. Virgin soil, clean sea, pure air, vastness by day, still deeper vastness in dark when beginnings and endings joined.

Our recreation in the Mission House was the pasting together of broken prayer- and hymn-books. It seemed the churches sent all their cripples to missions.

After the Missionaries blew out their candles and the ceiling blackened down to our noses, the square of window which the candle had made black against outside dark cleared to luminous greys, folding away mystery upon mystery. Out there tree boles pillared the forest's roof, and streaked the unfathomable forest like gigantic rain streaks pouring; the surge of growth from the forest's floor boiled up to meet it. I peered at it through the uncurtained window while the Missionaries prayed.

To attempt to paint the Western forests did not occur to me. Hadn't those Paris artists said it was unpaintable?

No artist that I knew, no Art School had taught Art this size. I would have to go to London or to Paris to learn to paint. Still those French painters who had been taught there said, "Western Canada is unpaintable!" How bothersome! I nibbled at silhouetted edges. I drew boats and houses, things made out of tangible stuff. Unknowingly I was storing, storing, all unconscious, my working ideas against the time when I should be ready to use this material.

Love and Poetry

IMMEDIATELY upon my return from the West Coast Mission, I tasted two experiences for the first time—love, and poetry. Poetry was pure joy, love more than half pain. I gave my love where it was not wanted; almost simultaneously an immense love was offered to me which I could neither accept nor return. Between hurting and being hurt life went crooked. I worked and taught for all I was worth. When my teaching for the day was over, with a book of poetry under my arm and with my dog, I went to the Beach or roamed the broom bushes on Beacon Hill. From the underscored passages in my poets, poetry did not touch love as deeply as it touched nature and beauty for me. Marked passages are all earth and nature.

Up to this time my painting had followed the ordinary Art School curriculum—drawing from the antique, still-life painting, portraiture, design and landscape. Now it took a definite list toward pure landscape.

When, dangling from the studio rafters, the old pair of hoarding shoes were crammed with money from my teaching, I announced, "I am going to London."

"You have friends or relatives there?" asked an old lady friend.

"I have neither, but for my work I must go."

"London is big, much noise, many people; you will miss your pine trees and your beaches, child."

"London will be beastly; all the same, I'm going."

"My sister, Amelia Green, accepts a few paying guests."

"What are paying guests—boarders?"

Love and Poetry

"My dear! Ladies of good family in England do not take boarders. If circumstances compel them to accept remunerative visitors, they call them paying guests," said the shocked old lady.

"PG's? Then all right, I'll be one of your sister's PG's."

It was arranged that Aunt Amelia, wearing something green in her buttonhole, should meet me at Euston Station.

Nearly everyone in Victoria gave me a life-size portrait photograph of himself or sometimes of the entire family grouped. I was supposed to cart them along as a preventative for homesickness. I locked them into my stow-away cupboard at home. But more friends brought more photographs to the boat-side. On entering my stateroom I was greeted by cardboard stares, male and female, propped against the tooth mug, the waterbottle, the camp stool; a family group rested on my pillow. The nicest family of all slid out the porthole. Undulating on a great green wave it smiled back at me. I gathered the rest into my cabin trunk, I could not be comfortably seasick with them looking on. I was provided also with a bale of introductory letters asking people to be kind. If England could not be kind for my own sake I did not want charity niceness from my friends' friends!

Canada's vastness took my breath. The up-and-downness of the Rockies, their tops dangled in clouds, thrilled and were part of natural me, though I had to steel myself as we glided over trestle-bridges of great height spanning gorges and ravines with rivers like white ribbons boiling far below, and lofty trees looking crouched and squat down there in the bottom of the canyon while we slid over their tops. We squeezed through rocky passes, hid in tunnels, raced roaring rivers, slunk through endless levels of dead, still forest, black-green and mysterious, layer upon layer of marching trees, climbing trees, trees burned, trees fallen, myriad millions of trees and loneliness intertwisted. Our engine gulped endless miles, each rail-length one bite. On, on, till the mountains ended and the train slithered over level land munching space rhythmically as a chewing cow.

Was there never to be an end? Did our engine spin track as she advanced like a monster spider? Would we finally topple over the brink into that great bonfire of a sunset when we came to the finish of this tremendous vastness?— No rocks, no trees, no bumps, just once in a great, great way a tiny house, a big barn, cattle in that great space sizing no bigger than flies—prairie houses, cows, barns, drowned in loneliness.

When at last we came to Canada's eastern frontier, just before she touched the Atlantic ocean, she burst into a spread of great cities, clean, new cities. The greedy, gobbling train turned back to regobble Canada's space, while we launched into sea-bounce that grieved the stomach, wearied the eye.—Nothingness, nothingness, till your seeing longed and longed—whale, bird, anything rather than nothing piled on top of nothing!

The Voyage and Aunt Amelia

THE WOMAN in the deck chair next to mine stroked a strand of red hair from her forehead with a freckled hand.

"Oh, my head!"

"Have my smelling bottle."

She took three long sniffs and then pointed the bottle across the deck.

"Awful woman!" indicating a loud, lounging woman in noisy conversation with the Captain.

"Discussing whisky! Irish against Scotch! Glad she prefers Irish, I should feel her preference for Scotch a desecration of my country."

Captain crossed the deck. He looked enquiringly from one to the other of us.

"Miss Carr?"

"Yes, Captain."

"This lady wants to meet you, her maiden name was Carr."

The Captain indicated the loud woman with whom he had been discussing whisky. The Captain's lady flopped noisily into the chair the smelling bottle and the Scotch lady had hastily vacated.

"Any London relatives?" she asked sharply.

"None."

"What are you by birth?"

"Canadian."

She beckoned the Captain back to her side. Irish versus Scotch was again discussed—they forgot me.

Suddenly I felt awful. The former Miss Carr made a

swift move. I felt the cold scratchy hardness of an immense sunburst which Mrs. Downey (the former Miss Carr) wore upon her breast, then I was in my berth, and my cabin was full of people but most full of Mrs. Downey. Sometimes I was there, sometimes not; finally I sailed out into blankness entirely.

In those times C.P.R. boats took ten days to cross the Atlantic. We were almost across before I woke. First I thought it was me crying, then I opened my eyes and saw it was Stewardess.

"Are you hurt?" She patted me and mopped herself. "How could your mother send you this great way alone?"

"Mother's dead. I am older than I look."

The Captain, doctor, Stewardess and Mrs. Downey had been in conference. A girl belonging to no one and for the moment not even to herself had to be landed. It was a problem. Stewardess had volunteered to take me home with her for the week that she was in port and nurse me, but now I had waked up.

They carried me to the upper deck for air. We were lying in the Mersey, not landing our passengers till morning. The air revived me. Doctor said I might take the special boat train in the morning providing there was anyone going my way who would keep an eye on me. There was not, until Mrs. Downey made it her business and changed her route. She sent stewards scuttling with wires. Miss Green was to meet me at Euston. Just because a girl had her maiden name, Mrs. Downey made it her business to see I was delivered safe and sound into competent hands.

The ship's little Irish Doctor saw us comfortably tucked into our train. I heard Mrs. Downey say, "Then come on up, I'll give you a time."

The Doctor waved his cap.

I could not lie back resting, as Mrs. Downey wanted me to. We were skimming across the Old World—a new world to me—entirely different, pretty, small. Every time I looked at Mrs. Downey she was looking at me. Suddenly she said, "You're not a-goin' to that Amelia person. You're a-comin' to me."

"I'm promised to Miss Green, Mrs. Downey."

"She's no relative—bust the promise; I'll fix 'er! 'Twon't cost you nothin' livin' with me. You c'n go to your school, but nights and Sundays you'll companion my little daughter."

"Have you a daughter?"

"Same age as you—'flicted, but we'll 'ave good times, you an' me and my girl. That doctor chap is stuck on you. 'E tole me so. I was lookin' for company for my Jenny. . . . Only jest 'appened . . . 'er 'fliction. . . ." She choked . . . snuffled.

As we pulled into Euston's sordid outskirts of grime and factories the station's canopied congestion threw a shadow of horror over me.

"That white-pinched little woman has green in her button hole, Mrs. Downey."

"She's no gittin' you."

Her fingers gripped my arm as in a vice.

"Miss Green?"

The two women stared at each other belligerently.

"She's comin' to me—been sick—not fit to be among strangers, she isn't. I'm 'er friend."

"I'm promised, Mrs. Downey. My people expect it."

The wiry claw of the lesser woman wrenched me away so that I almost fell. I was clutched fiercely back to the scratchy sunburst, then released with a loud, smacking kiss.

"Any 'ow, come an' see my little girl . . . she needs . . . ," the woman choked and handing me a card turned away.

"Frightful person! The entire platform must have heard that vulgar kiss," gasped Miss Green.

"I was very ill on board; she was kind to me, Miss Green."

"You must never see her again, one cannot be too careful in London."

She glanced at the address on the card in my hand. "Brixton! Impossible!"

"I shall have to go just once to thank her, and to return

her umbrella. She gave it to me to carry while she took my heavier things."

"You can post the umbrella. I *forbid* you to associate with vulgar people while living in my house."

"I am going once."

Our eyes met. It was well to start as I meant to continue. I was only Miss Green's PG. My way, my life were my own: it wa' well she should understand from the start.

Aunt Amelia's PG House

LONDON was unbearable. August was exceptionally hot. Aunt Amelia lived in West Kensington—one of those houses in a straight row all alike and smeared with smug gentility. I felt the shackles of propriety pinch me before the door was shut.

The six PG's without one direct look amongst them disdainfully "took me in" at lunch. "Colonial!" I felt was their chilly, sniffy verdict. I hated them right away. Their hard, smooth voices cut like ice skates, "dearing" each other while they did not really like each other one bit. The moneyed snob who had the big front room swayed the establishment; next came the opulent Miss Oopsey, a portrait photographer who only "portrayed" titles. The PG's dwindled in importance till at the tail came Miss Green's niece, a nobody who was the snootiest of the lot and earned her keep by doing unnecessary things that were good form around the PG house.

London stewed, incorporating the hot murk into her bricks all day and spitting it out at you at night. The streets were unbearable. Everyone who could get out of London had got and were not missed. I used to wonder where any more population could have squeezed. Certainly if there were many more people in London they would have to ration air for the sake of fairness.

"Miss Green, is there any place one can go to breathe?"

"There are London's lovely parks."

"Just as crammed—just as hot as everywhere else!"

Miss Green clicked, "Dear me! You Canadians demand

a world apiece. I have offered to take you to Hyde Park, show you our titled people riding and driving, but no, you Canadians have no veneration for titles—jealously, I presume."

"I'll admit I do prefer cool air to hot celebrities, Miss Green. Now, about a breathing place?"

"Kew—if it is roots and bushes you want, go to Kew Gardens."

To Kew I went.

The great gates of Kew Gardens were plastered with many notices—"Nobody is allowed in these gardens unless respectably attired."—"No person may carry a bag, parcel, or basket into the gardens; all such impedimenta to be checked at the porter's lodge."—"No one may carry food into the gardens; tea may be procured in the tea-houses." —"You must not walk upon the grass, or run or sing or shout."

Striding past the lodge, clutching my bag, I walked down the main way and, turning into a woodsey path, began to sing. First hint of Autumn was in the air, there were little piles of dead leaves and fallen twigs burning, shreds of blue smoke wandered among the trees deliciously.

Kew was a bouquet culled from the entire world. I found South America, and Asia, Africa, China, Australia—then I found Canada (even to a grove of pines and cedars from my own Province). I rubbed their greenery between my hands—it smelled homey. I stabbed my nose on our prickly blue-pine. I sat down on the grass beneath a great red cedar tree. From close by came the long-drawn cry of a peacock. Suddenly I was back in the old barn studio! I threw up my chin and gave the answering screech which my peacock had taught me—my beauty on the old barn roof. I waited for an ejecting keeper, but my teacher had taught well, no keeper came. I went back to stuffy West Kensington refreshed, happy.

Again Miss Green in company with that swell who snobbed it over her PG's offered to conduct me to see the Hyde Park Parade. The "swell" boarders, Miss Green told me, always sat on penny chairs.—"Much more refined than to sit on a free bench, my dear," drawled Miss Green.

"I'd rather go to the Zoo," I replied and went.

Resignation if not content was in the eye of the captive creatures. Having once acquired a taste for the admiration and companionship of man animals like it. Here and there you saw a rebellious or morose newcomer furiously pacing, but most of the creatures were merry and all were well tended. All here looked more satisfied with life than the weary "great" looked in Hyde Park. I loved Kew.

St. Paul's

WESTMINSTER School of Art did not open until September. When I was a little rested, a little steadier, I climbed the curving little iron stairways at the backs of omnibuses and, seated above the people, rode and rode, watching the writhe of humanity below me. I had never seen human beings massed like this, bumping, jostling, yet as indifferent to each other as trees in a forest.

I puzzled, wondering. What *was* the sameness with a difference between a crowd and a forest? Density, immensity, intensity, that was it—overwhelming vastness. One was roaring, the other still, but each made you feel that you were nothing, just plain nothing at all.

History always had bored me. *Little Arthur's History of England* in its smug red cover—ugh, the memory of it! And now here before me was the smugness of it ossified, monumented, spotted with dates thick as an attack of measles. The English had heads twisted round onto their backs like drowsy ducks afloat, their eyes on what they had passed, not on what they were coming to.

Dickens had taught me far more about England than had *Little Arthur*. Dickens' people still walked the streets, lived in the houses of old London. Little Arthur's Great were shut up in dull books, battered monuments.

Deep in the City I happened one day upon Paternoster Row, a dark narrow little way lined with book shops. All the Bibles, prayer-books, hymnals in the world began life here. I saw them sprawled open at the fly-page. All the religious books that I remembered had had Paternoster Row printed inside them.

I did not, as Miss Green's other PG's did, attend some fashionable church in the West End. Sunday was the day on which I crept into London's empty heart. Everyone had gone from it, all business houses were closed. The lonely old churches were open but empty; all the light was pinched out of them by the grim huddle of business establishments. The old churches still had their bells, still rang them. Empty London threw back their clamour in echo. Often an entire congregation consisted of me, sitting under a very indifferent preacher, ushered in and out by a very pompous verger in a black robe almost as cleric as the clergy. My coin looked pitiful in the pompous collection-plate. Echo made the squeaky old parson's whisper hit back at you from every corner of the bare church.

London's national religion was conducted either in St. Paul's Cathedral, the heart of London's heart, or in Westminster Abbey in the West End. All immense events were solemnized in one or the other of these churches.

The business houses and shops of St. Paul's Churchyard fell back from the cathedral allowing it breathing space and sunshine. The steps up to her great doors were very, very wide. Beginning from each side of the steps was a circle of space encompassing the cathedral. It was lightly railed but the gates were flung wide, flowers and shrubs and benches were about and always there were people, sitting on the benches, eating things out of paper bags, feeding the pigeons and resting.

St. Paul's is the kernel of London as London is the kernel of England.

Westminster Abbey is beautiful too but rather historical and it was made a little cheap by sightseers who whispered and creaked. It had not the unity of St. Paul's; there were chapels here and chapels there—all sorts of pokes and juts, tablets, monuments and statues, "great ones" bouncing from niches and banners flapping. St. Paul's was domed under one immense central round. High, pale light flooded down; roll of organ, voice of chorister, prayer trembled upward.

Always there were people in St. Paul's standing, sitting, praying, or doing nothing, not even thinking, wanting only to be let alone.

At five o'clock each afternoon the great organ played, flooding the cathedral with music. The prayer-soaked walls came alive. Great, small, rich and shabby Londoners crept into St. Paul's to find sanctuary.

Sightseers climbed hundreds of steps to look down from a high gallery running round the inside of the dome. It was considered a thing to do, one of London's sights. I did not want to "sight-see" St. Paul's. The people moving up there in the high gallery were black spots in the mystery. I remained among the solid, silent company on the paved floor of the cathedral.

Letters of Introduction

TURMOIL, crowding, too many people, too little air, was hateful to me. I ached with homesickness for my West though I shook myself, called myself fool. Hadn't I strained every nerve to get here? Why whimper?

Aunt Amelia's mock-genteel PG's galled me at every turn—high-bridged noses, hard, loud, clear voices, veneering the cold, selfish indifference they felt for each other with that mawkish, excessive "dearing". My turbulent nature was restive to be at work; it made me irritable and intolerant. Miss Green suggested the British Museum as a sedative.

To the British Museum I went and loathed it—the world mummified. . . . No matter which turn I took I arrived back in the mummy-room, disgusting human dust swaddled in rags, dust that should have been allowed centuries back to build itself renewingly into the earth. The great mummy halls stank of disinfectants. Visitors whispered and crept. . . . Place of over-preservation, all the solemnity choked out of death, making curiosity out of it, prying, exposing, indecent.

Miss Green said, "The British Museum is marvellous, is it not, my dear?"

"It's disgusting!—Good decent corpses for me, Miss Green, worms wriggling in and out, hurrying the disagreeables back to dust, renewing good mother earth."

Aunt Amelia screeched, "My dear, you are revolting!"

Recoiling from mummies I turned to parsons. Our clergyman at home had given me two introductory letters to

93

brother clergy—his own particular brand—in London's suburbs. One had a fancy name, the other was Rev. John Brown who lived at and parished in Balham. Balham was two hours out of London by train. In the same suburb I had been commissioned by a Victoria widow to call on her well-to-do sister-in-law. The widow's husband had just suicided and left his family in difficult financial circumstances. I was to furnish the well-to-do "in-law" with the distressing particulars and hint at the straitened circumstances facing the widow.

The sister-in-law received me in a hideous drawing-room. She rustled with silk from the skin out, and served tea, very strong, together with plum cake as black and rich as bog-earth. She said, "To suicide was very poor taste, especially if you had not first made comfortable provision for your family."

Then at my request she directed me to the residence of the Rev. John Brown.

I meandered through paved suburban streets that called themselves "groves", and along "terraces" sunk below ground level, and "crescents" that were as straight as knitting needles.

A slatternly maid, very frilly as to cap and apron, said, "Wite 'ere," and took my letter into a room where tea cups clattered. After a pause the Reverend came out holding my opened letter. He snapped his reading glasses into their case and adjusted a dangling pince-nez to his nose and looked me over from hat to shoes.

"What is it you want me to do for you, young woman?"

I felt myself go scarlet.

"Nothing! Nothing at all, sir! I *had* to come because our home parson would have been mad if I hadn't! They'd have fussed if I had not promised—my people I mean."

I rushed towards the door.

"Stop!"

His roar was as if he were thundering "amen" over a huge congregation. Again he changed glasses, scrutinized me and re-read my letter.

"You'd better have a cup of tea and meet my wife."

He said it ponderingly as if wondering if I would pour my tea into the saucer and blow it.

"I have had tea, thank you."

"But you have not met my wife."

He gestured me into the drawing room with furious authority. A voice, submerged in the vagueness that comes of deafness, called, "John, dear, your tea is getting cold. I've sugared it."

"My dear," he waited for her to adjust the tin ear-trumpet and close her eyes against the impact of his bellow . . . "Canadian, my dear!"

His shout must have filled the trumpet to make her realize that I was standing in front of her. He took her hand and held it out, at the same time tapping the side of the trumpet sharply.

Mrs. Reverend Brown winced, her mild, kind eyes smiled into mine, while she prepared for me a cup of tea, lavishly sugared. The Reverend then began to fire statistic questions at me, roaring them in duplicate into the trumpet.

I did not know the population of Ontario, nor how many cases of salmon British Columbia shipped in export each year. He began to look suspicious, then bellowed his final test watching my face narrowly.

"You have heard my brother, the Reverend Samuel Brown, preach in Chicago?"

"I have never been in Chicago."

"What! So few cities of importance in America and not know Chicago! Every American should be familiar with such cities as they have."

"But I do not live in America. I am Canadian."

"Same thing, same continent!"

Now he *knew* I was an impostor.

"You have finished your tea?"

He rose, took my cup, glanced towards the door.

I rushed back to London, burned the balance of my letters of introduction.

Westminster Abbey—Architectural Museum

I WENT to Westminster to hunt up my Art School.

I was to become very familiar with Westminster Abbey because the Art School lay just behind it, being housed in the Architectural Museum in Tufton Street. There stood the richly magnificent Abbey stuffed with monumental history, then a flanking of dim, cold cloisters, after that the treed, grassed dignity of Dean's Yard and then you passed through an archway in a brick wall and were in Tufton Street. Here was the Architectural Museum, a last shred of respectability before Westminster plunged into terrible slum. In the Architectural Museum was housed the Westminster School of Art.

I climbed the Museum's grimy steps, pushed my shoulder against the heavy swing-door, entered a dark, lofty hall smelling of ossification—cold, deadly, deadly cold.

"Wat'cher wantin'?"

"I am looking for the Westminster School of Art."

"'Ere, but 'olidayin'."

The old janitor thumbed to a door up two steps, muttered, "Orfice" and lighted a gas jet over the door. Down the entire length of the hall was lying a double row of stone couches, on each of which was stretched a stone figure.

"Who are these?"

"Them is Great Uns, Miss."

The janitor's grim, dirty face went proud.

In the office I found Mr. Ford, the Curator, a white-bearded, tall old man, gentle, clean, too lovely for this grim setting. He smiled kindly, pen poised over his figuring.

"Yes?"

"Please, may I join the Art School?"

He reached for his enrolment book, wrote, "Emily Carr, Victoria, B.C. . . . English?"

"No, Canadian."

"Ah! Canadian, eh?"

His smile enveloped Canada from East to West, warming me. So few over here accepted Canada. These people called us Colonials, forgot we were British. English colonists had gone out to America with a certain amount of flourish, years and years ago. They had faded into the New World. Later, undesirable not-wanteds had been shipped out to Canada. It was hoped that America would fade them out too—all the west side of the earth was vaguely "America" to England. This courteous old gentleman recognized Canada as herself—as a real, separate place.

"How soon can I start work?"

"As soon as the class rooms open next Monday, Miss Hurry."

The Museum was lighted when I came out of the Office. A dreary young man in rusty black was drawing in a little black book propped against a stone dove on a shelf, bits of cornices, stone lilies, and saints with their noses worn off. Why must these people go on, and on, copying, copying fragments of old relics from extinct churches, and old tombs as though those were the best that *could ever* be, and it would be a sacrilege to beat them? Why didn't they *want* to out-do the best instead of copying, always copying what had been done?

I walked down the centre of the hall between the rows of stone sofas. I could not see the faces of the "Great Uns". The crowns of their recumbent heads were towards me. Some had stone hair, some hoods of stone, the heads of some were bald. It chilled one to see their bareness against stone pillows—hands crossed over stone bosoms, feet exactly paired, chipped old noses sticking up from stone faces, uncosy stone robes draping figure and sofa.

97

Except for the Curator, the Westminster Architectural Museum was grim.

Something smelly was very close. The janitor was "shooing" the dreary young man out. He held wide the heavy door, beckoned me and cupped his filthy paw for a tip. . . .

"Closing time!"

Fog was in dirty Tufton Street. I did not put a tip into the dirtier hand. He banged the door after me. Newton expected a tip for every nothing he did or did not do. That janitor was loathsome—my first experience of that type of cockney.

Life Class

WHEN school opened Monday morning at nine sharp I was at the Westminster School of Art. I went first to the Office, enquiring how I was to act. Mr. Ford took me up the broad stairway leading to the balcony off which our class rooms opened. There were two "life" rooms for women. Mr. Ford introduced me to the head student, a woman dour and middle-aged.

"Ever worked from life?" she snapped.

"Only portrait."

"It is usual for new students to work first in the Antique Class."

"I have had three years study in antique and still life at the San Francisco School of Art."

The head student gave a mighty snort, grunted, "Colonial" with great disfavour. She had not the right to place me. Mr. Ford had put me into the Life Class.

"Stars in the West bump pretty hard when they compete with civilized countries!" she said acidly. "Well, Professor will put you where you belong when he returns."

She proceeded to put numbers on a lot of pieces of paper. The students were about to draw for a place in class. I, being the new student, had the last number and therefore no choice.

Around the model throne were three rows of easels—low, higher and high.

"Pose!"

The curtains of a little recess parted, out stepped the model and took her place on the throne.

I had dreaded this moment and busied myself preparing my material, then I looked up. Her live beauty swallowed every bit of my shyness. I had never been taught to think of our naked bodies as something beautiful, only as something indecent, something to be hidden. Here was nothing but loveliness . . . only loveliness—a glad, life-lit body, a woman proud of her profession, proud of her shapely self, regal, illuminated, vital, highpoised above our clothed insignificance.

The confusion of re-assembly after the holidays stilled. Every eye was upon her as she mounted the throne, fell into pose. Every student was tallying her with perfection, summing up balance, poise, spacing, movement, weight, mood. Charcoal began to scrape on paper and canvas . . . swishing lines, jagged lines, subtle curve, soft smudge. Tremblingly my own hand lifted the charcoal—I was away, lost in the subtlety, the play of line merging into line, curve balancing curve.

"Rest!"

I could not believe the first forty-five minutes had gone. The model broke pose, draped a kimono round herself and sat on the edge of the platform to rest for fifteen minutes. Students too relaxed, moving from easel to easel looking— saying little. No one looked at my work nor spoke to me. I was glad; nevertheless I was chilled by these cold students. In California there was comradeship from the first day and kindliness towards the new student. I was glad to hear "Pose!", to see that serene creature, with trembling life in every inch of her, snap back into model queen of the room. Everything was for her. The notice on the outside of the door, "Life Class, Keep Out" was for her. Heat, light, hush —all were for her. Unprotected flesh made us tender, protective, chivalrous. Her beauty delighted the artist in us. The illuminated glow of her flesh made sacred the busy hush as we worked.

At four o'clock the model stepped down from her throne, rubbed tired muscles a little, disappeared behind the curtain, emerged ordinary, a woman clothed shabbily, all the beauty she had lent us hidden.

The professor did not return to his class for two weeks. I had but one fear during that time—would I be turned back into the Antique Class? His criticisms were gruff, uninspiring; however, he let me stay in the Life Class.

Mrs. Radcliffe

MRS. RADCLIFFE was the aunt of friends of ours at home. They did not give me a letter of introduction but wrote direct to her. They said to me, "Go and see Aunt Marion," and their faces sparkled at her mention. So, while waiting for school to open, I went.

"I've heard all about you from my nieces," she said and accepted me as you accept a letter from the postman. It may contain good. It may contain bad. There I was. She received me kindly but without demonstration.

Mrs. Radcliffe was a widow with one son who was almost middle-aged, a London lawyer. She was Scotch by birth and raising, had spent her married life in Canada, but by inclination she was pure London through and through. Almost her first question to me was, "And how do you like London?"

"I hate it."

Her brown, starey eyes popped, grew angry, were hurt as if I had hit her pet pup. She said, "Dear me, dear me!" four times. "London is the most wonderful city in the world, child!"

"It is stuffy, hard and cruel—Canada . . . is . . ."

"Canada!" biting the word off sharp, "Canada is crude!"

She spread her hands as if she would drip all memories of Canada from her fingertips.

"London will soon polish Canada off you, smooth you, as your English parents were smooth. You are entitled to that. Make the most of your opportunities in London, child."

"I am Canadian, I am not English. I do not want Canada polished out of me."

"Dear me! Dear me!" said Mrs. Radcliffe, shifting the conversation to her Canadian cousins and nieces. "Come to me whenever you want to, child; I am always home on Sunday at tea time."

We parted, feeling neither warm nor cold towards each other.

I went to Mrs. Radcliffe's most Sundays. It got to be a habit. She liked me to come and I liked going. Usually I stayed and went with Mrs. Radcliffe and her son, Fred, to Evening Service in Westminster Abbey, then back with them to supper. Son Fred saw me safely home. Fred was nearly twice my age. He was kindly—teased me about Canada. In his mother's presence he pretended to be all English. She had educated him so—English schools, Cambridge University, taking him back to England as a small boy at the death of her husband. Down deep Fred loved to remember his early boyhood in Canada. If he saw that I was dreary or homesick he would chatter to me about the woods and the Indians.

One night Fred said, "Tell me about that comic old Indian who threw a tombstone overboard at the spot in the sea where his brother was drowned."

I had been feeling morose at England, homesick for Canada that week. We all started to laugh at the Indian story. Suddenly Fred, looking at me, said, "Now I see why the Indians called you 'Klee Wyck'—means laughing one, doesn't it?" After that the Radcliffes always called me "Klee Wyck".

Mrs. Radcliffe's Sunday tea parties were always masculine for friends of Fred's. Mrs. Radcliffe never asked girls; occasionally she had an old lady, a contemporary of her own. She gave out plainly that she intended to share her son's affections with no woman during her lifetime. She never thought of me as a woman; besides, Fred liked girls stylish and very English. She was not afraid of his liking me.

Mrs. Radcliffe was my English backbone. Her kind, practical strength of character was as a pole to a vine. In all my difficulties I went to her.

Mrs. Radcliffe had a dainty, little old lady friend called Mrs. Denny, who also was a widow with a son a good deal younger than Fred. The two men were warm friends.

Mrs. Denny had three little white curls dangling in front of each ear and wore widow bonnets with long crêpe weepers dangling behind. She was fragile, pink and white, and lowest low Evangelical in religion. Mrs. Radcliffe leaned towards the High Church. The ladies never discussed degrees of ritual, but confined conversation to their sons and to London. Mrs. Denny was as rabid a Londoner as Mrs. Radcliffe. She was as anxious to see "son Ed" happily married before she died, as Mrs. Radcliffe was determined that her son Fred should remain a bachelor. The ladies put their heads together and decided that, with some taming down and brushing up, I would be all right as a wife for Ed Denny. The first thing to be done was so to fill me with London that I would be quite weaned from the crudities of Canada.

Mrs. Denny said to me, "My dear, you stick far too close to that Art School; confinement is telling on your health. Now I tell you what we will do. Every Thursday my daughter Loo and I will call at your school at noon, take you out to lunch; then we will spend the afternoon exploring London. You will come back to dinner with us and Ed will see you home."

"But my work, Mrs. Denny!"

"One afternoon a week will make no difference. There is more to be learned in life than Art."

"Art is what I came over to London for."

"Who knows, you may find love here, may never want to go back to Canada—"

"Oh, I hope not! I would not want that."

She kissed me, very fondly pinching my cheek. Then her fingers took hold of a little cornelian cross that I wore.

"Don't wear this as an ornament, child, it savours of R.C."

She never said "Roman Catholics" out loud, only whispered, "R.C." Once I saw her take a half-crown from her purse to tip a "Beef-Eater" who had conducted us round the Tower of London. Her hand was half out when the sun glinted on a little cross dangling from his watch chain. She slipped the half-crown back into her purse, substituted a shilling for it.

Under Mrs. Denny's guidance I saw a lot of London. She always carted a little red *Baedeker* under her arm with the "sight" we were "doing" marked by a slip of paper. We stood before the sight and read *Baedeker* and tried to memorize the date. The wretched part of these excursions was Ed's meeting us for tea. When we came out of the tea shops Loo and her Mother always took a quick, wrong turn on purpose, and left me alone with him for the rest of the time.

I would say, "Oh dear!" in dismay and start hunting them but Ed only laughed and said, "Don't worry, Mother knows her way about London as well as the nose on her face. They will be waiting at home." But it provoked me.

English women were horrid about this marrying business. They seemed to think the aim of every girl was to find a husband. Girl students "adored" their stuck-up, autocratic art masters, or their clergy or their employers. Men and women students did not work together in the Westminster Art School. I was glad. English husband-seeking girls shamed me.

Miss Green's PG's were all women—all silly. Shortly after I came to Miss Green's two men came up to London to see me. One was an Englishman from Liverpool whom I had met out in Canada. The other was the ship's doctor, an Irishman. The Englishman was a brother of Frank Piddington whom I had so detested as a child at home. Clifton had visited Frank in Canada. He did not ask me to marry him there, but came home to think it over and wasted a postage stamp on it. I could not have been more emphatic in saying, "No", but, as soon as he found I was in London, he came from his home in Liverpool to see how I looked in English setting. He sat very uncomfortably on the edge of a chair in Miss Green's drawing room. The PG's were all in a twitter.

When Clifton had got as red as he could get, he said, "Shall we go out and see some sights?"

Anything was better than that horrible drawing room, so I said, "That would be nice . . . what shall we see?"

"I have always had a hanker to see Madame Tussaud's wax works," said Clifton.

Off we went. We punched the real policeman, asked the wax policeman the way, tried to buy a catalogue from the wax dummy, watched the chest of the Sleeping Beauty hoist and flop. Then we came to the head of a dark little stair and a man asked us for an extra sixpence. Over the drop into a cellar was the notice, "Chamber of Horrors. Expectant mothers and nervous persons warned."

"Need we, Clifton?"

"Of course."

Sinking into that dim underworld was horrid. Red glistened and dripped from a severed head in the guillotine, King Somebody was lying in a bath of red ink, having cut his veins in suicide, Indians were scalping, murderers murdering, villains being villainous. Once outside again, even the dirty London air seemed pure.

"What next, Clifton?"

"Well, I thought—Euston Station?"

"Must you be going so soon?" I said politely.

"Not for several hours yet . . . want to see the engines— very newest models, you know."

I said, "Oh!"

Clifton was an engineer; engines were meat and drink to him. He ran from platform to platform patting the snorting brutes as they slithered panting into their places, calling them "beauties", explaining their internals to me.

"You sit here. There is the four-thirty special. I must see her—the very, very newest."

I sat down on a luggage truck while he ran and dodged and ducked. Then I saw him engage the engineer in conversation. They investigated every bolt and screw of the miserable thing. He came back exhilarated. "Going to let me ride home in the cab with him! Starts in an hour, time for tea first."

We went to an A.B.C. and ate crumpets.

"Good-bye!" His hand was clammy with excitement, he gasped, "Very latest model!"

He grabbed my hand.

"It's been splendid! . . . the Chamber of Horrors, the engines—you."

I was relieved. It was so delightfully plain that this was to be our final meeting.

The Irish doctor's ship was in port. The doctor came to London and to the Art School.

"Impatient young man downstairs in the Museum waiting to see our young Canadian." Mr. Ford smiled at me and gave my arm an affectionate little pat. "Young man unable to wait till the janitor was free. Ordered my old bones to run upstairs and fetch you at once."

He rubbed a rheumatic knee. Dear old man! Descending the stair we saw that the janitor's amble was unusually brisk. He came lashing his feather duster and glowering down the aisle between the architectural tombs. There sat the little Irish ship's doctor on the stomach of a "Great One", impatiently kicking his heels against its stone sofa.

"Oh, doctor, their stomachs are sacred, please don't!"

He jumped down.

"Shall we go into St. James's Park and sit on a bench? It is quite close."

It was a wide bench. The doctor sat down on one end and I on the other. Soon he was so close to my end of the bench that I fell off. I walked round the bench and sat down on its other end,—he did not look nearly so nice or nearly so well-bred in plain clothes. He was ill-at-ease too, trying to make conversation.

I said, "Don't they squabble?" meaning the sparrows

who, down in the dust, were having a battle over a crust. A dove swooped down and took the crust.

"Gentlest of all birds!—a dove—" sighed the doctor. He was slithering up the bench again.

"Doves squabble like the dickens," I replied.

The doctor said, "Your tongue is losing its Canadian twist; you have changed in these few months."

"I should hope so! Wasn't I flabby and ghastly? Let's walk."

I jumped up just as his hand touched my arm. We strode silent three times round the duckpond.

"What time is it?"—Being late for dinner is one of the unpardonable sins in England.

"Good-bye."

I held out my hand. He hurried South, I North, neither looked back. Was it his uniform, not he, that had been a little attractive? Perhaps doctors, too, prefer girls meek and sick.

But for that hint, I was grateful to the doctor. I was trying to speak more like the English, ashamed a little of what they ridiculed as my colonialisms. Bless you, doctor, for the warning! Unconsciously I'd tried to be less different from the other students,—I who had seen many Canadian-born girls go to England to be educated and come back more English than the English. I had despised them for it. I was grateful for the doctor's visit and I swore to myself I would go home to Canada as Canadian as I left her.

Mrs. Simpson's

ACROSS from the dim archway of the Architectural Museum was a tiny grocer shop owned and run by Widow Simpson, a woman mild-voiced and spare. The little shop was darkly over-shadowed in the narrow street by the Architectural Museum. Pinched in between the grey of the street and the black of the interior, goods mounted to the top of the shop's misty window, pyramids of boxes and cans which Mrs. Simpson sold across a brown counter under a flickering gas jet, sold to ragged children and draggled women who flung their money upon the counter with a coppery clank. Mrs. Simpson's trade was "penny". She handed goods to children unwrapped but for the "lydies" she wrapped in old newspapers. At the back of the little shop was a door with a pane of glass inset. This door led into Mrs. Simpson's "Tea-room for Students". Here students, who wanted an entire light meal or to supplement their carried lunches, hurried at noon across Tufton Street, hatless, hungry and in paint-spotted pinafores.

The small Tea-room was centred by a round table on which stood a loaf, potted meat, jam, apples, biscuits, cheese and butter cut into ha'penny portions. In the middle of the table stood a handleless delft cup. Business was run on the honour system. You ate a penny's worth, hurled a penny into the delft cup, ate another pennyworth and hurled in another penny. Anyone mean enough to cheat Mrs. Simpson was very low.

Mrs. Simpson trusted us about the food but not with her "cats and her kettles". On either side of the bars of the grate fire were black hobs and on them sat copper kettles. On the floor before the fire was a spread of cats, black, tortoise-shell and tabby, so close packed that they resembled an immense, heaving fur rug. No footgear but Mrs. Simpson's old felts could judge its placing among tails and paws. So Mrs. Simpson herself filled the great brown teapot over and over from the kettles. No one else was allowed to for fear they might scald a cat. When a kettle was empty Mrs. Simpson picked her way among students and cats to a tiny door in the corner and climbed two steps. On the first step she "shoo'd", on the second she "hist" and was answered by a concerted meowing. In her bedroom Mrs. Simpson kept special cats, along with the great jugs of fresh water drawn from some public tap in the district. The jugs were ready to refill the tea kettles and the cats to dart to alley freedom.

The Tea-room boasted two chairs and a stool. Mrs. Simpson usually lunched some dozen or more students. The first three got the chairs and stool, the next six sat on the floor, the remainder squirmed a foothold among the sitters and stood. It took planning to reach the food and to make sure it found its way into your mouth before some-body's elbow jogged and upset it.

The Tea-room window was never open. It looked into a small yard, piled with "empties". This place was the cats' opera-house and sports-field. It was very grimy, a vista of dim congestion, that filtered to us through a lace curtain, grey with the grime of London.

Mrs. Simpson's was a cosy, affectionate institution, very close to the Art School's heart. From Mr. Ford down to the last student every one spoke gently of the little, busy wo-man, faded, work-worn cockney. There was a pink ridge prominent above her eye-hollows. It was bare of eyebrows. Above the ridge was a sad-lined forehead. The general drag of her features edged towards a hard little walnut of grizzled hair, nobbed at the rounding of her skull.

Even in that slum setting there was something strong, good and kindly about Mrs. Simpson that earned our respect, our love. The men-students helped her "stock-take" and shamble through some crude form of book-keeping. When the chattering, paint-daubed mob of us pressed through the shop into the little back-room Mrs. Simpson's smile embraced us—her young ladies and gentle-men—as sober and as enduring as the Abbey's shadow. We were the last shred of respectability before Westminster slummed. The Abbey had flung us over the Dean's Yard wall into Tufton Street. Too poor for the Abbey, too respectable for the slum, the Architectural Museum and the art students hovered between dignity and muddle.

Leaving Miss Green's—Vincent Square

THE MAKE-BELIEVE gentility of Miss Green's Paying-Guest-House became intolerable to me. An injury received to my foot out in Canada was causing me great pain. Transportation from Miss Green's to the Westminster School was difficult and indirect. I made this my excuse to change my living quarters. Miss Green was terribly offended at my leaving her house. She made scenes and shed tears.

I took a room in a house in Vincent Square where two other Art School students lodged. One of these girls, Alice Watkin, was the girl in the school I liked above any other. The other student was the disagreeable head of the Life room. We three shared an evening meal in their sitting room. The disagreeable student made it very plain that I was in no way entitled to use the sitting room, except to eat the miserable dinner with them, sharing its cost. The room was dismal. It was furnished with a table, three plain kitchen chairs of wood, a coal-scuttle and a sugar basin. The sugar basin was kept on the mantelpiece. It was the property of "Wattie" and me who kept it full to help to work our puddings down. Because the disagreeable student was on diet and did the catering our meals were sugarless and hideous. Our grate fire always sulked. Old Disagreeable would often pour some of *our* sugar on the black coals to force a blaze.

Vincent Square was grimly respectable though it bordered on the Westminster slums. The Square lay just behind Greater Victoria Street. You could reach the Architectural Museum in an entirely respectable way by cutting through a little street into "Greater Victoria" which was wide, important and mostly offices. When you came to the Abbey you doubled back through Dean's Yard into Tufton Street and so to the Architectural Museum but this way was circuitous. The others always took it, but I cut through the slums because every saved foot-step spared me pain. The slum was horrible—narrow streets cluttered with barrows, heaped with discards from high-class districts, fruit having decay-spots, wilted greens, cast-off clothing. Women brushed their hair in the street beside their barrows while waiting for trade. Withered, unwashed babies slept among shriveled apples on the barrows.

I tried not to see too much slum while passing through. It revolted my spirit. Wattie said, "Don't go that way, Carlight"—that was always her name for me. When I came to the School motor-cars were just coming into use; they were fractious, noisy, smelly things. It was not a compliment to be called "Motor". Wattie had invented her own name for me. She never called me "Motor" like the others, always "Carlight"!

"Carlight," Wattie pleaded, "don't go through the slum! How can you!"

"Oh, Wattie, my foot hurts so!"

I continued to limp through the murk, odours, grime, depravity; revolting ooze, eddying in waves of disgustingness, propelled by the brooms of dreadful creatures into the gutters, to be scooped into waiting Corporation waggons dripping in the street.

One raw, foggy morning, as I hobbled along, a half-drunk street-sweeper brought his broom whack across my knees. They bent the wrong way, my bad foot agonized! Street filth poured down my skirt.

"'Ere you! Obstructin' a gent's hoccipation."

"Yer mucked the swell good, 'Enery," chuckled a woman.

"Let 'er look out, what 'er 'ere for, any'ow? Me, I'm a doin' of me dooty."

I boiled but dared not speak, dared not look at the

creature. I could have fought. I think I could have killed just then. Doubling over, the nearest I could to a run, I managed to get to the school cloak-room.

Wattie found me crying over the wash-basin swishing my skirt about in the water, crying, crying!

"Carlight!"

"I got muddied, Wattie."

She groaned, "That wretched foot!" She thought I had tripped. She finished washing the skirt, took it off to the fire to dry, draped a cover-all apron over my petticoat, took me into her arms and rocked. That was Wattie's way. When one was in great tribulation she faced you, crooned, wound her arms round and rocked from side to side. She was such a pretty girl and gentle; had it not been for that clear-cut hardness of English voice, I could have forgotten her nationality.

Wattie would never have cried from being muddied. She would have squared her chin, stuck her high-bridged nose in the air but she would have kept out of slums and not have got herself muddied to begin with. English girls were frightfully brave in their great cities, but when I even talked of our big forests at home they shivered just as I shivered at their big, dreadful London.

While I lived in Vincent Square I breakfasted in my own room. The view from my window was far from nice. I looked directly across a narrow yard into a hospital. Nurses worked with gas full on and the blinds up. I saw most unpleasant things. I could not draw my own blind or I was in complete black—my landlady cut the gas off at dawn. She went by the calendar, not the weather, and daylight was slow piercing through the fogs of Westminster.

The landlady got a notion.

" 'Ere's wot," she said. "You eat in my 'sittin' ' downstairs; save me luggin' up, cosy fer yous."

I breakfasted there once only. Her "sittin' " window looked into a walled pit under the street which was grated over the top. The table was before it. Last night's supper remnants had been pushed back to make room for my cup and plate. A huge pair of black corsets ornamented the back of my chair. There was an unmade bed in the room. The air was foul. The "sittin' " was reached by a dreadful windowless passage in which was the unmade bed of the little slatternly maid-of-all-work. I rushed back up the stair, calling to the woman, "I prefer to breakfast in my own room."

The woman was angry; she got abusive. I did not know how to tackle the situation, so, as was now my habit, I went to Mrs. Radcliffe, who immediately set out and found nice rooms near to her own. Wattie and I moved into them. Old Disagreeable remained in Vincent Square.

I could scarcely bear to put my foot to the ground. I had to stay at home, penned in dreariness, eating my heart out to be back at work. Wattie was away all day. London land-ladies are just impossible! Lodgers are their last resort. This woman had taken to drink. She resented my being home all day; there was no kindness in her. I had to have a mid-day meal. She was most unpleasant about it. She got drunk. With difficulty I hobbled to Mrs. Radcliffe. She was seated under an avalanche of newspapers when I burst in. The Boer War was at its height. Mrs. Radcliffe followed its every up and down, read newspapers all day.

Flopping onto the piano stool I burst into tears. "I can't bear it!"

Mrs. Radcliffe looked up vexed.

"What now, Klee Wyck! Dear me, dear me, what a cry-baby! Pull yourself together. A brisk walk is what you need. Exercise—exercise—That stuffy Art School!"

"My foot is bad. I *can't* walk."

"Corns? Nonsense, every one has *them*."

"It is not corns. Where is there a doctor? My foot will have to be cut off or something—I *must* get back to school."

"Doctor, fiddlesticks! You homesick baby! Stop that hullabaloo! Crying over a corn or two!"

The portière parted—there stood Fred. He had heard.

I nearly died of shame. He was never home at this hour. I had not dreamed he would be in the dining room.

"Mother, you are cruel!"

I felt Mrs. Radcliffe go thin, cold, hard. Hiding my shamed, teary face in the crook of my arm I slithered off the piano stool. Fred held the door for me, patted my shoulder as I passed out.

"Cheer up, little Klee Wyck."

I did not cheer. Afraid to face the drunk landlady I crawled to a bus, scrambled to its top somehow, got close to the burly, silent driver, rode and rode. The horses were a fine pair of bays. I watched their muscles work. At the end of the route I put fresh pennies in the box and rode back to the start. Back and forth, back and forth, all afternoon I rode. The jogging horses soothed me. At dusk I went home.

"Mrs. Radcliffe has been twice," Wattie said. "She seemed worried about you—left these."

She held up a beautiful bunch of the red roses with the deep smell Mrs. Radcliffe knew I loved so well.

"I don't want her old roses. I hate her, I am never going near her again. She is a cruel old woman!"

"She loves you, Carlight, or else she would not bother to scold. She thinks it is good for you."

Wattie rocked, dabbing the red roses against my cheek as she rocked. Something scratched my cheek. It was the corner of a little note nestling among the blooms.

"Come to dinner tonight, Klee Wyck."

"Wattie, d'you know what hell would be like?"

"Father does not like us to joke about hell, Carlight; he is a clergyman, you know."

"This is not a hell joke, Wattie, at least it is only London hell! London would be hell without you and without Mrs. Radcliffe. But I must hurry or I shall be late for Mrs. Radcliffe's dinner, and she'll scold all over again."

"Good old Carlight. I am glad you are going."

All the houses in Mrs. Radcliffe's street looked exactly alike. I hobbled up the steps I thought were Mrs. Radcliffe's. A young man came out of the door. He stepped aside—I entered. The door closed, then I saw I was in the wrong house. I could not open the door so I went to the head of the stair and rang a bell. A woman came hurrying.

"I got in by mistake, please let me out."

"That's your yarn is it, Miss Sneak-thief; tell it to the police."

She took a police whistle from the hook and put it to her lips; her hand was on the door knob.

"Wait, really, honestly! A man came out and I thought he was the lodger above Mrs. Radcliffe, next house. I ran in before he shut the door. I am going to dine with Mrs. Radcliffe. Please let me out quick. She hates one to be late."

"A likely story!"

"It's true."

She opened the door but stood in front so there was no escape. Taking a leap in the dark, I said, "You know Mrs. Radcliffe; she often sends you roomers. Please ask Mrs. Radcliffe before you whistle the police."

The woman paused, she did not wish to lose custom. My chance leap had been lucky. I had not really known which side Mrs. Radcliffe lodged her visitors. I knew only that it was next door. The woman let me out, but she watched, whistle to lips, till I was admitted to Mrs. Radcliffe's.

Dinner had just been brought up. Fred laughed when I told my story. Mrs. Radcliffe frowned.

"You always manage to jump into situations, Klee Wyck! My nieces don't have these experiences when they come to London."

"They are not Canadian, perhaps."

"Some are."

"But Eastern Canadians. I come from far, far West."

Mrs. Radcliffe smiled, gentler than I had ever seen her smile.

"I have made an appointment with my surgeon-cousin. He is going to have a look at that foot of yours tomorrow," she said.

THE DOCTOR found my foot had a dislocated toe, a split bone—results of an old injury. His treatment made no improvement.

"We will have to amputate that toe," he said. "I do not care to do it, though, without the consent of your home people; your general condition is bad."

"To write home and wait an answer will take so long, do it this afternoon. I want to get back to school. Please do it quick."

"Not so fast. The fact is I do not care to take the responsibility."

"It's my foot. I have no parents."

"Tell cousin Marion to come and see me," said the surgeon. Mrs. Radcliffe went.

"I will accept the responsibility," she told her cousin. "If that toe must come off, do it." To me she said, prefacing her words as usual with "dear me!"—"My cousin is a good surgeon. If he says amputation is best, it is. You don't mind, I suppose, don't feel sentimental over a toe?"

"Goodness no! I only want to get back to work."

"Of course a toe is not like your hand or head. I've told Cory to go ahead," said Mrs. Radcliffe.

The foot went wrong. I suffered cruelly. Every day Mrs. Radcliffe tramped clear across London in fierce heat to sit by my bed. She kept a vase full of red roses, velvety red ones with the glorious smell, always fresh by my bedside. She sat close, rocking in a rocker. The toe of her shoe struck the bed with every rock, each vibration was agony, but I would not cry out. I bit my lips and my cheeks were scarlet.

She said to the nurse, "Klee Wyck looks fine! Such bright colour! That foot must be doing splendidly!"

"She is suffering," said the nurse.

"Oh, well! The restless creature—doubtless she bangs that foot about all night."

I longed to yell, "Turn the cruel old thing out!" and yet, when Mrs. Radcliffe had gone, I turned my face into the pillow crying, counting the hours until she would come again. She was my strength; without her I was jelly.

Mr. Ford sent his daughter with flowers. Aunt Amelia Green came, wagging her pinched little head, saying, "I told you. . . . You should never have left my house. My Canadian nieces were the same—wayward."

Wattie had won her diploma. She was down in Cambridgeshire, at her Father's vicarage. She wrote, "Come to us, Carlight, the moment they will let you leave the nursing home. You will love the vicarage garden, the wonderful old church. I will take such care of you."

When Wattie left London I had moved to Mrs. Dodds' big boarding house for students.

The vicarage garden was a tangled wilderness, the church and vicarage tumbling down. The Vicar had passed his eightieth year and was doddery. He was, however, still possessed of a beautiful intoning voice, so the Church retained his services. Wattie from her seat in the choir, her sister from the organ bench, agonizingly watched their father. After the Vicar had filled the solemn old church with his voice, reading lessons and intoning the service, his strength was spent. Tottering up the pulpit stair, gasping out the text of his sermon, his eye roved vaguely over the congregation. A halting sentence or two, a feeble lifting of his arms to bless, the congregation was dismissed to its dinner.

But for the old man's prattle Sunday dinner in the

vicarage would often have been very sad. One after the other his three daughters taking me aside said, "Father ought to be retired," but, in the next breath, "Isn't his intoning voice rich and mellow?" They were proud of him, but the Church was not being fair to the congregation.

The vicarage garden was high-walled with red brick circled by venerable elm trees in which was a rookery. Daws and starlings chattered around the disused stable. The Vicar could not afford to keep a horse. He had an old gardener, an old cook, and an old nurse to maintain as well as himself and three daughters. The daughters helped to eke out the living expenses by teaching drawing and music and by running his house. The cook was too old to cook, the gardener too old to dig, the nurse too old to be bothered with children; besides, the vicarage nursery had been empty for the last fifteen years.

Wattie, scouring the unpruned rose bushes for a house posy, said to me, "Our gardener is beyond work, besides which he is lazy and drunken."

"Why don't you sack him?"

"Carlight! Sack an old servant! In England servants remain with us until they die."

"What do they do?"

"Cook can still peel potatoes. The gardener sweeps up the paths, when he is not too drunk to hold the broom. Nurse dusts the nursery and makes our underwear all by hand."

"Can't she run a sewing machine?"

"Our family wearing machine-made body linen! Oh, Carlight!"

"Dozening hand stitches when you could million better, stronger ones by machine! Life's too short! Come to Canada, Wattie."

"Canada! Why, Carlight? England is the only place in the whole world to live."

"Your brothers have all gone abroad, haven't they?"

"Men are different, more adventurous. The world needs educated Englishmen. All my seven brothers went to college. It meant pinching a bit at home. They have all done so well for themselves in the Civil Service—India, China . . ."

"Why don't they do a bit for you girls now, make up for your pinch? Why should everything be for the boys and men in England?"

"Mother brought us up that way—the boys first always. The boys have wives now."

"I'm glad I'm Canadian! I don't like your English ways, Wattie!"

"Being English is my greatest pride, Carlight."

A narrow, walled way led from the side door of the vicarage to the church vestry, a sombre interlude in which to bottle secular thoughts and uncork sacred. Through a squeaky, hinged gate you could pass from vicarage garden to churchyard, from overgrown, shady green to sunny, close-clipped graves. Some of these had gay posies snuggled to the tombstones. Some stones staggered and tipped, almost as if they were dancing on the emerald turf. Everything was so sombre about the vicarage and church it made the graves seem almost hilarious. Gaiety accompanied you through the churchyard, but, at the threshold of the church the merry spirit fell back into the sunlight, sky, air of the graveyard. The church was too dead, too dreary for that bright spirit. It belonged to life, to perpetual living.

"Rebellious Carlight!" Wattie would say, with a shake of her head, and a few swaying rocks to my shoulders. "Rebellious little Carlight!"

There had been moments when I nearly envied Wattie's uneventful calm at Art School. We worked easel-to-easel. Wattie's work was stable, evenly good. Sometimes my work was better than hers, sometimes worse. She neither lifted nor sank. She had enough South Kensington certificates to paper the Vicarage. I had none. She knew Art History from the Creation to now. She knew the Elgin Marbles and the National Gallery, the South Kensington Museum, all the art treasures of London. She knew the anatomical structure of the human body, bone for bone. She stepped with reverent tip-toeing among the stone couches of the "Great Ones" in the Architectural Museum, but neither our Art nor our hearts had anything in common other than that we loved one another deeply. Each went her own way unfalteringly, staunch to her own ideals. When our ideals clashed, each jumped back into silence, because we wanted to keep both our friendship and our own opinion.

Kicking The Regent Street Shoe-Man

MRS. RADCLIFFE'S surgeon cousin advised a surgical support in my shoe.

"I will take her to my own shoe-man in Regent Street," said Mrs. Radcliffe and off we went.

My foot was very sore, very painful to the touch, for a long time after the operation.

I said to the fitter, "Do not handle the shoe when it is on my foot, I will put it on and off myself."

It was a very swell shop. The clerks were obsequious, oily tongues, oily hair, oily dignity and long-tail black coats like parsons. Our salesman was officious, he would persist in poking, prodding, pressing the shoe to my foot in spite of my repeated protests.

At last angry with pain, I shouted, "You stop that!"

Mrs. Radcliffe explained to him that I had recently had an operation on my foot which had left it tender. The man still persisted in pinching; after he had forced about seven squeals out of me, I struck with the well foot giving the princely creature such a kick square amidships that he sprawled flat and backwards, hitting his head against a pile of shoe boxes which came clattering down on him spreading him like a starfish. Every customer, every clerk in the store paused in consternation while the enraged shoeman picked himself up.

"Klee Wyck!" gasped Mrs. Radcliffe.

"Well, he would persist when I told him not to," I cried. "Serves him right!"

I dragged on my old shoe by myself and we left the

shop, Mrs. Radcliffe marching in stony, grim quiet while I limped beside her, silent also.

We waited for our bus, standing among all the Oxford Circus flower women on the island. The flowers were gay in their baskets, the women poked them under our noses, "Tuppence-a'penny a bunch, lydy! Only tuppence!"

"Um, they do smell nice, don't they, Mrs. Radcliffe?"

Mrs. Radcliffe's thoughts were back in the Regent Street shoe shop.

"Thirty years," she moaned, "I have dealt there! Dear me, dear me! I shall never be able to face those clerks again."

Our bus jangled up to the curb. We got in. I knew I was not a nice person. I knew I did not belong to London. I was honestly ashamed of myself, but London was . . . Oh, I wanted my West! I wasn't a London lady.

Are You Saved?

I TOOK my letter from the rack and read it while waiting for Mrs. Dodds, my landlady, to finish totting up a long row of figures. I liked going down to pay my weekly board. Mrs. Dodds' office was cosy, she was kindly. She knew London like a book and could tell every one of her fifty lady-student boarders all they wanted to know about everything and every place in the world.

"I won't!" I exclaimed, reading down the page. Mrs. Dodds looked up from her figuring.

"Won't what?"

"Pay a snob-visit in Upper Norwood over the week-end. I don't know the people."

"The Handel Festival is being held this week; it is in the Crystal Palace which is at Upper Norwood. Probably that is why your friends are inviting you down. Don't miss a treat like that, child."

"They are not my friends, I've never seen them. My sister did the woman a kindness when she was ill out in Canada. The woman thinks she ought to pay back."

"Well, let her.—Why not?"

"She does not owe me anything. They have money. I refused to bring over a letter of introduction to her. I won't have anybody feel they have got to be good to me because my sister was good to them. They don't owe me a thing!"

"Take all the fun that comes your way, don't be stupid. That foot operation has taken it out of you. Go, have a good time."

"I'd like to hear that festival all right!"

On reconsidering, I wrote, "I've had an operation on my foot. I still limp. If you will excuse a limp and a soft shoe, I would be pleased, etc. . . ."

I loathed the snoopy little woman with boiled-goose-berry eyes from the moment I saw her peering down the platform looking for something resembling my sisters. She knew all about my foot and that I was just out of nursing home—my sister had written her. They had corresponded ever since they met in Victoria.

"I suppose you can walk? It is only one mile."

"No, I am afraid I cannot."

"Then shall I call you a cab?"

She made it plain that it was *my* cab. When we got to her gate she turned her back till I had paid the cabby.

"You do not look the least like any of your sisters."

"So I believe."

They were people of very considerable means. On the way from the station she told me that her son had been in the Boer War. He got enteric. The whole family—father, mother, three sisters and the son's fiancée—had gone out to South Africa to bring him home. They were just back.

"It was such a nice little pleasure jaunt!"

That was the scale on which these people could afford to do things. Six passages to Africa cost a great deal of money!

All the way in the cab she had stared at me.

"No," she said, "I see no resemblance whatever. Three fine women—if ever there are fine women outside . . ." She stopped to consider and added, "Three Godfearing, fine women."

She led me into a tasteless, chapel-like, little drawing room, its walls plastered with framed texts and goody-goody mottos.

"Put your foot up!" indicating a hard shiny sofa in an alcove. As soon as I was settled, she drew a chair to the side of the sofa, also arranged a small table on which stood an aspidistra plant, that beastly foliage thing so beloved of English matrons, because it requires no care, will thrive in any dingy room. English boarding houses always have aspidistras. I think it is the only growing plant that I loathe; it is dull, dry, ugly. When the woman had securely barricaded me into the alcove by her disagreeable self and the hateful plant she turned full upon me her gooseberry-green stare, scummed over the green with suspicion, mistrust and disappointment.

Again she stabbed, "You differ from your family." Then in a voice, harsh, hateful, cruel, "Are you saved?"

Quite taken aback I faltered, "I ... I ... don't know..."

"That settles the matter, *you are not!* I know that I am saved. I know that my entire family—myself, my husband, our three daughters, my son, my son's fiancée—all are saved, thank God!"

She rolled her eyes over the aspidistra, as if she pitied the poor thing for not being included in family salvation.

The door opened, in marched her three daughters, two stumpy, one lank. Behind them came a maid carrying the tea tray. All the girls had strong, horsey, protruding teeth like their mother. Introductions followed. I was so shaken by my sudden shove into damnation that, not being yet fully recovered from my illness, tears came. I had to wink and sniff during the introductions to the daughters. For five minutes nobody spoke; strong, white teeth chewed insufficiently buttered muffins, hard lips sipped tepid tea. I did the same. The silence got unwelcome. I wanted to reinstate myself after my lack of self control. Mama was obviously upset that my salvation had been interrupted by tea. She drank three cups silently and straight off in long earnest gulps. Looking out of window, I cried, "Oh, is that the roof of the Crystal Palace glittering over there?"

"Yes."

"That is where the Handel Festival is being held, is it not?"

"Yes."

"Have you seen Beerbohm Tree in *Henry the Eighth?* I was taken last night, it was simply splendid!"

127

Silence.

"I heard the *Elijah* in Albert Hall last week. The vast enclosed empty space made me feel quite queer when we first went into the hall. Does it make you feel that way?" I turned to the lean daughter as being most human.

"No."

The girl was fingering the harmonium in the centre of the drawing room.

"Are you fond of music?" I ventured, and from Mama, in a tornado burst, came, *"Our music* is hymns at home. Of that, yes! Of concerts, theatres, NO! We are Christians."

"But . . . the *Elijah,* the *Messiah,* are sacred," I faltered.

"Sacred! The worst music of all! What do those professionals think of as they sing? Their own voices, their own glory, not the glory of God. We are Christians. We would not attend such performances."

A hymn book fell off the harmonium. Did I see the lean daughter's foot steal towards it as if she would kick it under the instrument? Mama stooped and replaced the book on the harmonium.

"I am very tired," I pleaded. "May I go to my room and rest a little?"

The lean daughter showed me the way, but she did not speak.

Next morning a letter was passed round at breakfast. The lean daughter tossed it across the table to Father when she had read it.

The eldest daughter remarked, "What luck, dear Mama!"

"Providence, not luck, my child!"

The lean daughter scowled and Mama announced, "Brother Simon and Sisters Maria and Therese will be with us for luncheon." Turning to her son, "It is my wish that you be here for lunch, my son. Brother Simon and the Sisters will wish to see you and ask about Africa."

In an aside the lean daughter whispered in my ear, "Relatives by faith, not by blood!"

"Certainly I will be present, dear Mama," said the son of the house.

Faint and chill the door bell tinkled under the hand of Brother Simon at noon. It was as if the pull were frozen by Brother's touch, but the maid heard and admitted. Mama left the drawing room; there were whisperings in the hall, whisperings that chilled me but made my ears burn. I was introduced. Six eyes tore me as a fox tears a rabbit.

"Let us pray," said Brother Simon, lifting fat red hands —the finger nails were very dirty. We all flopped where we were and ducked our noses into the seats of the chairs. My chair was in the bay window close to the street. I felt as if I were "praying on a housetop". I was sure passers-by could hear Brother's roar. At every footstep I peeped to see how pedestrians were taking it. Suddenly I heard my own name bellowed by Simon. He was explaining me to God as "the stranger within our gates". He told God mean things about me, such personal things as made me feel almost as if I were eavesdropping. He told God that I came of religious stock but that I was rebellious. I felt my face was crimson when I got up from my knees.

The maid was in the doorway waiting to announce lunch. She looked very sorry about something, either a beastly lunch or my sins.

The lunch was certainly dreadful. The three visitors bragged how they had defied nurses and doctors to crawl to the bedsides of dying men in Africa for a last remonstrance with them about their sins. They discussed fallen soldiers with the son of the house.

"Was he saved?"

"No, no! I said a few words but I fear. . . ." Not one of those dead soldiers did Brother Simon credit with being saved or deserving to be.

At last lunch was over. The three trailed drearily away; they were booked for a religious meeting. All embraced Mama and the girls effusively. I'd have done them a damage had any of their kisses attacked my cheek. Brother took my hand in a clammy grip. One of his hands below mine, the other on top, was like being folded between raw kippers. "I shall," he said, "continue to pray for you, my child!"

"Thank you, dear Brother," murmured Mama. The kippers fell apart, releasing me.

The lean daughter's hand slipped through my arm, her whisper was directed straight into my ear. "Brother and Sisters by faith, *not* by blood, thank God!"

Queen Victoria

ONE DAY when Wattie and I were crossing Leadenhall Street we were halted by a Bobby to let a carriage pass. The wheels grazed our impatient haste. We looked up petulantly into the carriage and our eyes met those of Queen Victoria, smiling down on us.

Chatter ceased, our breath held when Her Majesty smiled right into our surprised faces. She gave us a private, most gracious bow, not a majestic sweeping one to be shared by the crowd. The personal smile of a mother-lady who, having raised a family, loves all boys and girls. The carriage rolled on. Wattie and I stared, first after the carriage, then at one another.

"Carlight—the Queen!"

How motherly! was my impression. The garish, regal chromos on Mrs. Mitchell's walls had been Queens only. This kindly old lady in a black bonnet was woman as well as Queen.

Wattie had never before seen the Queen close. She had been only one of a bellowing multitude watching her pass. She was tremendously excited.

Having just won her final South Kensington teaching certificate she was tip-toey anyhow and she was going out to a married brother in India for a year. I had moved to Mrs. Dodds' big boarding house for students in Bulstrode Street. Wattie had run up to London to bid me goodbye.

Mrs. Radcliffe, surrounded by the daily newspapers,

was as near tears as I could imagine her being. Mrs. Denny opposite was openly crying, curls bobbing, handkerchief mopping, the delicate little face all puckered. In the students' boarding house all was silent, the usual clatter stilled. London had hushed, England was waiting and Queen Victoria lay dying. Bulletins were posted every hour on the gates of Buckingham Palace. We stole out in twos and threes all through the day to read them. The ones at home looked up on our return, saw there was no change, looked down again. Every one was restless. Fräulein Zeigler, the German, at present cubicled in our room in Bulstrode Street, was retrimming her winter hat. From his moth-ball wrappings she took a small green parrot with red beak and glassy eyes. Smoothing his lack-lustre plumage she said, "So, or so, girls?" twisting the mangy bird's stare fore, then aft. Advising heads poked out between cubicle curtains. Nobody's interest in the German woman's hat was keen.

"Extry! Extry! 'Er Majesty gorn!" shrilled the news-boys. Everyone took a penny and went out to buy a black-bordered "Extry". Then they read the bulletin posted on the gate which said,

> "Osborne, January 23, 1901.
> My beloved Mother has just passed away, surrounded
> by her children and grandchildren.
>
> Signed 'Albert Edward'."

The following morning, passing through St. James's Park on my way to school, I was halted for a passing carriage. In it sat the new, uncrowned King—Edward VII. He looked sad and old. When they had said to him, "The Queen is dead. Long live the King!" he had replied, "It has come too late!"

I remarked to Wattie, "Queen Victoria might have sat back and let Edward reign a little before he got so old."

"Carlight! It is poor taste to criticize England's Queen, particularly after she is dead."

"She was our Queen too, Wattie. All the same, I do not think it was fair to Edward."

London completely blacked herself. It was ordered so. Shops displayed nothing but black, lamp posts and buildings draped themselves in black rag which fog soon draggled. Bus-horses wore crêpe rosettes on their bridles. Black bands were round the drivers' arms, cab and bus whips floated black streamers. Crêpe was supremely fashionable. The flower women couldn't black the flowers so they favoured white and purple varieties, ignoring the gay ones. Dye-shops did a roaring trade; so many gay garments visited them and returned sobered. The English wallowed in gloom, glutted themselves with mourning.

On the first black Sunday Marie Hall, a young violinist in our house, asked to come to service in the Abbey with me. Young Marie, sure of herself since Kubelik had kissed her and told her she was the prodigy of the day, had just bought a new hat—bright cherry. "I don't care. It's my only hat; I shan't black it."

Instead of sitting in her usual seat beside me, Mrs. Radcliffe crossed to the far side of the Abbey. After service she whispered coldly in my ear, "How could you, Klee Wyck! The whole loyal Abbey blacked—that screaming hat!"

"Can I help it, Mrs. Radcliffe, if an English girl won't kill her hat in honour of her dead Queen?"

In the boarding-house Fräulein angrily removed the green parrot. "I don't see why I should," she grumbled, rolling "Polly" back in his moth-ball wrappings, slapping a black bow in his place and sulking under it.

The funeral preparations were colossal. Every Royalty in Europe must be represented. Mouse-like queens no one had ever heard of came creeping to the show—and Kaiser William with his furious moustachios! Hundreds of bands throbbed dead marches, the notes dragging so slow one behind another the tune was totally lost. London's population groaned and wept.

I did not want to go to the Queen's funeral procession —Little Kindle, my cubicle neighbour in the new boarding house, begged, "Come on, you may never see such another."

133

We rose at five; at six we took position in the Piccadilly end of St. James Street, front row. The procession was not due till eleven. In one hour we had been forced back to the sixth row by soldiers, police and officials who planted themselves in front of us. In defiance of the law, I carried a little camp-stool, but by the time I was sitting-tired the crowd was too tight to permit my doubling to sit. You could not even raise an arm. St. James Street had a gentle rise, the upper crowd weighted down on those below. Air could only enter your mouth, you were too squashed to inflate. Each soul was a wedge driven into a mass as a tightener is forced into an axe handle.

Those with seats reserved in upper windows along the route came much later than the crowd. Police tore a way for them through the people. The seat-holders hanging on to the Bobby, the crowd surged into the gap to better their position. They fought tooth and nail.

"Kindle!"

She half-turned, looked, groaned, pounded a Bobby on the vertebrae, said, "My friend, get her out quick, Bobby."

"Way there! Lydy faintin'!" shouted the policeman.

A great roaring was in my ears—then nothing. I recovered, draped over an area railing in a side street. I was very sore, very bruised.

"My camp-stool, Kindle?"

"Back among the legs—rejoicing in the scoop it took out of my shin. I told you not to bring the thing!"

She bound a handkerchief round her bloody stocking.

"Come on," she growled.

"Home?"

"Not after we have waited this long! The Mall, it's wide; hurry up!"

I dragged. I know exactly how a pressed fig feels.

I saw a corner of the bier, Kindle saw the Kaiser William's moustachios. Oh, the dismal hearing of those dead-march bands, which linked the interminable procession into one great sag of woe, dragging a little, old woman,

who had fulfilled her years, over miles of route-march
that her people might glut themselves with woe and souse
themselves in tears on seeing the flag that draped the
box that held the bones of the lady who had ruled their
land.

English Spring

THE WESTMINSTER Art School closed for a short Easter recess, when I had been nine months in London, nine months of hating the bustle, the crowd, the noise, the smell.

I said, "Mrs. Radcliffe, is there a little village that you know of where I could go and be in real country?"

"There is the village of Goudhurst in Kent. It has a comfortable Inn; I have stayed there myself."

There was another student in the school who came from Victoria. She decided to come to Goudhurst for the holiday, too.

The village was a tiny sprawl of cottages on the top of a little hill. We were met and wavered up the Goudhurst Hill by the Inn's ancient host and his more ancient horse and chaise. The village was all of a twitter because tomorrow the Butcher's daughter was to marry the Baker's son. Everyone was talking of the coming event.

The Inn parlour was low-ceiled, and beamed. There was a bright fire on the open hearth and its glow pinked the table cloth, the teacups, and the cheeks of our host and hostess, who were garrulous about the wedding.

My bedroom was bitterly cold, the bed felt clammy with damp. I woke to a sharp spring rain next morning, but the sky did not want to wet the wedding, clouds scuttled away and soon the sun shone out. Villagers swallowed hasty breakfasts and hurried with flowers to decorate the church which was just across from the Inn.

I too hurried across the churchyard but not to the wedding. I saw a wood just beyond the graves. There was a stile across the graveyard fence. Thrushes, blackbirds, every kind of song bird was shouting welcome. From the centre of the graveyard two larks rose up, up—wings and song twinkling. The notes scattered down to earth clear as rain drops. I sat one moment on top of the stile. The church bells began to peal such a merry jangle. They must have seen the bride coming down the village street and were reporting to the people. Dog carts, pony carts, chaises from all over the neighbourhood nosed up to the church-yard fence, dogs barked, a donkey brayed—long, derisive, melancholy brays. I climbed over the stile. The gravestones were blackening with sitters waiting the bride.

I heard enough churchbells, saw enough people in London. I pressed hurriedly into the wood, getting drenched by the dripping greenery. Deeper, deeper I penetrated among foliage illuminated by the pale, tender juices of Spring. There were patches of primroses pale as moon-light, patches of bluebells sky colour, beds of softest moss under my feet. Soon my feet were chilled and wet.

"Cuckoo, cuckoo!" Live throats uttered the call I had heard voiced only by little wooden painted birds connected with a mechanical apparatus, unmannerly birds who shrieked "cuckoo!", burst open a door in the front of the clock and slammed it shut again. Violent little birds!

"Oh, London! Oh, all you great English cities! *Why* did you do this to England? Why did you spoil this sublime song-filled land with money-grabbing and grime?"

Baby daffodils hooked the scruffs of their necks up through the moss under my feet; those whose heads were released from the moss were not yet bold enough to nod. Spring was very young. I was so happy I think I could have died right then. Dear Mrs. Radcliffe, I loved her for directing me to Goudhurst. I would gather a big boxful of bluebells, primroses and daffodils, post them for her Easter in London. Oh, the spring smells! The lambs bleat-ing in the field beyond the graveyard! The shimmer of the greenery that was little more than tinted light! How ex-quisite it all was! How I hated to go back to London!

I burst in on Mrs. Radcliffe, reading the war news as usual.

"Mrs. Radcliffe! Oh, oh, oh!"

"You like our English Spring, Klee Wyck?"

Mrs. Radcliffe was not a kissy person. I was shy of her, but I could not help what I did. I attacked from behind her chair. Her cheek was not soft, nor used to being kissed —my hug knocked her hat crooked.

"Dear me, dear me!" she gasped. "What a—what a 'Klee Wyck' you are, child!"

My Sister's Visit

I HAD BEEN a year in England when my favourite sister came from Canada to visit me.

Wild with excitement I engaged rooms in the centre of the sightseeing London. Houses and landladies had to be approached through a rigorous reference system of Mrs. Radcliffe's. I pinned my best studies on the wall of the rooms, thinking my sister would want to see them.

She came in the evening. We talked all through that night. At five a.m. my senses shut off from sheer tiredness. My last thought was, "She will want a pause between travel and sightseeing."

At seven the next morning she shook me.

"Wake! What sight do we see today?"

"Won't you want to rest a little after travel?"

"The trip was all rest. I am a good traveller."

We started off. She entered the sights in her diary every night—date, locality, description.

At the end of a week I remarked, "Not interested in my work, are you?"

"Of course, but I have not seen any."

"I suppose you thought these were wallpaper?" pointing to my studies on the wall. My voice was nasty. I felt bitter. My sister was peeved. She neither looked at nor asked about my work during the whole two months of her visit. It was then that I made myself into an envelope into which I could thrust my work deep, lick the flap, seal it from everybody.

Martyn

MARTYN came all the way from Canada to London just to see me and with him he lugged that great love he had offered to me out in Canada and which I could not return. He warned of his coming in a letter, carefully timed to be just too late for me to stop him even by wire. For I would have pleaded, "Dear Martyn, please don't come."

I had been spending the long summer holiday with friends in Scotland. I got his letter there. I had been on the point of returning to London, but, on receipt of that letter, I dallied. It made me unhappy. I wanted time to think.

Martyn got to London first. He was on the platform at Euston waiting for me, had been in London for three days rampaging round, nearly driving my landlady distracted by his frequent—"Have you heard anything of her yet?"

But Martyn on the platform at Euston Station was like a bit of British Columbia, big, strong, handsome. I had to stiff myself not to seem too glad, not to throw my arms round him, deceiving him into thinking other than I meant. He gave me all sorts of messages from everybody at home. Then he searched my face keenly.

"How tired you look!"

"I am, Martyn; please take me straight home."

In the cab we were silent. On my doorstep he said, "What time tomorrow?"

"I am meeting Mrs. Radcliffe at the Abbey door at five to eleven—join us there."

He frowned. "Must she be along? Must anyone but you and me?"

"Mrs. Radcliffe and I always sit together in church. She is fine—you will like her."

Mrs. Radcliffe and Martyn impressed each other at once. Martyn was Canadian born but his parents had raised him ultra-English. After service Mrs. Radcliffe, with a coy smile and one or two "dear me's", left us, taking her way home by a route entirely different to the one that was her habit.

"Goodbye, children!" I don't know how many "dear me's" her eyes twinkled as she said it.

"Bring your friend in to tea with me this afternoon, Klee Wyck." In one of her piercing, tactless whispers she spilled into my ear, "Poor Eddie!"

Martyn and I were alone, Mrs. Radcliffe's back fading down Great Victoria Street.

Martyn asked, "Who is Eddie?"

"The friend of Mrs. Radcliffe's son, Fred."

Martyn frowned. We walked along quiet and stupid.

After lunch Martyn called for me and we went to Kensington Gardens and got things over, sitting uncomfortably on a bench near the lake side. Everywhere was black with children and their nurses. The children sailed boats on the lake and shrieked. The roar and rumble of London backgrounded all sounds. I was glad of London's noise that day and of her crowds.

Martyn had three months' leave. I undertook to show him London. Mrs. Denny and Eddie, Mrs. Radcliffe and Fred, as well as my many solitary pokings round the great city, had made me an efficient guide. Every day at four o'clock I found Martyn ambling among the tombs of the "Great Ones" down below our workrooms at the Architectural Museum, his eyes always directed to the doors leading off the upper balcony of the great hall, closed doors behind which we studied. From his office old Mr. Ford gave us a kind smile as we passed, politely amused smiles but never objectionable nor coy like the ones English ladies and the students lipped at you when they saw you with a man.

I showed Martyn every sight I thought would interest him. We went to the theatres. Martyn liked Shakespearian plays best, but it did not matter much what the play was, whenever I took my eyes off the stage I met Martyn's staring at *me*.

"What's the good of buying tickets!" I said crossly— "you can see my face for nothing any day." He asked me on an average of five times every week to marry him, at my every "No" he got more woebegone and I got crosser. He went to Mrs. Radcliffe for comfort and advice. She was provoked with me about Martyn, she kept his time, while I was at school, divided between intercession services and sentimentality. I wished she would tell him how horrid, how perverse I really was, but she advised patience and perseverance, said, "Klee Wyck will come round in time."

We used to go to tea at the Radcliffes' every Sunday afternoon, stay on and go with her to the Abbey for evening service. One night Mrs. Radcliffe and I were putting on our hats in her bedroom. She returned unexpectedly to the sitting room for her scarf and surprised Martyn on his knees before the fire warming my cloak. He was patting the fur collar as if the thing were a live kitten. Mrs. Radcliffe was delighted.

"Dear me! So romantic, Klee Wyck! Don't be a fool, child!"

"He's a silly goat!" I snapped.

Ever after that night, when Mrs. Radcliffe spoke to me of Martyn, she called him the Knight of the Cloak.

Martyn and I had one perfect day during his stay in London—the day we went to Epping Forest. For a long, long day Martyn promised me that he would not *ask* that day. You could depend on Martyn to keep his promises.

First we pretended that Epping Forest was our Canadian woods, but it was no good, there was not one bit of similarity. We gave up and sipped England's sweetness happily. Here were trees venerable, huge and grand but tamed. All England's things were tame, self-satisfied, smug and meek—even the deer that came right up to us in the forest, smelled our clothes. There was no turmoil of undergrowth swirling round the boles of the trees. The forest was almost like a garden—no brambles, no thorns, nothing to stumble over, no rotten stumps, no fallen branches, all mellow to look at, melodious to hear, every kind of bird, all singing, no awed hush, no vast echoes, just beautiful, smiling woods, not solemn, solemn, solemn like our forests. This exquisite, enchanting gentleness was perfect for one day, but not for always—we were Canadians.

We hired a pony and cart and drove through the straight *made* roads of the forest, easy, too easy. Soon we returned the pony and went on foot into the forest's lesser ways. Here greenery swished against us, rubbed shoulders with old tree boles. It was good to get our feet on the grass-grown paths and against the cool earth. When we came into the wider ways again, we took hands and ran. Martyn gathered some sprigs of holly for me in the forest.

The woman who hired us the pony said, "Keepers would jail ye shure, ef they sawed you with that there 'olly."

It had never occurred to us we could not gather a twig. At home we might take anything we wanted from the woods.

Epping Forest was honey sweet—rich as cream. That was a perfect day, but too many days like that would have cloyed. We ate our picnic lunch among the trees, enjoying it thoroughly, but all the while there was a gnaw in us for wild, untrimmed places. This entranced, the other satisfied; this was bounded, the other free.

Martyn and I made a great many mistakes in England not realizing that we were doing wrong according to English standards.

One evening we took a bus ride and at the terminus got off to walk in the cool. Tiring, we stepped inside a wide open gateway and sat down on a bench to rest. The place appeared to be a park, no house was in sight. Very soon a man came and walked round our bench several times, staring at us. He went away and brought another man. They both stood staring at us. Simultaneously they shouted, "How dare you!"

Seeing they meant us, Martyn asked, "How dare we what?"

"Trespass."

"We are only resting a few moments, the gate was open."

"Do you think select tennis clubs are for the resting of vagabonds?"

They drove us out and locked the gate. I had difficulty keeping Martyn cool.

"Hateful snob-country! Emily, come home," he begged.

After Art School one late autumn day we went to walk in Kensington Gardens. It was one of Martyn's *asking days*; they always depressed us.

"Come," I said, "it must be near closing time."

Martyn looked at his watch—"Half an hour yet." We sauntered to the great gates; to our horror we found them shut, locked. Nobody could possibly scale that mile-high iron fence. There we stood between the dusking empty gardens and the light and roar of Piccadilly.

I said, "There is a keeper's lodge close to the Albert Memorial, Martyn. He has a tiny gate. I've noticed it."

We tapped at the door of the lodge and explained that, being strangers, we did not know about winter hours—this it seemed was the first day of the winter change; the time had been hurried on by half an hour. The man said vile things, was grossly insulting. Martyn boiled at the things the man said, the language he used before me. It was all I could do to hold him back.

"Don't," I whispered, "let us get out first."

The man led to the little gate, stood before it with out-stretched palm. We must tip before he would open.

"Lend me sixpence," whispered Martyn. "I have only big coin in my pocket. I will not give the brute more than sixpence!"

In my flurry I took half a sovereign from my purse, thinking it was sixpence. The lodge keeper became polite and servile at once when he saw gold. I never dared tell Martyn about my mistake.

We were always doing things that were right for Canada but found they were wrong in England.

"Martyn, I hate, hate, hate London!"

"Come home, Emily; marry me; you don't belong here."

"I can't marry you, Martyn. It would be wicked and cruel, because I don't love that way. Besides—my work."

"Hang work; I can support you. Love will grow."

"It is not support; it is not money or love; it's the work itself. And, Martyn, while you are here, I am not doing my best. Go away, Martyn; please go away!"

"Always that detestable work!"

Dear Martyn, because he loved me he went away.

"Martyn's gone back to Canada."

Mrs. Radcliffe's eyes bulged.

"When are you marrying him, Klee Wyck?"

"Never."

Mrs. Radcliffe jumped to her feet. "Little silly! What more do you want? Is it a prince you wait for?"

"I wait for no one; I came to London to study."

The Radcliffes' Art and District Visiting

THE WESTMINSTER Art School students did not discuss Art in general very much. They soberly drudged at the foundations, grounding themselves, working like ditch-diggers, straightening, widening, deepening the channel through which something was to flow—none were quite sure what as yet.

I never wrote home about my work nor did my people ask me about it. A student said to me once, "Are any of your people Artists?"

"No."

"Take my advice, then—don't send any of your nude studies home."

"Goodness gracious, I would never dream of doing so! Why, they'd have me prayed for in church. My family are very conservative, they suppose I only draw clothes. If my drawings intimated that there was flesh and blood under the clothes they'd think I'd gone bad!"

The other girl said, "My people wrote begging me, 'Send us home some of your studies to see.' I did. They wrote again, 'Oh, please do not send us any more; we wanted to be able to show your work to our friends—well, the only place we could hang them was in the bathroom.' "

Mrs. Radcliffe and Fred were Art-lovers but they only liked or tolerated old masters or later work of the most conservative type. They knew every continental gallery by heart, had volumes of photos of the masterpieces of the world. The modern school of painting was as indecent to them as my nude studies would have been to the home folks. The Radcliffes had arty cousins, studying in Paris and in Rome. They talked about the Art exploits of these cousins till I was sick of them. Perhaps a little of my disgust came from jealousy, for I was beginning to feel that Paris and Rome were probably greater centres for Art than London. The Art trend in London was mainly very conservative. I sort of wished I had chosen to study in Paris rather than in London. What had decided me was the difficulty my tongue had always experienced in crawling round foreign words; even the difference in English and Scotch words from those we used in Canada was perplexing at times. The students ridiculed what they called my colonialism.

Fred asked, "Klee Wyck, do you go often to the National Gallery?"

"I did at first, but not now. It is a dreary place. Besides, one wet day, when the rooms were dark and empty, I was alone in a big gallery. One of the guards came into the room and said something horrid to me. I have never been back to the National Gallery since."

"The man should have been reported," said Fred angrily. "Come with Mother and me next Saturday."

I went. Mrs. Radcliffe and I stood, one on either side of Fred. Fred told us what pictures to look at, the date of each picture's painting. Fred knew every date of every happening in the world. He knew why the artist painted the picture and how. The older they were and the more cracked and faded, the better he loved them. He loved the Old Masters like blood brothers. If he had eaten and shaken hands with them he could not have seemed more intimate with the artists.

Every year the Radcliffes swallowed the Royal Academy show, a week of steady gulping, as if it were a great pill. They went on opening day, bought their catalogues and ticked off just how many pictures they had to do a day. They knew to a minute just when they would *finish* the Academy and were scrupulously conscientious, giving even the more modern canvases (though there were very few with even a modern taint in the Academy show) an honest stare before passing on. They liked sentiment, something that told a story. The more harrowng the story the better. "The Doctor" by Luke Fields was a great favourite of theirs. They wracked themselves over the dying child, the agonized mother, the breaking dawn and the tired doctor. They liked "The Hopeless Dawn" too. I forget whom that was by. It showed the waiting wives and mothers in a fisherman's cottage on the night after a terrific storm. And the Radcliffes liked Arnesby Brown's cow pictures very much—billows of breath bursting from the cows' nostrils like steam from tea kettles. The dark spots in the dewy grass where the milkmaid's feet had smudged the wet, making the grass a deeper green, nearly brought tears to Mrs. Radcliffe's eyes, though, of course, she would have said, "Dear me, dear me! No, *I* am not the least sentimental."

I found on the whole that it was better not to discuss Art with the Radcliffes. We did not agree about London. We conversed a good deal about churches—not as to their degree of highness or lowness as much as about their mellow old beauty. Even the jump from high to low ritual was not so violent as that between ancient and modern Art. Mrs. Radcliffe leaned towards the high but all churches were more or less acceptable to her. She and I both attended morning service at an unfashionable old church behind Westminster Abbey. It was called St. John's and Canon Wilberforce preached grand sermons there. In the evening we went to Westminster Abbey and Fred came with us.

It provoked Mrs. Radcliffe that I would not cut morning school by an hour every day to attend intercession services for the troops in the Boer War.

Canon Wilberforce called for district visitors in the parish. Mrs. Radcliffe volunteered and said to me, "Klee Wyck, I think you should offer to take a district too."

"Oh, I couldn't, Mrs. Radcliffe. I think it is beastly to go poking into the houses of the poor, shoving tracts at them and patting the heads of their dirty babies, pretending you are benevolent."

"That is not the idea. A district visitor simply calls in a friendly spirit and reports any cases of sickness or distress to the visiting curate, asks if they would care to have him visit them. Don't let Art be a selfish obsession, Klee Wyck. Art is all very well, but be of some real, practical use in the world, too."

"All right, I'll try to swallow a lump of Westminster slum, but I don't like it and I know the slummers will hate me."

I was to visit two long stacks of three-storey tenements in a dirty court—deadly places. Each family's quarters opened onto a long landing or balcony. Door, window— door, window, down the whole row, monotonous as "knit, purl, knit, purl". All the doors had the most aggressive bangs, all the windows had dirty curtains.

When I knocked, the curtain waggled and a stare peered out. If they *did* open the door it was only so that they might bang it harder against my nose, as they shouted through the keyhole, "Don't want no visitors pokin' round 'ere."

"Mrs. Radcliffe, I tremendously loathe slumming!"

"Dear me! you have only just started, Klee Wyck. You will get fond of the unfortunate creatures by and by."

So I sneaked out of school one afternoon every week, telling no one where I was going. I'd have died of shame if the students had known I was district-visiting in the Westminster slums. At last, after a week or two, a girl twice my own age in what she knew about life, and half my span of years, opened a door after I had passed it and called, " 'Ere you! Ma says, 'Come,' she's took bad."

I went into the tiny stifling room. An enormous, roaring coal fire burned in the grate. Besides that in the tiny room there was a great bed, a chair and a half eaten pie on a tin plate. The pie sat on the bed beside the woman; it was black with flies. The girl flipped the pie onto the floor. The swarm of flies rose and buzzed angrily up to the tight-closed dirty windows as if they were all going to be sick and wanted to get out immediately. I felt that way myself, especially when the morose, aggressive woman in the bed discoursed on her symptoms. She had dropsy and rolled her great body round in the bed so that I might hear her dropsy swish.

"Tell that there Curate feller 'e can come see me ef 'e wants ter."

I came away and the filthy court seemed as a pure lily after that fetid room.

I rushed round to the door of St. John's church and got the address of the visiting curate from the notice board.

"Reverend be 'ome," said the slattern who opened the door to me, adding, "foller!"

We went upstairs, the slattern flung the door back. The Curate was having tea at a littered, messy table, reading as he ate, his book propped against the sugar basin. There was no fire in the room. Late afternoon had dimmed London; it was cold, drab and full of fog, yellow fog that crowded up to the window panes.

A flickering gas jet was over the Curate's head—it "haloed" him. He was ugly and so lean you saw the shape of his teeth through his cheeks. The Curate's bed was draped with brown cotton hangings. Table, bed, chair, were loaded with books. He stopped chewing to stare at me, first over, then under, finally through his spectacles.

"Mrs. Crotch in Catfoot Court says you can go and see her if you want to. Here's my district card; I can't district-visit any more. It is beastly, how can you!"

The Curate's face twisted into a sighing little smile. He stretched a bloodless hand and took my card. He said. "You are young," and looked as if it were a long time since he had felt young.

"Mrs. Radcliffe, I'm through with slumming!"

"Oh, Klee Wyck!" She looked disgustedly at me.

"Yes, I have abandoned good works; they never were in my line. Ugh, those revolting creatures, rude, horrible!

I am much sorrier for the Curate in his wretched lodging than for those slum people with their roaring fires, their dropsies, their half-eaten pies swarming with flies."

"What do you know about the Curate's lodging?"

"Went there, to hand in my district visitor's card."

"You went to the Curate's room!"

"Had to give my card in, didn't I?"

"You should have taken it to the Church House."

"Church House! What's that? I never heard of one, and goodness, my sisters were churchy enough, too."

"All parish work is conducted through the Church House in London parishes. Workers never go direct to the clergy."

"Well, I did and he was the miserablest human I ever saw."

Mrs. Radcliffe assumed a sly simper. "I wonder what he thought of you?" She looked so coy, so hinting, I wanted to hit her. Mrs. Radcliffe twitted me so about that wretched visit to the Curate that I stopped going to St. John's.

To Mrs. Denny I was frankly a disappointment. She had taught me London, pointed out the wrongness of Roman Catholicism, had even intimated that she was willing to share with me the love of her very precious son. And London's history bored me! I continued to wear Mother's little cornelian cross, to go to the Brompton Oratory on occasion to hear magnificent music. Most astounding of all I did not want Ed's love! No wonder she was disappointed. At least I had the decency to be honest with Ed, to show him and his mother, too, that I had no intention of marrying him, that I did not want his love! I spared Ed the humiliation of a "No" by not allowing him to ask me.

The heads of Mrs. Denny and Mrs. Radcliffe nodded a duet of amazement and sorrow. Next to Martyn as a husband for me, Mrs. Radcliffe favoured Eddie. The two old ladies had tried to remodel me. I was so difficult to mould. After a couple of years they gave up, concluding that after all I had really come to London seeking Art, not a husband. By this time they had got to love me a little for myself, had accepted me as an assorted bundle of good and bad. Everyone was much more comfortable when at last they realized that love won't be pushed into contrary channels.

Good Ed did not marry; he cared devotedly for his old mother till she died. Fred wrote out to Canada at the time of the World War, "Ed is over-age for active service but he drives himself beyond human limit on the home front to release younger men."

London Tasted

NOW THAT my sister's visit was over, now that Martyn had come and gone, foot troubles were straightened out, London explored, and now that I was comfortably settled in Mrs. Dodds' boarding house for students in Bulstrode Street, it seemed that things were shaped for steady, hard work.

Besides all-day Life Class at the Westminster School of Art, I joined night classes—design, anatomy, clay modelling. Against London I was not quite so rebellious, though I did not like life in a great city.

I made a few friends in the school and some in the boarding house. Wattie was out in India. I plunged into work, not noticing that my face had become pasty; but, because I was always tired, I pushed and goaded myself harder. It was a long way I had come to get what London had to give. I must make the best of it, learn all I could.

I knew London well—not the formal sights only, but I knew her queer corners too. Mrs. Denny and Mrs. Radcliffe had shown me national astonishments, great sights, picture-galleries, Bank of England, British Museum, Mint, Guildhall, Tower of London, Buckingham Palace, and Windsor. I had canoed with Fred and his mother up the Thames and down. London had instructed, amazed, inspired, disgusted me. The little corners that I had poked into by myself interested me most. My sight-showers would have gasped had they known the variety and quality of my solitary wanderings. It would have puzzled them that I should want to see such queernesses.

The orthodox sights I found wearing. The Zoo I never tired of, nor of Kew Gardens, St. Paul's, the Abbey cloisters.

I took endless rides on bus-tops, above the crowd yet watching intently the throngs of humanity. I went into the slums of Whitechapel, Poplar, and Westminster and roamed the squalid crookedness of Seven Dials, which is London's bird-shop district, entering the dark stuffiness of the little shops to chirp with bird prisoners, their throats, glory-filled and unquenchable, swelled with song even in these foul captive dens. There was Paternoster Row too—the street of books, Lincoln's Inn Fields—the world of Dickens, haunted by Dickens' houses, Dickens' characters, as St. Bartholomew's, Smithfield was haunted by smell of fire and the burning flesh of martyrs. From the "gods" of the great theatres I saw Shakespeare's plays, cried over Martin Harvey in *The Only Way*, roared over *Charlie's Aunt*, saw Julia Neilson in *Nell Gwyn*. That play I saw first from the "gods"; afterwards I saw it from stalls with swell friends from home. I liked it best from the "gods", distance dimmed the make-up, the sham. In the "gods" it was vision and carried me away.

So I looked at London from different sides, mostly hating it; cities did not sit on me comfortably. There were a few little tag ends I loved, insignificant things that most Londoners scorned, but the oldness and history of it made little appeal to me.

There were fifty-two women and girls in Mrs. Dodds' boarding house, every kind of student and all nationalities. Once I counted fourteen countries dining at one table of sixteen souls. Sometimes nationalities clashed but not often. Many foreigners were here to learn English. They learnt squabble English and slang as well as the pure language in our boarding house.

We had two large sitting rooms; one was talkative and had a piano, the other was silent for writing and study. Occasionally I went into the silent room and always got into trouble for drawing caricatures and rhyming, not for talking. Another student would look over my shoulder, see some of our queer ones—giggles were forbidden in

154

the silent room. I would be ejected. But, being out at classes most nights, the sitting room students were not bothered by me much.

The few private rooms at Mrs. Dodds' were small and very dismal. The other rooms were very large and were divided into cubicles by red and yellow curtains.

The girl in the cubicle next mine was a North Country farm girl, jolly and wholesome. We drew back the dividing curtains, so making our cubicles one, and had fun. We kept a big box of goodies and had feasts, making cocoa on a spirit lamp after night-school. My cubicle had a private window—windowed cubicles cost a shilling a week extra. There was a curtained alley down the middle of the big room; a window was at one end of the through alley, the door with a ventilator over it at the other.

There were five cubicles in our room. Three of us were permanent, the other two cubicles were let to transients. It was amusing to wonder who would come next into the transients' cubicles. We had a Welsh singer, a German governess, a French mademoiselle, some little Swedish girls. Often we had two Scotch sisters in the spare cubicles. They quarrelled over the shutting and opening of the public ventilator in the aisle and sneaked on each other when one thought the other asleep. Each had to stand on her bed to reach the hook of the ventilator using her umbrella handle. Stealthily, stealthily they sneaked, but the other always heard—clash! whack! whack! whack! went umbrellas over the curtain tops!

"Ye hurrt me," Little Scot would whimper.

"A' meant ta," Big Scot would reply.

Bed springs squeaked impatiently, the three permanents were disturbed. Three "shut-ups!" came from their cubicles.

The food at Mrs. Dodds' had no more variety than a calendar. You knew exactly what the kitchen saucepans were doing without the help even of your nose. Sunday's supper was the peak of misery. The maids were out; we helped ourselves to the everlasting monotony—same old cold ham, same salad, same cake, same sliced pineapple.

Why couldn't the salad have been other than beet-root and lettuce? Why must the cake always be raspberry slab? Why not another canned fruit than pineapple? Everyone who could wangle an invite to sup out on Sunday wangled.

When it came to bed time, one cubicle would brag, "I had roast beef and Yorkshire."

Groans!

"I had duck and green peas," from another cubicle.

More groans.

"Must you gloat over your greed!" from a cubicle who had suppered at home. Bedclothes dragged over heads, there was savage, "goody-hungry" quiet.

The Other Side of Life

WHEN Westminster School closed for the long summer vacation I, with other students, joined a sketching class at Boxford down in Berkshire. The quaintness of thatched cottages in the village delighted me. The sketching master was a better teacher than painter, I learned a lot from him. It was the first time I had sketched out-doors in England. Even across one field there was soft hazy distance, distance gradations were easier here to get than in our clear Canadian atmosphere and great spaces; everything was faded, gentle here. Colour did not throb so violently. English landscape painting was indolent seeing, ready-made compositions, needing only to be copied. I was very happy in my work, sorry when the summer ended.

The other students went home. I lingered, hating to leave woods and fields for chimney-pots and clatter. The weather grew sharp and a little wet. The master and his wife lived in another village. The man was drinking. He forgot his lesson dates, smelled beery. I stopped taking lessons from him and worked on alone.

I had given the landlady my week's notice. She came to me in distress.

"A lady from Westminster Art School wants accommodation immediate. 'Er wants comin' afore weather's broke. I got no 'sittin' ' till you goes!—Plenty bedrooms, no 'sittin's'."

"Who is the lady?"

"Miss Compton."

"I know her; she may share my sitting room, if it is any convenience for you and her."

"Thanks, miss."

Mildred Compton came. At school I knew her only slightly; she was older than I, wealthy, stand-offish, prim.

"We will have little in common, but any way I shall only be in Boxford one week," I thought.

Mildred Compton was a society girl. I decidedly was not. We ate together, sat together, worked together— amiable, not intimate.

"I'm going back to London tomorrow," I said one night.

Mildred looked as if I had loosed an evil upon her.

"Oh! I did want to get two whole weeks sketching here, in Boxford."

"Does my going make any difference?"

"Of course, I could not *possibly* stay in a strange village all alone. Nothing but villagers!"

"They are quite tame."

"Queer things happen in out-of-the-way places!"

Mildred had been born condensed. Space alarmed her. She was like a hot loaf that had been put immediately into too small a bread-box and got misshapen by cramping. She was unaware of being cramped, because she was unconscious of any humans except those of her own class. The outer crowd propped her, but she was unaware of them. Away from crowds Mildred flopped.

I said, "I am in no hurry; I can stay another week if you like."

"Would you? How very kind!"

She was glad to have me. I was glad to elude London a little longer. Gladness drew us into companionship in spite of our different upbringings.

Cows and cobwebby barns terrified Mildred as history and crowds terrified me. The weather broke, there was nothing but cowbarns and sheds to shelter in against wind and rain while we worked. Smartly-dressed, lily-fair Mildred crouched on a campstool, set on a not too clean stable floor, hens scratching in the straw about her feet, a sow and litter penned in the corner, did seem unnatural, topsy-turvy, I'll confess.

Mildred, hurrying her things into her sketch-sack, asking breathlessly, "Doesn't the cow come home about this time, Motor?" Mildred saying, "I had no idea hens had such a vocabulary. The speckled thing has made six entirely different squawks in as many minutes. She makes me nervous, Motor!"

"Not as nervous as you make her."

"Ouch! there's a mouse!—behind that barrel—ouch, ouch!" She pinched her skirt in close.

"Mice much prefer the bran barrels to you!" I laughed. She gathered up her things.—"Let's go."

"Motor, will you visit us for a week when we go back to London?"

"Me! Why, your life would scare me worse than the barn and hen scare you, Mildred. Besides . . . I couldn't."

"Why not?"

"Clothes!"

"*You* would be inside the clothes, Motor. We don't love our friends for their clothes. I want you to know my mother; I want my mother to know you. She is an old lady, a little lonely, a very lonely old lady sometimes!"

"Thank you, Mildred, I'd be a sparrow in a peacock house,—still—if a washed-to-bits muslin dress won't shame your dinner-table, I'll come. I would love to meet your mother."

I dreaded the ordeal, but I'd see London from another side. Yes, I'd go to Mildred's.

The Comptons lived in a dignified mansion in Belgrave Square. Every house in that square was important, wealthy, opulent. A little park was in the centre of the Square; none but residents were permitted a key to the gate in its high iron fence. Belgravians seldom walked. Very few of the Belgrave Square people were aware of having legs, all owned horses. You could not drive in the little park; there were no roads, only trees, shrubs, grass, seats, and gravel paths.

The Compton family consisted of Mrs. Compton, her companion, an elderly lady named Miss Bole, who was a family institution—began as governess, continued as secretary till Mr. Compton died and was now companion to Mrs. Compton. Mildred divided her time between being a society girl and an Art student of Westminster. A staff of twelve servants attended to the creature comforts of the three women.

The Compton mansion was enormous and not half as cosy as one of our Western homes—thousands of stairs, no elevator, no telephone, no central heating. There were roaring grate-fires in every room but the halls and passages were like ice.

There was a marble swimming bath, a glass-topped billiard room, a conservatory and a walled garden through which I longed to run, unlock an arched doorway in the wall and pass into the mews where the Compton carriages lived. I hinted to Mildred about wanting to visit the horses, but Mildred hinted back that it was not done by London ladies, and I did not want to shame Mildred before her family.

The servants ran the house like clockwork, but they upset me dreadfully. The maids were so superior, and I wanted to push the footmen out of the way to save tumbling over them, rushing to do things for me I had rather do for myself. They made me feel as stupid as a doll.

Mildred's mother was beautiful. She was plump, with a tiny waist and great dignity, white hair, blue eyes, pink cheeks. I loved her the moment she took my hand and said, "So this is *our* little Motor." I was always "our" little Motor to her.

Miss Bole was plump too, with bright brown eyes like a robin's, black hair smoothed back. She always dressed in plain, rich black.

Belgrave food was marvellous, each help faded into your appetite without effort, like a tiny dream, not like the boarding-house stuff. This was food which, somehow, you never connected with a kitchen or a cook. The butler juggled it off the sideboard like a magician. A footman slid the silver dishes noiselessly to your elbow. Sometimes I remembered the heavy plates of heaped monotony slapped down in front of us by a frowsy maid at Mrs. Dodds' student home and laughed to myself.

Besides three table-meals a day we ate snacks in other rooms—wine and biscuits in the library at eleven in the morning, afternoon tea in the drawing-room, a little something in the library before going to bed, the early morning tea in bed that destroyed your loveliest sleep and from which I begged to be excused.

When I asked, "Must I have that early tea, Mildred?" she exclaimed, "No early morning tea, Motor! Oh, you'd better."

So a prettiness in a frilly cap and apron stole into my room very early. She pulled back the heavy silk curtains, lit a fire in the grate, laid a downy pink rug before it; on that she set a white bath, half pudding-basin and half arm-chair. On either side of the tub she stood a great covered can of hot water, draped over the top with a snowy bath towel. Then she fetched a dainty tea tray, put it on a little table at the bedside, and, bending close, whispered, "Tea, Miss," and was gone. At Bulstrode Street yawns and groans would that minute be filtering through the cubicle curtains. The dressing bell—we called it the distressing bell—would clang, there would be pandemonium. And yet this wealth of luxury weighted me, not being born to it.

I had not dreamt that social obligations *could* be so arduous. After breakfast we marched soberly into the library to write notes, notes of inviting or of accepting. Every dinner, tea, house-party, call, must be punctiliously returned. I was rather sorry for these rich, they could so seldom be themselves; even their smiles were set, wound up to so many degrees of grin for so much intimacy. Their pleasures seemed kept in glass cases just out of reach. They saw but could not quite handle or feel their fun, it was so overhung with convention.

When later I told Mrs. Radcliffe where I had been

staying, her eyes popped. She said "dear me!" six times, then she exclaimed, "Fred, Klee Wyck in Belgravia!" and again, "dear me!" After that she had nothing more to say.

While the ladies attended to the answering of the morning notes, Miss Bole took me and the key and went into the Park in the centre of the Square. This was the time I felt I really had got ahead of London. In the middle of the little park, among the trees and bushes, you were quite hidden from London and London was quite hidden from you. There was no traffic in Belgrave Square, only the purring roll of carriages and the smart step of dainty horses outside the railing of the little park. Even London's roar was quite cut off by great, high mansions all round. Every house-front was gay with flower-boxes. There was no grime, scarcely any sparrows—only a few very elegant pigeons who strutted in the park cooing. Miss Bole and I watched them, we did not talk much but we liked each other.

Mildred had a married sister who despised me for one of Mildred's "low-down student friends". When she came to the house I was unhappy. She talked over my head and made me feel so awfully naked, as if I had no clothes on at all. I felt ugly, shy, shabby and nervous the moment she came into the house, and feeling that way made me so.

One night Mrs. Compton gave a dinner party. The married daughter came. I slunk from my bedroom in the old white muslin, to find Mildred waiting for me on the stairs. She looked lovely, dressed in a gown all colours yet no colour at all, just shimmer. She held her hand to me. "Come, my poppet!"

"Oh, Mildred, I am so shabby in this wretched old muslin!"

"Motor, you are *Spring*."

She caught me up and kissed me. Suddenly I did not care about the old muslin any more. Mildred had sent Spring bubbling up into my heart, I knew she loved me for me, not for my clothes.

We "Noah-arked" into the dining-room. The men's coat

tails swished so elegantly, the silks of the women rustled and billowed. Then came Miss Bole in her rich black, very quiet and clinging to her arm was me, just a little cotton rattle. Mrs. Compton placed me close to her. I watched, shy and very quiet till Mrs. Compton said, "Tell that little Indian story you told us at lunch, Motor." My face burned —I thought I should have died, but to please her I tried. It went all right till a beastly footman slithered a dish of peas close to my elbow and made me jump—the peas upset. The married daughter began to talk and laugh very loud. I wanted to hurl the peas, along with a frightful face, at her. I wish now that I had.

"Look at my face, Mildred."

"It is rather greeny white, isn't it? It's those stuffy rooms in the Westminster Art School, Motor."

"Is there any part of England where one can work outdoors all the year round?"

"At St. Ives there is an Art Colony who work outdoors nearly all the year."

"I'm going there."

Mrs. Compton ordered a great hamper to be packed for me. In it were four bottles of wine, a great plum cake, biscuits, nuts and fruit—the kind she knew I liked. I was to stay at the Temperance Hotel in St. Ives until I found rooms.

I went to say goodbye to Mrs. Radcliffe and to Mrs. Denny. Mrs. Radcliffe was a little glad; I think she resented the Comptons having me. Perhaps she thought Mrs. Compton would make me soft with too much petting. I did love Mrs. Compton, but I could not have got along without Mrs. Radcliffe's bullying and strength.

Mrs. Denny shook her head. "My dear," she said, "the R.C.'s are strong in Cornwall, beware!" She frowned at the little cornelian cross I still wore in spite of her protests. The next day Ed staggered to Belgrave Square carrying two huge books, one under each arm—*Roman Catholicism Exposed, Volumes I and II!*

"Mother wants you to take these with you to read in your spare time."

"I shan't have any spare time, I am going to St. Ives to work like blazes, Ed. I have more luggage now—work things and food—than I can manage."

Kind Ed tucked the volumes under his arms again saying, "I understand." I liked Ed better that moment than I ever had before, loyal to his mother—understanding both to his mother and to me.

St. Ives

AS OUR train slithered through the small prettiness of Devonshire I was angered. My parents had so lavishly praised its beauty to us when we were children. I wondered if after many years in Canada it would have seemed as small and pinched to them as it did to me seeing it for the first time—something one could fold up and put in his pocket, tiny patches of grass field hemmed about with little green hedges.

When we came to Cornwall, the land grew sterner and more jagged—stony fields, separated by low stone walls, stunted, wind-blown trees, wild but not with the volume of Canada's wildness. Cornwall's land had been punished into tameness, but her sea would always be boisterous, stormy. From Devonshire to Cornwall the land changed; Devon was, as it were, pernickety check, while Cornwall loosened to broader plaid.

My luggage looked sneaky and self-conscious wheeled into the Temperance Hotel. I knew Mrs. Compton's red wine blushed in its middle. I tried to forget its presence as I entered the Hotel, a sour-faced structure down in the old town. Never having stayed alone in a hotel before, I entered timidly.

The old town of St. Ives lay low, its rocky edges worn by the violence of the sea. On the hillside above was a smarter, newer St. Ives, composed of tourist hotels, modern houses and fine studios of Artists who had inherited wealth or made names—few students could afford the heights. Most students other than snobs and the ultra-smarts lived

165

down among the fisherfolk in the old town. Fisherfolk packed themselves like sardines in order to enlarge their incomes by renting rooms to student lodgers. Many of the old sail lofts were converted into studios.

A few students lived at the Temperance Hotel and from them I made enquiry about studios.—Did I want *work* or studio tea-parties?—Work? Then go to Julius Olsen's Studio; he worked you to the last gasp!

To Julius Olsen I presented myself.

Julius Olsen's studio had been an immense sail loft overlooking the sea. The massive, blue-eyed Swede carelessly shoved my fee into the sagging pocket of his old tweed jacket, waved a hand towards the beach and left me stranded like a jelly fish at low tide, he striding off to criticize canvases which some boy students were turning from the walls.

"I'll show you," said an Irish voice at my elbow.

Hilda was the only girl student in the room.

"You will want to outfit?" she asked.

"I have my kit."

She looked at it with disapproval.

"Too light—'Jo' insists on weight,"—she exhibited her own equipment.

"Gracious! That easel is as heavy as a cannon and that enormous brass-bound paintbox! I can't, I *won't* lug such heaviness."

"Jo bellows if you cross his will," warned Hilda.

"Let him roar!"

She led me to the open front of the studio. Great doors folded back, creating an opening which was wide enough to admit three or four fishing boats abreast. A bar was fixed across the opening, we leaned on it looking at the busy fisher life buzzing on the beach below. Morning fish market was in progress. Buyers raced down from London on swift express trains, bartered for the night's catch, raced it back to London's markets.

Not Cornwall ate St. Ives' fish, but London. In St. Ives you could not buy so much as one herring.

Shrill-voiced fish-wives bargained, children yelled, cats yowled. Every house-roof, every street, every boat, swarmed with cats.

> *Each wife had seven sacks,*
> *Each sack had seven cats,*
> *Each cat had seven kits!*

This was obviously the *cat* St. Ives of our nursery rhyme book.

The tide was far out. Looking down on it all, I was suddenly back in Mrs. Compton's drawing room standing before Moffatt Linder's picture, "St. Ives' Beach". Sky, sea, mudflats were shown but he had left out the bustle and the smell.

"Now," said Hilda, "to the sands and work!"

"Not work on those sands amid that turmoil!"

"Jo insists—white boats in sunlight—sunlight full on the canvas, too."

"Jo will find me in a shady street-end sitting with my back to the wall so that rubbernoses can't overlook."

Hilda's head nodded forebodings beyond wording. "I'd advise that you don't let him see you work sitting," was her parting headshake. Leaving me to my fate she went off, lugging her heavy kit.

Stump, stump, I heard Jo's heavy footfalls on the cobbles and trembled, not scared of Jo, the man, but of Jo's artist eye, a splendid eye for colour, space, light. Nervous as a cat, I waited.

"Sitting to work!"

"Bad foot, sir."

"Huh! I said the sands, didn't I? Sunshine on sea and white boats. With the first puff that thing will blow out to sea," pointing to my easel. "Get the weighty 'Standard'."

"Too heavy to lug, sir. Mine is weighted. See!"

I showed him a great rock suspended in a paint rag and hung from my easel top.

"If you please, sir, the glare of sea and white sand blind me with headache."

Jo snorted, strode away—adoring English students

never argued with their masters. He came back by-and-by, gave a grunt, made no comment and was away again! That was my first day of study under Julius Olsen. We remained antagonistic always. I believe each admired the other's grim determination but neither would give in.

The St. Ives students were a kindly lot—ready to give, ready to take, criticism. We numbered ten or more in the studio. Three Australian boys, a Frenchman, an ultra-Englishman, and an ultra-Englishwoman, (swells rooming up on the hill), a cockney boy, the Irish girl, myself, and the nondescript old women who are found in most studios just killing time.

We met in the big studio at eight each morning to receive "crits" on the work done the afternoon before. Olsen gave us criticisms three times a week, his partner, Talmage, the other three days. What one taught the other untaught; it was baffling but broadening. After "crit" we dispersed. The master came wherever we were working to examine our work on the spot. From eight in the morning till dusk we worked outdoors, in all weathers except during hurricanes. The great studio doors were shut then and we huddled under the studio skylight and worked from a model. But St. Ives was primarily a school for land- and seascape painting.

I found living quarters next to the churchyard. My host was a maker of antiques; he specialized in battering up and defacing old ship's figure-heads and grandfather clocks. Six grandfathers higgledy-piggledyed their ticks in my sitting room. When they all struck high-count hours simultaneously your hands flew to your ears, and your head flew out the window.

My window opened directly onto the cobblestoned street with no mediating sidewalk. Heavy shoes striking cobblestones clattered, clattered day and night.

Student heads, wrapped in student grins, thrust themselves through my window announcing, "We are about to call!" Then I rushed like a flurried hen to protect "the complete beach". This object was an enormous mahogany and glass cabinet in which was displayed everything nautical except a mermaid—shells, coral, seaweed, fish bones, starfish, crabs—all old and brittle as eggshell. My foot and that of every student who called on me itched to thrust through the prominent glass corporation of this rounded glass monster, to crush, to crackle. My hosts, the Curnows, valued the thing highly. When a student warned through the window, I pushed the six straight-backed leather chairs whose leather laps were usually under the big mahogany dining-table (as if the chair feet had corns and were afraid of having them tramped on) and circled the chairs, round "the complete beach". The room was not any too large. What with this massive furniture, a fireplace, the cat and me in it, it was over-full.

My bedroom was marvellous! You reached it through an ascending streak of black between two walls. The treads were so narrow that they taught your toes the accuracy of fingertips on a keyboard. But glory dawned when I opened my bedroom door. Two large windows overlooked the sea. In the centre of the room stood an enormous bed—mahogany, carved with dolphins galloping on their tails. Mrs. Curnow told me this treasure-antique was built in the room by Pa Curnow himself. It would have sold many times over, only it had been built in the room, and could never be moved because no door, no window, certainly not our stair, would have permitted the passage of its bulk! There were four posts to the bed and a canopy of pink cotton. I was solemnly warned not to lay so much as a pocket handkerchief across the foot-board for fear of scratching or otherwise defacing a dolphin. Even on the side-boards dolphins galloped. I had to taut myself, run and vault in order to avoid touching one, when at night I retired to rest on the hard unbouncy mattress. Beside the bed there was little else in the room—a meagre washstand, a chair, a clothes closet set in the wall. The closet contained all the family's "best". This is a Cornish way; rental of a room does not include its cupboards.

My Curnow family were reputed the cleanest folk in St.

Ives because for years they had threatened to install a bath in their house. No other family had gone that far. I bargained for a hot wash once a week. The three women, mother and two girls who would never see forty again, gravely consulted. It could be managed, they said mournfully, but Saturday was always an anxious and disturbed day for the Curnow family.

Ma tiptoed into my room after supper and, carefully shutting the door, whispered, "The cauldron, Miss, it is heated to wash your feet."

She would not have allowed "the girls" to hear mention of such a thing as a bath. No one suspected me of such indecency as taking an "all-over"! The tin foot-bath was set as far as possible from the dolphins, who were draped in pink calico for the event. Greatest secrecy was exercised in getting the bath down the dark stair and through the kitchen without old Curnow or a visitor seeing. The girls frankly admitted they preferred men lodgers. If they must bathe they did it in the sea.

When storms came the whole St. Ives Bay attacked my room with fury and with power. The house was built partly on the sea-wall, and waves beat in thuds that trembled it. The windows, of heavy bottle-glass stoutly braced, were dimmed with mazed green lights. I was under the sea. Sea poured over my roof, my windows were translucent, pouring green, which thinned, drew back receding in a boil of foam, leaving me amazed that the house could still be grounded. Water raced up the alley between the graveyard wall and our house, curled over the cobble-street to meet the flood pouring over the low roof-top of the house on the other side of ours. We were surrounded by water. Privies, perched on the sea wall, jaunted gaily off into the bay. Miles inland bundles of white fluff, dry as wool, clung to the trees; it was beaten foam, carried inland by tearing wind. These storms were, of course, exceptional but there was usually breeze in St. Ives, though she had many, many bright, glistening days—sea sparkling, air clear, mudflats glowing.

Tides ruled the life of the town and of the fishermen. All night lanterns bobbed, men shouted, boats clattered over cobbles, cats prowled the moonlight, their eyes gleaming.

The Irish girl Hilda and I were warm friends. Outdoors we did not work together—she was for sea, I for land. But we hired fisher children to pose for us in the evenings, working by a coal-oil lamp in my sitting-room. The boy students jeered at our "life class" but they dropped in to work with us off and on.

The atmosphere of Julius Olsen's studio was stimulating. He inspired us to work. He was specially nice to his boy students, inviting them up to his own fine studio on the hill, showing them his great seascapes in the making, discussing an artist's problems with them, treating them as fellow workers.

Mrs. Olsen was a billowy creature who only called on those of her husband's students who were worth while; she did not call on me.

I never liked Jo much, but I respected his teaching and the industry which he insisted that his students practise and which he practised himself.

Christmas came, everyone went home except me. The Olsens went to Sweden on their yacht. Noel, a nice English student, came to bid me goodbye.

"I say, it's going to be beastly lonely for you with everybody gone—studio shut. What shall you do with yourself?"

"Explore. Albert will still be here, he will pilot me, he knows Cornwall."

"Albert! That wretched little cockney!" said the autocrat, Noel, with a lift of his nose.

"I *could* visit, too, if I wanted." I tossed a letter across for Noel to read.

"Whew—horses to ride and all and you turned this down!" he exclaimed.

"Don't like the outfit, connections by marriage, snobs, titled too!"

171

"What matter? Put likes and dislikes in your pocket, silly; take all the good times you can get."

"Take and hate the giver?"

Noel shrugged, "I *was* going to ask Mother to invite you to visit us in the summer holidays. How about it, Miss Snifty?"

"Try."

"Tell me, what are you doing at this present moment?" asked Noel. "Hat, felt slipper, snipping, sewing—it's beyond my figuring entirely!"

"Felt from under hat ribbon provides patch for toe of slipper. See, Mr. Dull-Head?" I fitted the patch.

Noel's roaring laugh—"Canadian thrift!" He vaulted through the window shouting, "I'll ask Mother about the summer visit."

Cornish people love a wrench of misery with every joy. The Curnows wept all through Christmas. I came upon Pa, Ma, and both girls, stirring the plum pudding, eight eyes sploshing tears down into the mixing bowl.

"Anything wrong?"

"Always something wrong for we," wailed Ma.

It seemed some relative preferred to Christmas elsewhere than with the Curnows. Their grief seemed so disproportionate to the cause that I laughed. Eight mournful looks turned upon me.

"You be awfu' merry, Miss. Thousands of miles betwixt you and yours, yet you larf!" There was reproach in the voice.

Under the guidance of Albert I saw Polperro, Mousehole, St. Earch, St. Michael's Mount and more places. Little cockney Albert enjoyed having company. He was not quite one of us—no one bothered about him.

For one week Albert and I holidayed, then I fell on work with doubled fury. I knew I was a fool, grinding, grinding, but I had so much to learn, so little time.

They all came trooping back to the studio. Olsen outstayed himself by a matter of six weeks. Talmage took charge. High on the hill I had discovered Tregenna Wood

—haunting, ivy-draped, solemn Tregenna. Talmage saw what I had been doing up there during the holidays, away from the glare and racket of St. Ives. He was a calm, gentle man, one who understood.

"Trot up to your woods; that's where you love to be. I will come there and give you your lesson."

I gave a delighted squeal. "Oh, but, Mr. Talmage, wouldn't it be too far for you to come for my lesson alone. None of the other students work there."

"Trot along; one works best where one is happy."

Tregenna Wood was solemn, if not vast. A shallow ravine scooped through its centre. Ivy crept up the tree-trunks to hang down in curtains. No students worked here, few people passed this way. A huge white sow frequented Tregenna, a porky ghost, rustling through the bushes. She aimed always to pass at lunch hour so that she might share my lunch. If I had any form of pigmeat (Mrs. Curnow often gave me fat pork sandwiches), then, out of delicacy, I did not offer anything but the breadcrust.

The students teased me about my "lady friend in Tregenna" but I loved my sow. I wrote a poem and made a skit about the students and her. It was more complimentary to the sow than to the students.

I said to Talmage, "I don't care if Jo never comes back; I learn much more from you than from him."

"Jo is the better artist," replied Talmage. "Jo is a genius. What I have got has been got through grind. Probably that helps me to understand my students' problems better."

He praised my woods studies highly, so did the students. Jo came home.

"Jo's home! 'Crits' in the studio at eight tomorrow!" A student's head thrust the news through my window.

I had a vast accumulation to show Jo. I knew the work was good—happy, honest stuff. I swung into the studio with confidence. Jo was pacing the floor. The Frenchman sat crying before his easel. Jo gave me a curt nod, "Fetch your stuff."

I turned my canvases face out, waited—silence, except for Jo's snorts through a dead pipe.

"Maudlin! Rubbish!" he bellowed, pointing his dead pipe at my canvases. "Whiten down those low-toned daubs, obliterate 'em. Go out *there*," (he pointed to the glaring sands) "out to bright sunlight—PAINT!"

Kicking the unlucky canvases into a corner, I bolted. No one was going to see me as I had seen Frenchie.

On a desolate road far beyond the town I came to my unhappy self. On either side the way were fields of frosted cabbages. I crept among them to sit down on a boulder, rocking myself back and forth, crying, crying till I was very hideous and very hungry.

I got up. I'd see how the others came out. I dragged myself back to town.

Burgess, one of the Australians, studied under Jo, but he had a studio of his own. Burgess and I had a pact. He had chased away a fisherman who had religious mania and tormented any student he could find working in a quiet corner, as to their views on purgatory. In return I went to Burgess' studio when the Frenchman had declared his intention of giving him a "crit", because, unless Burgess had company, the Frenchman *would* kiss him, not only on one but on both cheeks.

It took three knocks to rouse a dreary, "Come in." When I pushed open the door Burgess was seated on a three-legged stool before a dead grate, his red hair wild, his hands shaky. He kicked forward another stool.

"Poor Mother, she will be so disappointed. Do you suppose Grant's will take back that gold leaf frame?"

"The one for your Academy picture?"

"Academy! I'm returning to Australia right away. You may have the pile of canvas stretchers."

"Thanks, but I'm thinking of leaving for Canada myself immediately."

Shamed grins spread over our faces.

"Let's call on the rest, see what Jo did to them."

We met Ashton; he was whistling.

"Get a good 'crit', Ashton?"

"You bet."

"Liar," muttered Burgess. "Hello! There's Maude, . . . morning, Miss Horne, taken your 'crit'?"

"Criticism first morning after Jo's vacation! Not I. Jo always returns in a rage. This time it is two rages—his usual and a toothache. You pair of young fools!" she grinned at our grief-wracked faces. "Poor children, I s'pose you knew no better." Maude put on airs.

"I'm hungry as a hunter, Burgess. I'll run home for a bit, then the sun will be just right for painting those cottages in the Diji. Oh, about those canvas stretchers?"

"Needing them myself!"

We exchanged grins. Burgess had forgotten Australia. I had forgotten Canada. With noses and hopes high we were off again to work.

When long vacation came I went back to London.

A sneezing creature sitting next to me in the train gave me 'flu. When that was through with me, I crawled to Westminster. 'Flu had sapped the energy I had forced so long. Mildred found me huddled on a bench in the Architectural Museum, among the tombs—idle.

"Why, Motor!"

"After 'flu, Mildred."

"If we were not just starting for Switzerland I'd take you home right now."

Mrs. Radcliffe groaned, "You'd best take a strong tonic, Klee Wyck. Why you should fall to pieces the moment you come to London I can't imagine. London suits *me* all right."

Always kind, Fred said, "Try Bushey, Herts, Klee Wyck—Herkomer's Art School, a big art colony. Bushey is an easy run up to London for exhibitions and galleries. You just don't thrive as Mother does in London."

To Bushey I went.

Bushey

THE STATION Master's direction was accurate. "Bushey? Turn by that 'ere pub and keep a-goin'."

The road was a long squirm without any actual turnings.

Herkomer had built a theatre in connection with his Bushey art school; more time was now devoted to drama, they said, than to Art. For earnest Art I was advised to go to John Whiteley, Number 9, Meadows Studios.

The Meadows Studios stretched in a long row. Of unplaned lumber, linked together like stitches in a chain of crochet, they ran across a hummocky field, spattered with kingcups. Each frame building was one room and a thin corridor wide. Each had a door into the emaciated passage and a large north window.

The land around Bushey dipped and rose pastorally and was dotted with sheep, cows and spreads of bluebells. Everything was yellow-green and pearly with young spring. Larks hurried up to Heaven as if late for choir practice. The woods in the hollows cuckooed all day with cuckoos; the air melted ecstatically into the liquid of nightingale music all night.

John Whiteley was a quiet man and shy, his teaching was as honest as himself. There were sixteen students in his class, men and women. We worked from costumed models, often posed outdoors among live greenery. The students were of the Westminster type—cold, stand-offish. They lodged in the village. Being mid-term, all rooms were full, so I had to climb the hill to a row of working men's houses to find accommodation. Many in the row were glad to let rooms. The man and wife in my house kept the kitchen and the front bedroom for their own use, renting the front room downstairs, into which the house door opened, and the back, upstairs bedroom. The back door was their entrance. They were expecting their first baby—and were singing happy about it, so happy that they just had to do something for somebody. They showed me many kindnesses. When there was nothing else she could think of the woman would run into their tiny patch of back garden and pull half a dozen rosy, tender-skinned radishes for my tea. The man, returning from labouring as a farm hand, would ask of me, "Can 'er go through you, Miss; it be a long round from back. 'Er's not spry jest now. Us likes listenin' to nightingales down to valley"—and, passing hand in hand through my room, they drifted into the dimness of the dusky fields.

Mr. Whiteley's was a silent studio. No one talked during pose; few spoke during rests. To English girls Canadians were foreigners. A snobby trio in the studio were particularly disagreeable to me. They rented a whole cottage and were very exclusive. The bossiest of the three was "Mack", an angular Scotch woman. The other two were blood sisters and English. They had yellow hair and black eyes and were known as "The Canaries". After an ignored week, I came into the passage one morning to find a scrawny youth trying to make up his mind to knock on Mr. Whiteley's door.

"This Mr. Whiteley's studio?"

"Yes."

"Can I see him?"

"He does not come for 'crit' before ten."

The youth fidgeted.

"What'll I do? I'm a new student."

"Come on, I'll show you."

He threw a terrified look round the room when I opened the door, saw the work on the easels and calmed. I think he had expected a nude model. I got him an easel and board, set him in a far corner where he could not be overlooked, showed him where to get charcoal and paper. He was very grateful, like a chicken from a strange brood that an old hen has consented to mother. He stuck to me. The Canaries and Mack froze, throwing high noses and cold glances over our heads.

That night there was a tap at my door. A tall, loose-knit boy stood there. He said, "I'm from St. Ives. The students said to be sure to look you up. My name is Milford and do you mind if I bring Mother to see you? I'm going to Whiteley's too. Mother's come to settle me in—she's two doors off."

Milford had a stepfather who considered both stepsons and art unnecessary nonsense. The mother doted on Milford. "That dear boy won't chew, such poor digestion. Keep an eye on his eating," she pleaded, "insist that he chew and, if you would take charge of his money. He spends it all the first day, afterwards he starves!"

I said I would do my best over Milford's chewing and cash. I felt very maternal with two boys under my wing.

Milford lived down the street; his table was pushed close to the window. I passed at mealtimes whenever possible and yelled up, "Chew, Milford, chew!" He kept his weekly allowance in a box on my mantelpiece.

"Can I run up to London this week-end?"

We would get the box down and count. Sometimes I would say, "Yes," and sometimes, "No, Milford, you can't."

Milford and I sketched around the Bushey woods. Little Canary followed us. Presently we would find her easel set close to ours. Milford and I humanized those Canaries. (We never tackled Mack.) Little Canary soon ate out of my hand; she was always fluttering around me, and I gave her a hard flutter too. I made her smoke, damn, crawl through thorny hedges, wade streams. I brought her home in such tatters as made Big Canary and Mack gasp. They were provoked at Little Canary for accepting my lead. I behaved outrageously when Mack and Big Canary were around; I wanted to shock them! I was really ashamed of myself. The boys grinned; perhaps they were ashamed of me too—they were English. Mack would say, "Where *were* you brought up?" and I would retort, "In a different land from you, thank Heaven!"

One Saturday morning I came to Studio late. The door banged on me and I "damned". I felt shudders and tension in the room, then I saw two strangers—a doll-pretty girl, and an angular sourness, who knitted beside the doll while she drew.

Kicking Little Canary's shin, I mouthed, "Who?"

"Wait till rest," Little Canary mouthed back.

It seemed that the silk-smocked, crimp-haired girl was titled and a tremendous swell, an old pupil of Mr. Whiteley's. The other was her chaperon. They had been abroad. This was their first appearance since I had been at Mr. Whiteley's studio. The girl only "arted" on Saturday mornings and was always chaperoned. The chaperon had been heard to allude to Mr. Whiteley's Studio as "that wild place!" Her lips had glued to a thread-thin line when I "damned". She stopped knitting, took a shawl from their various luggages, draped it over the doll's shoulder that was nearest to the wind which had rushed in with my entry. She took the doll's spectacles off her nose, polished them and straddled them back again, sharpened six sticks of charcoal neatly into her pocket-handkerchief, then shook the dust and sharpenings over the other students and resumed knitting. After class they were escorted to their waiting carriage by a footman bearing the girl's work gear. The Canaries and Mack bowed as they passed.

I laughed all the way home, then I drew and rhymed a skit in which we all decided that we must bring chaperons to this "wild place". Even the Master had to "bring his loving wife and she their children three."

> *The model said, "I will not sit*
> *In solitude alone,*
> *My good old woman too must come*
> *And share the model throne!"*

I took my skit to class on Monday. The Canaries were

very much shocked,—a student caricaturing a master!

"Suppose he saw!" they gasped.

"It would not kill him," I grinned.

At rest I was sittting on the fence, giggling over my skit with the boys when Mr. Whiteley came by.

"Can I share the joke?"

The boy holding the sketch wriggled, "It does not belong to me, sir, it is Miss Carr's."

Mr. Whiteley looked enquiringly at me.

"Just some nonsense, but certainly if you wish to, Mr. Whiteley."

He took the skit in his hand, called "Pose"; it was the last pose of the morning. Dead silence in the studio, Canaries very nervous. Noon struck, model and students filed out, Mr. Whiteley settled himself to read, to look. The Canaries hovered; they were going to be rather sorry to see me evicted from the class—in spite of my being colonial and bad form it had been livelier since I came, they said.

Chuckle, chuckle, laugh, roar! Great knee-slap roars! No one ever dreamed Mr. Whiteley could be so merry. The hovering Canaries stood open-mouthed.

"May I take this home to show my wife?"

"Certainly, Mr. Whiteley."

"This chaperon business has always amused her."

He did not bring my skit back next morning, instead he took from the wrapping a beautiful sketch of his own.

"Will you trade?" he held out the sketch—"My wife simply refuses to give your skit up!"

"She is most welcome to it, Mr. Whiteley, but it is not worth this."

"We think so and, anyway, I should like you to have a sketch of mine to take back to Canada."

There was wild jealousy. Mack happened to be home ill. Little Canary asked, "May I take Mr. Whiteley's picture to show Mack?"

Mack said, "Huh! I doubt *that Canadian* is capable of appreciating either the honour or the picture!"

In the little wood behind the Meadows Studio, where the cuckoos called all day, I learned a lot. Like Mr. Talmage, Mr. Whiteley said, "Trot along to your woods; I will give you your 'crit' there, where you are happy and do your best work."

That was a luscious wood, lovely in seeing, smelling and hearing. Perpetual spring seemed to be there.

I remember with affection and gratitude something special that every Master taught me. Mr. Whiteley's pet phrase was, "The coming and going of foliage is more than just flat pattern." Mr. Talmage had said, "Remember, there is sunshine too in the shadows," when my colour was going black. Sombreness of Tregenna! Sunshine of Bushey! Both woods gave me so much, so much, each in its own splendid way, and each was interpreted to me by a good, sound teacher.

Birds

I WORKED in Bushey till late Autumn, then decided to winter again in St. Ives. But first I must return to my London boarding house and get my winter clothing from a trunk stored at Mrs. Dodds'. (We were allowed to store trunks in her basement at tuppence a week, a great convenience for students like me who were moving around.)

Always, when approaching London, a surge of sinking awfulness swept over me as we came to its outskirts, and the train began slithering through suburban manufacturing districts. Open country turned to human congestion, brick and mortar pressed close both sides of our way—ache of overcrowded space, murk, dullness stared from behind the glazed fronts and backs of brick houses. No matter how hard I tried, I could not take interest in manufacturing districts—they wilted me. Love of everything, that swamped me in the country, was congealed here, stuffed away like rotten lettuce. Nothing within me responded to the hum of machinery.

A crawling slither and the train oozed into the allotted slot, opened her doors and poured us into Euston's glare and hurry. Worry about luggage came first. To me the wonder is that any ever *was* found—no checking system, identification established solely by means of a pointing finger. The hot, hard pavements of London burned my foot soles.

"Why must you fuss so immediately upon coming to town?" I enquired angrily of my aching feet, and took a huge china water-pitcher from my cubicle to the floor below for hot water. The stair was straight and very long, the jug of water heavy. Only one step more, but one too many! I reeled; every step registered a black bump on me. There I lay in a steaming pool, among pieces of broken pitcher. I might have been an aquatic plant in a fancy garden.

The steaming water seeped beneath the doors of rooms. I hurt terribly, but the water must be mopped up. My groans brought students to doors which they slammed too quick and grumpily to keep the water out of their rooms.

I was unable to rise next morning. I sent a wire to Mildred, "Tumbled downstairs, can't come." Mildred sent the carriage and insisted. So I went. I managed to keep going till bedtime. That night is a blur of awfulness. When Mildred came into my room next morning she sent quickly for the doctor. Two nurses came, straw was laid on the pavement to dull the rumble even of those elegant, smooth-rolling carriages. For six weeks I lay scarcely caring which way things went.

"Send me to a nursing home," I begged. But Mrs. Compton's cool hand was over mine, "Go to sleep, little Motor, we're here." She always wore three rings—a hoop of rubies, a hoop of sapphires, and a hoop of diamonds. Even in the darkened room the gems glowed—they are the only gems I have ever loved. They were alive and were on a loved hand.

The doctor came and came. One day after a long, long look at me, he said, "You Canadians, I notice, don't take kindly to crowded cities. Try the sea-side for her, Mrs. Compton."

"There will be trees and air," I thought, and was glad.

There were no trees. The small, private convalescent home was kept by a fool. Because she had nursed in the German Royal Family she fancied herself. Every day she took their Royal Highnesses' photographs from the mantelpiece and kissed their ugly faces before us all. It made us sick. She was the worst kind of a snob ever made.

The sea was all dazzle and the sands white. My room

was white, even the blinds. I asked for dark—the glare hurt my head. If I sat in dark corners Nurse said I was morbid! From my window I saw a scrub willow-tree. I took a rug and lay in the little back lane under the willow. Looking up into its leaves rested my eyes. Nurse rushed out, furious.

She shrieked, "Morbid nonsense! Get out onto that beach, let sunshine burn the germs out of you!"

I was wretched but I shammed robust health to get away from her house. I fooled the nurse so that she let me travel to Noel's mother. She had come several times to Belgrave Square and said, "Come to us as soon as they will let you travel. Don't wait to be well, come and get well in our garden—my four boys to wait on you!"

The journey relapsed me. I was so desperately ill that they wired to Canada. I did not know that until my sister Lizzie marched into the room. They sent her because she was on the edge of a nervous breakdown and they thought the trip would do her good. It was bad for both of us. This sister and I had never got on smoothly. We nearly sent each other crazy. She quarrelled with my doctor and my nurse, got very homesick, wanted to take me home immediately. The doctor would not let me travel. She called him a fool, said he knew nothing. She scolded me. I went to a London specialist. He was as determined about the travel as my own doctor.

"Complete rest, freedom from worry and exertion for at least one year."

He recommended an open-air Sanatorium, and, above all, that my sister go home, leave me.

Lizzie was very, very angry. She refused to go because of what people would say. By luck my guardian and his wife came tripping to the Old Country. When my guardian saw me all to bits, tears ran down his cheeks.

"Anything to get you well, Millie," he said, and prevailed on my sister to return home leaving me in a Sanatorium—no work for me for at least one year!

East Anglia Sanatorium was primarily for tuberculosis.

They also took patients like myself, who required rest, good feeding and open air. The Sanatorium was situated in a beautiful part of England. I was there for eighteen months, surrounded by slow-dyings, and coughing! . . . But for birds I doubt I could have stood it.

The countryside was alive with song-birds. It was gentle, rolling country, open fields, little woods, such as birds love. There were wild rabbit warrens too, so undermined with rabbit-holes that few humans walked there. The birds had it all to themselves and let me share.

I could not walk as the lung patients were made to under doctors' orders, slow, carefully timed walks. I was kept in bed a good deal. When up, I was allowed to ramble where I would, my only restriction was, "Do not overtire." I would lie in the near woods for hours, watching the birds.

Everyone was very good to me. The Sanatorium was run entirely by women—women doctors, women gardeners. The head doctor came down from London twice a week. Often she talked with me about Canada—she had a desire to go there.

"England beats Canada in just one thing," I said.

"What is that?"

"Song-birds."

"Why don't they import some?"

"They did, but in such a foolish way they all died— poor trapped, adult birds, terrified to death."

"Could it be successfully done?"

"I know how I'd go about it. First, I would hand-rear nestlings, take them to Canada, keep them in semi-captivity in a large, outdoor aviary. I would never liberate those old birds, but let them breed till there was a strong band of young ones to free."

"Sounds reasonable, go ahead," said the doctor.

"You mean I could raise my little birds here?"

"Why not, open air, birds in plenty!"

My life began again. I sent to London for books on how to hand-raise English song-birds. I decided to concentrate on thrushes and blackbirds. One month now and they would start nesting. Buds on hedge-rows were no more than reddish bulges when blackbirds and thrushes began hurrying twigs and straws into the larger crotches and firming sticks for foundations, lining the nests with mud. Mother thrush and I were friends long before the eggs hatched; she did not suspect me of being a sneak-thief.

I took young birds, nest and all, just before consciousness chased the blank from the fledglings' eyes. Once they saw, it was too late, for they cowered down in the nest and would not feed. My hand must be the first idea in their brains connected with food. Had they seen their feathered mother before me, they would have preferred her. Mother thrush was delighted to be relieved of her responsibility. She was already planning her next nest. If you went out after a steal early next morning, she was busy building again, quite happy. Had I taken but half of her family, left the rest for her in the old nest, she would have let them die.

My nurse was co-operative. Anything that relieved the flat monotony of San life was welcomed by the patients. They were all twittery over the birds for Canada. Suddenly they became interested in ant hills and grubs. Offerings were left for my birdlings on my window ledges when patients came from walks. Soon I had all the nestlings I could care for.

The nests stood on a table by my bedside; I fed the birds every two hours between dawn and dusk, poking the food into their gaping mouths with a tiny pair of pincers I made out of wood. My nestlings grew with such furious intensity you almost saw the feathers unfold. The biggest suprise was when inspiration first touched the wings and, wriggling to be free from the crowding of brothers, the fledgling rose to his feet, flopped one wing over the side of the nest. Then suddenly he knew the ecstasy of flight. Once having spread his wings, never again could he endure the crowded nest. Oh, I knew how it felt! Hadn't I been thrilled when first I felt freedom? Now London had winged me, but I had once known what it was to be free! When they had mastered flying and feeding, the birds were put into a big cage built for them in the yard.

All the San loved my birds. Old Mr. Oakley, broken by the Boer War, wracked by coughing, crawled, by the aid of a nurse and a stick, to the cage every morning to watch my birds take their bath. Therese, the dying child in the room next mine, tapped in our special code, "How are the birds?" I would scrabble little taps all over the wall to describe their liveliness. Gardeners left tins of grubs and worms on my window sill, cook sent things from the kitchen. Patients took long-handled iron spoons on their walks and plunged them into ant-hills to rob the ants of their eggs for my thrushes. Kitchen maids donated rhubarb and cabbage leaves to lay on the grass. These, watered, drew little snails to their underneath cool—bird delicacies.

When the thrushes and blackbirds were out of hand, I took two nests of bullfinches to rear. These were the San darlings. If a patient was feeling sad, a nurse would say, "Lend the soldiers;" and off would go the cage with a row of little pink-breasted bullies sitting, singing and dancing with the bullfinch comic shuffle to cheer somebody's gasping despondency. Oh, the merry birds did help!

The big Scotch house-doctor christened me "Birdmammy" because one day she paid her rest-hour visit to find five baby bullfinches cuddled under my chin. Their wings had just become inspired. This was their first flight and made to me, the only mother they had ever known.

What birds meant to the East Anglia San only those who have lain helpless among slow-dying know. The larks, hoisting their rippling songs to Heaven, sinking with fluttering pause back into an open field! The liquid outpourings from thrush and blackbird throats! A great white owl, floating noiselessly past our open rooms, turned her head this way and that, the lights of our rooms shining her gleaming eyes. A sudden swoop—another field-mouse's career finished! Birds of East Anglia! You almost compensated for torn lungs and overwork breakdowns.

On her weekly visits to the Sanatorium the London

specialist scuttled past the door of my room, ashamed to face me. For months she had promised to write home to my people. (It took six weeks for an answer to a letter in those days.) Every week the little house-doctor pleaded with the big specialist.

"Don't forget to write to Canada about Mammy's condition." I was getting nowhere, nothing was being tried to help me.

Each week the "Big One" would say, "Dear me, I have been too busy to think of it. I will do it this week."

Then she would neglect writing again. Little house-doctor was bitter about it—I was disheartened. Had my check to the San not come regularly the "Big One" would have stirred herself to look into matters at once. Had I been a celebrity or possessed of a title she would have remembered. I was only a student who had overworked. The East Anglia Sanatorium was a company. The London doctor was its head. She snivelled over me, pretending devotion. My faith in this country was broken. I had no faith or confidence in the big, bragging doctor. She was a tuberculosis specialist. I saw patients contract all sorts of other troubles in that San. As long as their lungs healed and added glory to her reputation! Nothing else mattered.

Bitter Goodbye

WHEN THEY were about nine months old, my birds began to get very quarrelsome, damaging each other by fighting. From my bed I heard trouble in the cage but I could not go to them. I had now been in the Sanatorium for over a year. I was losing, not gaining. At last, to my dismay, I found that all my contemporaries were either dead or had gone home to continue the outdoor treatment there. A few, a very few, were cured.

The big Scotch house-doctor who was at the San when I came had been succeeded by a little English woman doctor of whom I was very fond. Most of the old nurses, too, were gone, new ones had come.

One day the London doctor introduced me to a visiting physician she had brought down with her for the week-end. She said of me, "This is the San's old-timer." Shame swept me as she said, "Sixteen months, isn't it, Mammy?" She turned to the visitor, explaining, "She's Mammy to every bird in the neighbourhood, raising nestlings to take back to Canada where they have few songsters."

Canada! Why, I was no nearer the voyage than I had been sixteen months back. I knew by everyone's gentleness to me, by the loving, evasive letters I received from old patients, it was not expected I would ever get back to Canada.

I was troubled about my birds. The old friends, who had always been willing to lend a hand with them when I was laid up, were gone—newcomers were indifferent. They did not know the birds, did not know me. The birds themselves were increasingly quarrelsome. The whole situation bothered, worried me. I pondered, unhappy.

At last the doctor had written to my people in Canada. It was decided to try a severe, more or less experimental, course of treatment. A special nurse was brought down from London, a masseuse, callous, inhuman, whom I hated. The treatment consisted of a great deal of massage, a great deal of electricity and very heavy feeding. This nurse delighted in telling horrible stories, stories of deformities and of operations while she worked over me. Her favourite story was of a nephew of hers, born without a nose. One hole in the middle of his face served as both nose and mouth; it sickened me. I appealed to the doctor who forbade nurse talking to me during the long hours of massage. This angered the woman; she turned mean to me.

The day before treatment started I said to the little house-doctor whom I was fond of, "What about my birds?"

The treatment was to last from six to eight weeks. Doctor was silent. I went silent too.

I asked, "May I get up for half an hour today?"

"You are too weak, Mammy."

"There is something I must attend to before treatment starts."

"Your nurse will do anything."

"This thing only I can do."

She gave a humouring consent. I knew she thought it made little difference. Her eyes filled; she was a dear woman.

In the quiet of the rest hour, when nobody was about, I slipped from my room, out through a side door in the corridor, into the yard where my birdcage stood. The birds heard my stick, my voice—they shrieked delightedly. I caught them every one, put them into a box which I took back into my bedroom.

Panting heavily I rang my bell, "Send doctor!"

Doctor came hurrying.

"Chloroform my birds."

"Oh, Mammy! Why not free them?"

"I love them too much! Village boys would trap the tame things—slow starvation on a diet of soaked bread and earth worms! Please, doctor! I've thought it all out."

She did what I asked.

The next day I was moved into a quiet, spacious room —treatment under the new nurse began. She would allow no one to come into the room but the doctor. I was starved on skim milk, till they had brought me as low as they dared. Gradually they changed starvation to stuffing, beating the food into my system with massage, massage, electricity— four hours of it each day. The nurse was bony-fingered, there was no sympathy in her touch; every rub of her hand antagonized me. The electricity sent me nearly mad. I was not allowed to read, to talk, to think. By degrees I gained a little strength but my nerves and spirit were in a jangle. By and by I got so that I did not want to do anything, to see anybody, and I hated the nurse. I had two months of this dreadful treatment—eighteen months in the East Anglia Sanatorium all told! Then the doctor said, "Now we will try letting you go back to work."

Work! I had lost all desire to work now. When first ill I used to ask, "When can I get back to work, when can I get back to work?" continually, and they had answered, "When you have ceased wanting to." I suppose they had got me in that place now—thought they had killed eagerness and ambition out of me.

Nurse took me up to London. I spent a wretched day or two in the house of the "Big One". At the time she was in a burst of exhilaration because she had been summoned to attend the wife of the Dean of St. Paul's. If it was not Lady this or Lord that, it was the Very Reverend Dean. Stretching after Big Pots, yearning to hang on to the skirts of titled, of "worthwhile" people—English worship of aristocracy! Oh, I loathed it! I left the doctor's house and went down to Bushey, forbidden ever to attempt working in London again.

The Bushey Studios were closed; classes would not re-open for two weeks. I took rooms in the village, disheartened, miserable, broken, crying, always crying, couldn't stop.

The San's little house-doctor took a long, round-about, cross-country journey from the San to Bushey specially to see me. I cried through her entire visit. She was deeply distressed at my condition, and I was shamed.

Through my tears and a pouring rain, I watched her wash down Bushey High Street. Yet doctor's parting words had done me vast good. This it what they were,—"I realize how hard it is after eighteen months of absolute inertness to find yourself again adrift, nobody, nothing, weak as a cat! I am proud of the fight you are putting up." After she had gone she ran back up the steps again to take me in her arms, hold me a moment tight, tight, say again, "I am proud of you!"

Oh how could she be proud of such a bitter-hearted, sloppy old coward? In my room she saw evidence of trying to pick up life's threads again. She guessed the struggle. I wished I had not cried *all* the time she was there! I'd make her laugh yet. "I'll make Little Doctor and all of them laugh!" I vowed and, running to my trunk, dug up a sketch book and fell to work.

Two weeks I laboured incessantly over a satire on the San, and on the special treatment. I wrote long doggerel verses and illustrated them by some thirty sketches in colour, steadily crying the while. The paper was all blotched with tears. I just ignored the stupid tears. The skit was funny—*really funny*; I bound the pages together, posted them off to Little Doctor—waited—.

Promptly her answer came.

"Bravo! How the staff roared!—all the staff but matron and me, we knew its price."

The world was upside down! The ones I had aimed to make laugh cried. I loved doctor's and matron's tears all the same and, believe it or not, their tears dried mine.

I went back to Mr. Whiteley's studio and slowly got into work again. It was not easy. I was weak in body, bitter in spirit. In about three months I was to be allowed to travel.

Five years and a half in London! What had I to show for it but struggle, just struggle which doesn't show, or does it, in the long run?

Mrs. Radcliffe, Mrs. Denny, Mildred had all been down to the San, from time to time, to visit me. Just now I could not bear Mrs. Radcliffe's bracing, Mrs. Denny's religion, Mrs. Compton's and Mildred's love. No, my pride could not face them, not just now. Without good-byes, I slipped through London, straight to Liverpool. Good-bye to my high hopes for work, to my beautiful birds, to my youngness! Good-bye, good-bye, good-bye—surely enough good-byes. Yet my ungracious creeping past those in London who were so kind to me has always left deep down in me a sore feeling of shame and cowardice.

I did not know the land which haze was swallowing was Ireland. I only knew I was glad to be leaving the Old World.

"Sure, it's Ireland is your home, too?" an Irish voice said at my side. I looked into the blue eyes of an Irish boy, homesick already.

"Canada is my home," I replied.

He faded into the crowd. I never saw but I thought often again of that kind boy who took for granted that my sadness was homesickness, same as his. Sad I was about my failures, but deep down my heart sang: I was returning to Canada.

Part III

Cariboo Gold

JUST BEFORE I left England a letter came from Cariboo, out in British Columbia. It said, "Visit us at our Cariboo Ranch on your way west." The inviters were intimate friends of my girlhood. They had married while I was in England. Much of their love-making had been done in my old barn studio. The husband seconded his wife's invitation, saying in a P.S., "Make it a long visit. Leave the C.P.R. train at Ashcroft. You will then travel by horse-coach to the One Hundred and Fifty Mile House up the Cariboo Road, a pretty bumpy road too. . . . I will make arrangements."

I had always wanted to see the Cariboo country. It is different from the coast, less heavily wooded, a grain and cattle-raising country. Coming as the invitation did, a break between the beating London had given me and the humiliation of going home to face the people of my own town, a failure, the Cariboo visit would be a flash of joy between two sombres. I got happier and happier every mile as we pushed west.

I loved Cariboo from the moment the C.P.R. train spat me out of its bouncy coach. It was all fresh and new and yet it contained the breath and westernness that was born in me, the thing I could not find in the Old World.

I will admit that I did suffer two days of violence at the mercy of the six-horse stage-coach which bumped me over the Cariboo Road and finally deposited me at the door of One Hundred and Fifty Mile House where my friend lived, her husband being manager of the Cariboo Trading

Company there. It had been a strange, rough journey yet full of interest. No possible springs could endure such pitch and toss as the bumps and holes in the old Cariboo road-bed played. The coach was slung on tremendous leather straps and, for all that it was so ponderous, it swayed and bounced like a swing.

A lady school-teacher, very unenthusiastic at being assigned a rural school in the Cariboo, shared the front top seat with the driver and me. She did not speak, only sighed. The three of us were buckled into our seats by a great leather apron. It caught driver round the middle and teacher and me under our chins. We might have been infant triplets strapped abreast into the seat of a mammoth pram. If we had not been strapped we would have flown off the top of the stage. At the extra-worst bumps the heads of the inside passengers hit the roof of the coach. We heard them.

We changed horses every ten miles and wished we could change ourselves, holding onto yourself mile after mile got so tiresome. The horses saved all their prance for final show-off dashings as they neared the changing barns; here they galloped full pelt. Driver shouted and the whip cracked in the clear air. Fresh horses pranced out to change places with tired ones, lively and gay, full of show-off. When blinkers were adjusted on the fresh horses so as not to tell tales, the weary ones sagged into the barn, their show-off done. The whole change only took a minute, scarcely halting our journey. Sometimes the driver let us climb a short hill on foot to ease the load and to uncramp us.

It was beautiful country we passed through—open and rolling—vast cattle ranges, zig-zag snake-fences and beast-dotted pasturage with little groves of cotton-poplars spread here and there. There were great wide tracts of wild grazing too.

The cotton-poplars and the grain-fields were turning every shade of yellow. The foliage of the trees was threaded with the cotton-wood's silver-white stems. Long, level sweeps of rippling gold grain were made richer and more luscious by contrast with the dun, already harvested stubble fields. Men had called this land "Golden Cariboo" because of the metal they took from her soil and her creeks, but Cariboo's crust was of far more exquisite gold than the ore underneath—liquid, ethereal, living gold. Everything in Cariboo was touched with gold, even the chipmunks had golden stripes running down their brown coats. They were tiny creatures, only mouse-big. They scampered, beyond belief quick, in single-file processions of twinkling hurry over the top rail of the snake-fences, racing our stage-coach.

At dark we stopped at a road-house to eat and sleep. Cariboo provides lavishly. We ate a huge meal and were then hustled off to bed only to be torn from sleep again at two a.m. and re-mealed—a terrible spread, neither breakfast, dinner, nor supper, but a "three-in-one" meal starting with porridge, bacon and eggs, and coffee, continuing with beef-steak, roast potatoes, and boiled cabbage, culminating in pudding, pie, and strong tea. The meal climaxed finally on its centre-piece, an immense, frosted jelly-cake mounted on a pedestal platter. Its gleaming frosting shimmered under a coal-oil lamp, suspended over the table's centre. At first I thought it was a wedding-cake but as every meal in every road-house in Cariboo had just such a cake I concluded it was just Cariboo. The teacher's stomach and mine were taken aback at such a meal at such an hour. We shrank, but our hostess and the driver urged, "Eat, eat; it's a long, hard ride and no stop till noon." The bumps would digest us. We did what we could.

At three a.m. we trembled out into the cold stillness of starry not-yet-day. A slow, long hill was before us. The altitude made my head woozey. It wobbled over the edge of the leather apron buckled under our chins. Between teacher and driver I slept, cosy as jam in a "roly-poly".

The One Hundred and Fifty Mile trading post consisted of a store, a road-house where travellers could stop or could pause between stages to get a meal, and a huge cattle barn. These wooden structures stood on a little rise and, tucked below, very primitive and beyond our seeing and hearing (because the tiny village lay under the bluff on which sat

199

the Cariboo Trading Company) were a few little houses. These homes housed employees of the Company. On all sides, beyond the village, lay a rolling sea of land, vast cattle ranges, snake-fenced grain-fields—space, space. Wild creatures, big and little, were more astonished than frightened at us; all they knew was space.

My friend met the coach.

"Same old Millie!" she laughed. Following her point and her grin, I saw at my feet a small black cat rubbing ecstatically round my shoes.

"Did you bring her all the way uncrated?"

"I did not bring her at all; does she not belong here?"

"Not a cat in the village."

Wherever she belonged, the cat claimed me. It was as if she had expected me all her life and was beyond glad to find me. She followed my every step. We combed the district later trying to discover her owner. No one had seen the creature before. At the end of my two months' visit in the Cariboo I gave her to a kind man in the store, very eager to have her. Man and cat watched the stage lumber away. The man stooped to pick up his cat, she was gone—no one ever saw her again.

I can never love Cariboo enough for all she gave to me. Mounted on a cow-pony I roamed the land, not knowing where I went—to be alive, going, that was enough. I absorbed the trackless, rolling space, its cattle, its wild life, its shy creatures who wondered why their solitudes should be plagued by men and guns.

Up to this time I had always decorously used a side-saddle and had ridden in a stiff hat and the long, flapping habit proper for the date. There was only one old, old horse, bony and with a rough, hard gait that would take side-saddle in the Cariboo barns. My friend always rode this ancient beast and used an orthodox riding-habit. I took my cue from a half-breed girl in the district, jumped into a Mexican cow-boy saddle and rode astride, loping over the whole country, riding, riding to nowhere. Oh goodness! how happy I was! Though far from strong yet, in this freedom and fine air I was gaining every week. When tired, I threw the reins over the pommel and sat back in the saddle leaving direction to the pony, trusting him to take me home unguided. He never failed.

I tamed squirrels and chipmunks, taking them back to Victoria with me later. I helped my host round up cattle, I trailed breaks in fences when our cattle strayed. A young coyote and I met face to face in a field once. He had not seen nor winded me. We nearly collided. We sat down a few feet apart to consider each other. He was pretty, this strong young prairie-wolf.

The most thrilling sight I saw in the Cariboo was a great company of wild geese feeding in a field. Wild geese are very wary. An old gander is always posted to warn the flock of the slightest hint of danger. The flock were feeding at sundown. The field looked like an immense animated page of "pothooks" as the looped necks of the feeding birds rose and fell, rose and fell. The sentinel honked! With a whirr of wings, a straightening of necks and a tucking back of legs, the flock rose instantly—they fell into formation, a wedge cutting clean, high air, the irregular monotony of their honking tumbling back to earth, falling in a flurry through the air, helter-skelter, falling incessant as the flakes in a snow storm. Long after the sky had taken the geese into its hiding their honks came back to earth and us.

Bands of coyotes came to the creek below our windows and made night hideous by agonized howlings. No one had warned me and the first night I thought some fearfulness had overtaken the world. Their cries expressed woe, cruelty, anger, utter despair! Torn from sleep I sat up in my bed shaking, my room reeking with horror! Old miners say the coyote is a ventriloquist, that from a far ridge he can throw his voice right beside you, while from close he can make himself sound very far. I certainly thought that night my room was stuffed with coyotes.

In Cariboo I did not paint. I pushed paint away from me together with the failure and disappointment of the last five years.

There was an Indian settlement a mile or two away. I used to ride there to barter my clothing for the Indians' beautiful baskets. At last I had nothing left but the clothes I stood in but I owned some nice baskets.

My friend was puzzled and disappointed. We had known each other since early childhood. She had anticipated my companionship with pleasure—but here I was!

"Millie!" she said disgustedly, "you are as immature and unsophisticated as when you left home. You must have gone through London with your eyes shut!" and, taking her gun, she went out.

She seldom rode, preferring to walk with gun and dog. She came home in exasperated pets of disgust.

"Never saw a living creature—did you?"

"All kinds; the critters know the difference between a sketching easel and a gun," I laughed.

We never agreed on the subject of shooting. She practiced on any living thing. It provoked her that creatures would not sit still to be shot.

"London has not sophisticated you at all," she complained. "I have quite outgrown you since I married."

Perhaps, but maybe London had had less to do with retarding my development than disappointment had. She was bored by this country as I had been bored by London. Quite right, we were now far apart as the poles—no one's fault. Surfacely we were very good friends, down deep we were not friends at all, not even acquaintances.

Winter began to nip Cariboo. The coast called and Vancouver Island, that one step more Western than the West. I went to her, longing yet dreading. Never had her forests looked so solemn, never her mountains so high, never her drift-laden beaches so vast. Oh, the gladness of my West again! Immense Canada! Oh, her Pacific edge, her Western limit! I blessed my luck in being born Western as I climbed the stair of my old barn studio.

During my absence my sister had lent the studio to a parson to use for a study. He had papered the walls with the *Daily Colonist,* sealed the windows. There were no cobwebs, perhaps he had concocted them into sermons. As I ran across the floor to fling the window wide everything preached at me.

Creak of rusty hinge, the clean air rushed in! The cherry tree was gone, only the memory of its glory left. Was everything gone or dead or broken? No! Hurrying to me came Peacock, my Peacock! Who had told him I was come? He had not been up on the studio roof this last five years. Glorious, exultant, he spread himself.

Victoria had driven the woods back. My sister owned a beautiful mare which she permitted me to ride. On the mare, astride as I had ridden in Cariboo, my sheep-dog following, I went into the woods. No woman had ridden cross-saddle before in Victoria! Victoria was shocked! My family sighed. Carrs had always conformed; they believed in what always has been continuing always to be. Cross-saddle! Why, everyone disapproved! Too bad, instead of England gentling me into an English Miss with nice ways I was more *me* than ever, just pure me.

One thing England had taught me which my friends and relatives would not tolerate—smoking! Canadians thought smoking women fast, bad. There was a scene in which my eldest sister gave her ultimatum. "If smoke you must, go to the barn and smoke with the cow. Smoke in my house you shall not."

So I smoked with the cow. Neither she nor I were heavy smokers but we enjoyed each other's company.

And so I came back to British Columbia not with "know-it-all" fanfare, not a successful student prepared to carry on art in the New World, just a broken-in-health girl that had taken rather a hard whipping, and was disgruntled with the world.

Of my three intimate school friends two were married and living in other places, the third was nursing in San Francisco. I made no new friends; one does not after schooldays, unless there are others who are going your way or who have interests in common. Nobody was going my way, and their way did not interest me. I took my sheep-dog and rode out to the woods. There I sat, dumb as a plate, staring, absorbing tremendously, though I did not realize it at the time. Again I was struck by that vague similarity between London crowds and Canadian forests; each having its own sense of terrific power, density and intensity, but similarity ceased there. The clamorous racing of hot human blood confused, perhaps revolted me a little sometimes. The woods standing, standing, holding the cool sap of vegetation were healing, restful after seeing the boil of humanity.

It did me no harm to sit idle, still pondering in the vastness of the West where every spilled sound came tumbling back to me in echo. After the mellow sweetness of England with its perpetual undertone of humanity it was good to stand in space.

Vancouver

EVERYTHING was five and a half years older than when I left home but then so was I—five of the most impressionable years of life past. I was glad some things had changed, sorry others had. I was sorry to say good-bye to my little self—I mean the little self that is always learning things without knowing that it is doing so.

It was nice now to go to church by choice and not be pushed there. It was nice even to miss occasionally without feeling "helly". The Y.W.C.A were now firmly established in a fine new building of their own and did not have to pray all over our floors. My sisters belonged to many religious and charitable societies. The choice was left to me— Ladies' Aid, Y.W.C.A., King's Daughters, a dozen others. I joined none.

There were no artists in Victoria. I do not remember if the Island Arts and Crafts Club had begun its addled existence. When it did, it was a very select band of elderly persons, very prehistoric in their ideas on Art.

It was nice to be home, but I was not there for long because the Ladies' Art Club of Vancouver asked me to accept the post of Art teacher to their Club. So I went to live in Vancouver. The Vancouver Art Club was a cluster of society women who intermittently packed themselves and their admirers into a small rented studio to drink tea and jabber art jargon.

Once a week I was to pose a model for them and criticize their work. I had been recommended by one of their members who was an old Victorian and who had known me all my life. She was abroad when I accepted the post.

The Art Club, knowing I was just back from several years of study in London, expected I would be smart and swagger a bit. When they saw an unimportant, rather shy girl they were angry and snubbed me viciously, humiliating me in every possible way. Their President was a wealthy society woman. Floating into the studio an hour or more late for class, she would swagger across the room, ignoring me entirely and change the model's pose. Then she would paint the background of her study an entirely different colour to the one I had arranged. If I said anything, she replied, "I prefer it so!"

Other members of the class, following her lead, and tossing their heads, would say with mock graciousness, "You may look at my work if you would like to, but I wish no criticism from you." At the end of my first month they dismissed me. Perhaps I did look horribly young for the post.

On her return to Vancouver my sponsor sent for me.

"I hear the Ladies' Club have dismissed you, my dear."

"Yes. I am glad!"

"All were unanimous in their complaint."

"What was it?"

"Millie, Millie!" she smiled, "You tried to make them take their work seriously! Society ladies serious! My dear, how could you?" she laughed.

"They are vulgar, lazy old beasts," I spluttered. "I am glad they dismissed me and I am proud of the reason. I hate their kind. I'd rather starve."

"What shall you do now?"

"I have taken a studio in Granville Street. The only woman in the Art Club who was decent to me (an American) has sent her little daughter to me for lessons. The child has interested her schoolmates. Already I have a class of nice little girls."

"Good, with them you will be more successful. The Club's former teacher was 'society'. She understood the Club ladies, complimented and erased simultaneously, substituting some prettiness of her own in the place of their daubs, something which they could exhibit. They liked that. She was older, too."

The snubbing by the Vancouver Ladies' Art Club starched me. My pride stiffened, my energy crisped. I fetched my sheep-dog and cage of bullfinches from Victoria, added a bunch of white rats, a bowl of goldfish, a cockatoo and a parrot to my studio equipment and fell into vigorous, hard, happy work, finding that I had learned more during those frustrated years in England than I had supposed—narrow, conservative, dull-seeing, perhaps rather mechanical, but nevertheless honest.

Because I did not teach in the way I had been taught, parents were sceptical, but my young pupils were eager, enthusiastic. Every stroke was done from objects or direct from life-casts, live-models, still life, animals.

Young Vancouver had before been taught only from flat copy. I took my classes into the woods and along Vancouver's waterfront to sketch. A merry group we were, shepherded by a big dog, each pupil carrying a campstool and an easel, someone carrying a basket from which the cockatoo, Sally, screeched, "Sally is a Sally." That was Sally's entire vocabulary. If she was left in the studio when the class went sketching she raised such a turmoil that the neighbours objected. Out with the class, joining in the fun, Sally was too happy even to shout that Sally was a Sally.

We sat on beaches over which great docks and stations are now built, we clambered up and down wooded banks solid now with Vancouver's commercial buildings.

Stanley Park at that time was just seven miles of virgin forest, three quarters surrounded by sea. Alone, I went there to sketch, loving its still solitudes—no living creature but dog Billie and me, submerged beneath a drown of undergrowth. Above us were gigantic spreads of pines and cedar boughs, no bothersome public, no rubbernoses. Occasional narrow trails wound through bracken and tough salal tangle. Underfoot, rotting logs lay, upholstered deep in moss, bracken, forest wastage. Your feet never knew how deep they would sink.

I loved too the Indian reserve at Kitsilano and to the North Vancouver Indian Mission Billie and I went for long days, our needs tucked into my sketch-sack and great content in our hearts.

Vancouver was then only a little town, but it was growing hard. Almost every day you saw more of her forest being pushed back, half-cleared, waiting to be drained and built upon—mile upon mile of charred stumps and boggy skunk-cabbage swamp, root-holes filled with brown stagnant water, reflecting blue sky by day, rasping with frog croaks by night, fireweed, rank of growth, springing from the dour soil to burst into loose-hung, lush pink blossoms, dangling from red stalks, their clusters of loveliness trying to hide the hideous transition from wild to tamed land.

The foundationless Ladies' Art Club of social Vancouver was crumbling; their President came to me, asking that I give up my studio and share theirs thereby lessening their rental. I refused. Then she said, "Shall we give up ours and come to share yours? Our teas of course—but," smirked the lady, "prestige of the Vancouver Ladies' Art Club behind your classes!"

"No, no, no! I don't want your prestige—I won't have the Ladies' Art Club in my studio!"

The President tore down my stairs. I had not imagined Presidents could rush with such violence.

The first year that I lived and taught in Vancouver my sister Alice and I took a pleasure trip up to Alaska.

The Klondyke rush had been over just a few years. We travelled on a Canadian boat as far as Skagway, end of sea travel for Klondyke. Prospectors had left steamers here and gone the rest of the way on foot over a very rough trail. Those who could afford to, took pack-beasts; those who could not, packed their things on their own backs.

The mushroom town of Skagway had sprung up almost overnight. It consisted of haphazard shanties, spilled over

half-cleared land. The settlement lay in a valley so narrow
it was little more than a ravine heading the shallow, muddy
inlet. Three tipsy plank walks on crooked piles hobbled
across the mud to meet water deep enough to dock steam-
boats. Each runway ended in a blob of wharf.

Jumping gaps where planks had broken away, I went
out on to the end of one wharf to look back at Skagway.
Bits of my clothing and sketching equipment blew off into
the sea.

Wind always moaned and cried down the little valley,
smacking this, overturning that shanty. The little town
was strewn with collapsed buildings. Crying, crying, the
valley was always crying. There was always rain or mist or
moaning wind. It had seen such sadness, this valley—high
hopes levelled like the jerry-built shanties, broken, crazed
men, drinking away their disappointments.

A curious little two-coach train ran up the valley twice
a week. Its destination was White Horse. It followed the
old Klondyke trail. We took it up as far as the summit.
Here, side by side, where their land met, fluttered two
flags, British and American. The train jogged and bumped
a good deal. We passed through valleys full of silence,
mocking our noisy little train with echoes because our black
smoke dirtied the wreaths of white mist which we met in
the valleys.

A stark, brooding, surly land was this, gripping deep
its secrets. Huddles of bones bleached by the wayside—
bullock bones, goat and horse bones, beasts for whom the
lure of gold did not exist but who, broken under burdens
of man's greed, had fallen by the way, while man, spurred
on by the gold glitter, shouldered the burdens of the dead
beasts and pushed further. In the valley, drowned under
lush growth, we stumbled upon little desolate log shanties,
half built. The finger of the wild now claimed the cabins,
saying, "Mine, mine!", mossing them, growing trees
through the mud floors and broken roofs.

"How do these come to be here?" I asked.

"Failures—men who lacked the courage to go home

beaten. Most drank themselves to death. For many, a gun was their last, perhaps their best, friend."

No wonder the valley cried so! Of those who stayed in Skagway it was seldom said, "He made good. He struck it lucky!" The lucky ones went down to the cities, scarred by their Klondyke experience, seldom happier for their added gold.

We stayed one week in Skagway; then, taking an American steamer, crossed to Sitka on Baronoff Island.

Sitka had an American army barracks, a large Indian village, and an ancient Russian church. It also had many, many very large, black ravens, sedate birds but comical. They scavenged the village, calling to one another back in the woods. The male and the female made different squawks; the cry of one was a throaty "Qua", the other answered, "Ping!", sharp and strident as a twanged string. At the top of its flagpole the barracks had a gilt ball which had great attraction for the ravens. There were always three or four of them earnestly trying to get firm foothold on the rounded surface. It was amusing to watch them.

As we walked through the little town of Sitka I saw on a door, "Picture Exhibition—Walk In". We did so.

The studio was that of an American artist who summered in Sitka and wintered in New York where he sold his summer's sketches, drab little scenes which might have been painted in any place in the world. He did occasionally stick in a totem pole but only ornamentally as a cook sticks a cherry on the top of a cake.

The Indian totem pole is not easy to draw. Some of them are very high, they are elaborately carved, deep symbolical carving, as much or more attention paid to the attributes of the creature as to its form.

The Indian used distortion, sometimes to fill spaces but mostly for more powerful expressing than would have been possible had he depicted actualities—gaining strength, weight, power by accentuation.

The totem figures represented supernatural as well as natural beings, mythological monsters, the human and animal figures making "strong talk", bragging of their real or imagined exploits. Totems were less valued for their workmanship than for their "talk".

The Indian's language was unwritten: his family's history was handed down by means of carvings and totemic emblems painted on his things. Some totems were personal, some belonged to the whole clan.

The American artist found me sketching in the Indian village at Sitka. He looked over my shoulder; I squirmed with embarrassment. He was twice my age and had had vastly more experience.

He said, "I wish I had painted that. It has the true Indian flavour."

The American's praise astounded me, set me thinking.

We passed many Indian villages on our way down the coast. The Indian people and their Art touched me deeply. Perhaps that was what had given my sketch the "Indian flavour". By the time I reached home my mind was made up. I was going to picture totem poles in their own village settings, as complete a collection of them as I could.

With this objective I again went up north next summer and each successive summer during the time I taught in Vancouver. The best material lay off the beaten track. To reach the villages was difficult and accomodation a serious problem. I slept in tents, in roadmakers' toolsheds, in missions, and in Indian houses. I travelled in anything that floated in water or crawled over land. I was always accompanied by my big sheep-dog.

Indian Art broadened my seeing, loosened the formal tightness I had learned in England's schools. Its bigness and stark reality baffled my white man's understanding. I was as Canadian-born as the Indian but behind me were Old World heredity and ancestry as well as Canadian environment. The new West called me, but my Old World heredity, the flavour of my upbringing, pulled me back. I had been schooled to see outsides only, not struggle to pierce.

The Indian caught first at the inner intensity of his subject, worked outward to the surfaces. His spiritual conception he buried deep in the wood he was about to carve. Then—chip! chip! his crude tools released the symbols that were to clothe his thought—no sham, no mannerism. The lean, neat Indian hands carved what the Indian mind comprehended.

Indian Art taught me directness and quick, precise decisions. When paying ten dollars a day for hire of boat and guide, one cannot afford to dawdle and haver this vantage point against that.

I learned a lot from the Indians, but who except Canada herself could help me comprehend her great woods and spaces? San Francisco had not, London had not. What about this New Art Paris talked of? It claimed bigger, broader seeing.

My Vancouver classes were doing well. I wrote home, "Saving up to go to Paris."

Everybody frowned—hadn't London been a strong enough lesson but I must try another great city?

But I always took enough from my teaching earnings to go north and paint in the Indian villages, even while saving for Paris.

One summer, on returning from a northern trip, I went first to Victoria to visit my sisters. There I received a curt peremptory command: "Hurry to the Empress hotel. A lady from England wishes to see you on business connected with your Indian sketches."

The woman was screwed up and frumpy, so stuffed with her own importance that she bulged and her stretched skin shone.

"I wish to see those Indian sketches of yours."

"For the moment that is not possible; they are stored in my Vancouver studio and it is rented," I replied.

"Then you must accompany me to Vancouver tonight and get them out."

"Do you wish to buy my sketches?"

"Certainly not. I only want to borrow them for the purpose of illustrating my lectures entitled 'Indians and Artists of Canada's West Coast'."

"Where do I come in?"

"You?—Publicity—I shall mention your work. Oxford! Cambridge!"

Her eyes rolled, her high-bridged nose stuck in the air. I might have been a lump of sugar, she the pup. Oxford and Cambridge signalled. Pup snapped, Oxford and Cambridge gulped—me.

"I shall see you at the midnight boat, then? You may share my stateroom," magnanimously.

"Thanks, but I'm not going to Vancouver."

"What! You cannot be so poor spirited! My work is patriotic. I am philanthropic. I advance civilization—I educate."

"You make nothing for yourself exploiting our Indians?"

"After expenses, perhaps just a trifle.... You will not help the poor Indian by lending the Alert Bay sketches? My theme centres around Alert Bay."

My interest woke.

"You have been there? Are you familiar with it?

"Oh, yes, yes! Our boat stopped there for twenty minutes. I walked through the village, saw houses, poles, people."

"And you dare talk and write about our Coast Indians having only that much data! The tourist folders do better than that! Good-bye!"

"Stop!"

She clutched my sleeve as I went out the hotel door— followed me down the steps hatless, bellowed at me all the way home, spluttering like the kick-up waves behind a boat. She stalked into our drawing room, sat herself down.

I said, "Excuse me, I am going out."

She handed me a card.

"My London Club. It will always find me. Your better self will triumph!"

She smiled at, patted me.

I said, "Listen! England is not interested in our West.

213

I was in London a few years ago, hard up. A well known author wrote a personal letter for me to a big London publisher.

'Take this to him with a dozen of your Indian sketches,' she said, 'and what a grand calendar they will make! England is interested in Canada just now.'

A small boy took my letter and returned, his nasty little nose held high, his aitchless words insolent.

'Leave yer stuff, Boss'll look it over *if* 'e 'as toime.'

I started down the stair.

"Ere, where's yer stuff? Yer ha'n't left any?'

'It is going home with me.'

At the bottom of the third flight the boy caught up with me.

'Boss says 'e'll see you now.'

The elegant creature spread my sketches over his desk.

'America, eh? Well, take 'em there. Our British public want this.' He opened a drawer crammed with pink-coated hunting scenes. 'Indians belong to America; take 'em there.'

'Canada happens to be British,' I said, 'and these are Canadian Indians.'

I put the sketches back in their wrappings.

Teach your English people geography, Madam! Then maybe they will be interested in British things. Half the people over here don't know that all the other side of the Atlantic does not belong entirely to the Americans."

France

"TWO PARROTS out in Canada waiting your return! Is it absolutely necessary that you buy another, Millie?"

"Those at home are green parrots; this in an African-grey. I have always wanted an African-grey frightfully. Here we are in Liverpool, actually at Cross's, world-wide animal distributors—it is the opportunity of a lifetime."

Perhaps pity of my green, sea-sick face softened my sister's heart and opened her purse. Half the price of the "African-grey" stole into my hand.

We called the bird Rebecca and she was a most disagreeable parrot. However, nothing hoisted my spirits like a new pet, the delight of winning its confidence!

Hurrying through London, we crossed the Channel, slid through lovely French country—came to Paris.

My sister knew French but would not talk. I did not know French and would not learn. I had neither ear nor patience. I wanted every moment of Paris for Art.

My sister studied the history of Paris, kept notes and diaries. I did not care a hoot about Paris history. I wanted *now* to find out what this "New Art" was about. I heard it ridiculed, praised, liked, hated. Something in it stirred me, but I could not at first make head or tail of what it was all about. I saw at once that it made recent conservative painting look flavourless, little, unconvincing.

I had brought with me a letter of introduction to a very modern artist named Harry Gibb. When we had found a small flat in the Latin Quarter, Rue Campagne Premier, off Montparnasse Avenue, I presented my letter.

Harry Gibb was dour, his wife pretty. They lived in a studio overlooking a beautiful garden, cultivated by nuns. I stood by the side of Harry Gibb, staring in amazement up at his walls. Some of his pictures rejoiced, some shocked me. There was rich, delicious juiciness in his colour, interplay between warm and cool tones. He intensified vividness by the use of complementary colour. His mouth had a crooked, tight-lipped twist. He was fighting bitterly for recognition of the "New Art". I felt him watching me, quick to take hurt at even such raw criticism as mine. Mrs. Gibb and my sister sat upon a sofa. After one look, my sister dropped her eyes to the floor. Modern Art appalled her.

Mr. Gibb's landscapes and still life delighted me— brilliant, luscious, clean. Against the distortion of his nudes I felt revolt. Indians distorted both human and animal forms—but they distorted with meaning, for emphasis, and with great sincerity. Here I felt distortion was often used for design or in an effort to shock rather than convince. Our Indians get down to stark reality.

I could not face that tight-lipped, mirthless grin of Mr. Gibb's with too many questions. There were many perplexities to sort out.

Strange to say, it was Mrs. Gibb who threw light on many things about the "New Art" for me. She was not a painter but she followed the modern movement closely. I was braver at approaching her than her husband with questions.

I asked Mr. Gibb's advice as to where I should study. "Colorossi," he replied. "At Colorossi's men and women students work together. At Julien's the classes are separate. It is often distinct advantage for women students to see the stronger work of men."—Mr. Gibb had not a high opinion of the work of woman artists.

The first month at Colorossi's was hard. There was no other woman in the class; there was not one word of my own language spoken. The French professor gabbled and gesticulated before my easel—passed on. I did not know whether he had praised or condemned. I missed women; there was not even a woman model. I begged my sister to go to the office and enquire if I were in the wrong place. They said. "No, Mademoiselle is quite right where she is. Other ladies will come by and by."

I plodded mutely on, till one day I heard a splendid, strong English "damn" behind me. Turning, I saw a big man ripping the lining pocket from his jacket with a knife. I saw, too, from his dirty brushes how badly he needed a paint rag.

I went to the damner and said, "Mr., if you will translate my lessons I will bring you a clean paint-rag every morning."

Paint-rags were always scarce in Paris. He agreed, but he was often absent.

The Professor said I was doing very well, I had good colour sense.

That miserable, chalky, lifelessness that had seized me in London overtook me again. The life-class rooms were hot and airless. Mr. Gibb told me of a large studio run by a young couple who employed the best critics in Paris. Mr. Gibb himself criticized there. Students said he was dour and very severe, but that he was an exceedingly good teacher. I would also have the advantage of getting criticism in my own language.

I studied in this studio only a few weeks and, before Mr. Gibb's month of criticism came, I was flat in hospital where I lay for three hellish months and came out a wreck. The Paris doctor said, as had the London one, I must keep out of big cities or die. My sister and I decided to go to Sweden.

While gathering strength to travel, I sat brooding in an old cemetery at the foot of our street. Why did cities hate, thwart, damage me so? Home people were wearying of my breakdowns. They wrote, "Give Art up, come home—stay home."

I showed some of my Indian sketches to Mr. Gibb. He was as convinced as I that the "New Art" was going to help my work out west, show me a bigger way of approach.

We enjoyed Sweden. She was very like Canada. I took hot salt-baths. In spring we returned to France, but I never worked in the studios of Paris again. I joined a class in landscape-painting that Mr. Gibb had just formed in a place two hours run from Paris. The little town was called Cressy-en-Brie. Mrs. Gibb found me rooms close to their own. My sister remained in Paris.

Cressy was quaint. It was surrounded by a canal. Many fine houses backed on the canal; they had great gardens going to the edge of the water and had little wash-booths on the canal—some were private, some public. The women did their laundry here and were very merry about it. Shrill voices, boisterous laughter, twisted in and out between the stone walls of the canal. Lovely trees drooped over the walls to dabble their branches. Women knelt in wooden trays, spread washing on flat stones before the washing-booths, soaped, folded, beat with paddles, rinsed. Slap, slap, went the paddles smacking in the soap, and out the dirt, while the women laughed and chatted, and the water gave back soapy reflections of their rosy faces and white coifs.

The streets of Cressy were narrow, and paved with cobblestones. Iron-rimmed cartwheels clattered noisily, so did wooden shoes. Pedlars shouted, everybody shouted so as to be heard above the racket.

Opposite my bedroom window was a wine-shop. They were obliged to close at midnight. To evade the law the wine vendors carried tables into the middle of the street and continued carousing far into the night. I have watched a wedding-feast keep it up till four in the morning, periodically leaving the feast to procession round the town, carrying lanterns and shouting. Sleep was impossible. I took what fun I could out of watching from my window.

Distant from Cressy by a mile or by a half-mile, were tiny villages in all directions. Each village consisted of one street of stone cottages, whitewashed. A delicate trail of grape-vine was trained above every cottage door, its main stem twisted, brown and thick as a man's arm, its greenery well tended and delicately lovely.

They grow things beautifully, these Frenchmen—trees, vines, flowers—you felt the living things giving back all the love and care the growers bestowed on them. A Scotch nurseryman of wide repute told me arboriculturists went to France to study; nowhere else could they learn better the art of growing, caring for, pruning trees.

I tramped the country-side, sketch sack on shoulder. The fields were lovely, lying like a spread of gay patchwork against red-gold wheat, cool, pale oats, red-purple of new-turned soil, green, green grass, and orderly, well-trimmed trees.

The life of the peasants was hard, but it did not harden their hearts nor their laughter. They worked all day in the fields, the cottages stood empty.

At night I met weary men and women coming home, bent with toil but happy-hearted, pausing to nod at me and have a word with Josephine, a green parrot I had bought in Paris and used to take out sketching with me. She wore an anklet and chain and rode on the rung of my camp-stool. The peasants loved Josephine; Rebecca was a disappointment. She was sour, malevolent. Josephine knew more French words than I. I did flatter myself, however, that my grin had more meaning for the peasants than Josephine's French chatter.

Mr. Gibb took keen interest in my work, despite my being a woman student. His criticisms were terse—to the point. I never came in contact with his other students. They took tea with Mrs. Gibb often. Mr. Gibb showed them his work. He never showed it to me. Peeved, I asked, "Why do you never allow me to see your own work now, Mr. Gibb?"

The mirthless, twisted grin came, "Don't have to. Those others don't know what they are after, you do. Your work must not be influenced by mine. You will be one of the painters,—women painters," he modified, "of your day." That was high praise from Mr. Gibb! But he could never let me forget I was only a woman. He would never allow a woman could compete with men.

One day I ruined a study through trying an experiment. I expected a scolding. Instead, Mr. Gibb, grinning, said, "That's why I like teaching you! You'll risk ruining your best in order to find something better."

He had one complaint against me, however. He said, "You work too hard. Always at it. Easy! Easy! Why such pell-mell haste?"

"Mr. Gibb, I dare not loiter; my time over here is so short! Soon I must go back to Canada."

"You can work out in Canada—all life before you."

I replied, "You do not understand. Our far West has complete art isolation ... no exhibitions, no artists, no art talk. . . ."

"So much the better! Chatter, chatter, chatter—where does it lead?" said Mr. Gibb. "Your silent Indian will teach you more than all the art jargon."

I had two canvases accepted and well hung in the Salon d'Automne (the rebel Paris show of the year). Mr. Gibb was pleased.

My sister returned to Canada. The Gibbs moved into Britanny—I with them.

St. Efflamme was a small watering place. For six weeks each year it woke to a flutter of life. People came from cities to bathe and to eat—the little hotel was famed for its good food. The holiday guests came and went punctually to the minute, then St. Efflamme went to sleep again for another year.

The Gibbs' rooms were half a mile away from the hotel. I had no one to translate for me. Except for talk with my parrots I lived dumb. Madame Pishoudo owned the hotel, her son cooked for us, her niece was maid. All of them were very kind to the parrots and me.

I was at work in the fields or woods at eight o'clock each morning. At noon I returned to the hotel for dinner, rested until three. Mr. Gibb, having criticized my study of the morning out where I worked, now came to the hotel and criticized the afternoon work done the day before. My supper in a basket, I went out again, did a late afternoon sketch, ate my supper, then lay flat on the ground, my eyes on the trees above me or shut against the earth, according as I backed or fronted my rest. Then up again and at it till dark.

I had a gesticulating, nodding, laughing acquaintance with every peasant. Most of them were very poor. Canadian cows would have scorned some of the stone huts in which French peasants lived. Our Indian huts were luxurious compared with them. Earth floor, one black cook-pot for all purposes—when performing its rightful function it sat ouside the door mounted on a few stones, a few twigs burning underneath—cabbage soup and black bread appeared to be the staple diet. The huts had no furniture. On the clay floor a portion framed in with planks and piled with straw was bed for the whole family. There was no window, no hearth, what light and air entered the hut did so through the open door. Yet these French peasants were always gay, always singing, chattering.

I watched two little girls playing "Mother" outside a hut one day. For babies one dandled a stick, the other a stone. They sang and lullabied, wrapping their "children" in the skirt of the one poor garment clinging round their own meagre little figures. Whatever they lacked of life's necessities, nature had abundantly bestowed upon them maternal instinct.

I stuffed paint rags with grass, nobbed one end for a head, straw sticking out of its top for hair. I painted faces on the rag, swathed the creatures in drawing paper, and gave each little girl the first dolly she had ever owned. She kissed, she hugged. Never were grand dolls so fondly cherished.

On a rounded hill-top among gorse bushes a little cowherd *promenaded* her *vache*. I loved this dignified phrase in connection with the small, agile little Breton cows. The child's thin legs were scratched by the furze bushes as she rustled among them, rounding up her little cows. She had but one thin, tattered garment—through its holes you saw bare skin. She knitted as she herded. Shyly she crept nearer and nearer. I spoke to her in English. She shook her head. Beyond *promener la vache* I could not understand her. She came closer and closer till she knelt by my side, one grimy little hand on my knee. All the time she watched my mouth intently. If I laughed, her face poked forward, looking, looking. Did the child want to see my laugh being made? I was puzzled. There was great amazement in her big, dark eyes. Presently she fingered her own white teeth and pointed to mine.

"D'or, d'or," she murmured. I understood then that it was my gold-crowned tooth which had so astonished her.

There was an aloof ridge of land behind the village of St. Efflamme. I climbed it often. On the top stood three cottages in a row and one stable. Two of the cottages were tight shut, their owners working in the fields. In the third cottage lived a bricklayer and his family. The woman was always at home with her four small children. They ran after her like a brood of chicks. The children sat round me as I worked; always little Annette, aged four, was closest, a winsome, pretty thing, very shy. I made the woman understand that I came from Canada and would soon be returning. She told the children. Annette came very close, took a corner of my skirt, tugged it and looked up beseeching.

The mother said, "Annette wants go you Canada."

I put my arm round her. With wild crying the child suddenly broke away, clinging to her mother and to France.

This woman was proud of her comfortable house; she beckoned me to *come see*. The floor was of bare, grey earth, swept clean. Beds were concealed in the walls behind sliding panels. There was a great open hearth with a swinging crane and a huge black pot. There were two rush-bottom chairs and four little wooden stools, a table, a broom and a cat. On the shelf were six Breton bowls for the cabbage soup smelling ungraciously this very moment as it cooked. A big loaf of black bread was on the shelf too.

They were a dear, kind, happy family. I made a beautiful rag doll for Annette. It had scarlet worsted hair. Annette was speechless—she clutched the creature tight, kissing its rag nose as reverently as if it had been the Pope's toe. She held her darling at arm's length to look. Her kiss had left the rag nose black. Laying the doll in her mother's arms she ran off sobbing. . . . We saw her take a little bucket to the well in the garden. When Annette came back to us there was a circle round her mouth several shades lighter than the rest of her face. The front of her dress was wet and soapy. She seized her doll—hugged and hugged again.

There was a farm down in the valley—house, stables and hayricks formed a square. The court sheltered me from the wind. I often worked there. A Breton matron in her black dress and white cap came out of the house.

"Burrr! pouf! pouf!" she laughed, mocking the wind. Then, pointing to my blue hands, beckoned me to follow. She was proud of her cosy home. It was well-to-do, even sumptuous for a peasant. Fine brasses were on the mantel-shelf, a side of bacon, strings of onions, hanks of flax for spinning hung from the rafters. There was a heavy, black table, solid and rich with age, a bench on either side of the table, a hanging lamp above. There was a great open hearth and, spread on flat stones, cakes were baking before the open fire—a mountain of already baked cakes stood beside the hearth. The woman saw my wonder at so many cakes and nodded. Laying three pieces of stick on the table, she pointed to the middle one—"Now", she said; to the stick on the left she pointed saying, "Before"; to the right-hand stick, "After". She went through the process of sham chewing, pointing to the great pile of cakes, saying "threshers". I nodded comprehension. The threshers were expected at her place tomorrow. The cakes were her preparation. She signified that I might sketch here where it was warm instead of facing the bitter wind. Again she sat herself by the hearth to watch the cakes and took up her knitting.

The outer door burst open! Without invitation, a Church-of-England clergyman and two high-nosed English women entered. Using English words and an occasional Breton one, the man said the English ladies wished to see a Breton home. The woman's graciousness congealed at the unmannerly entry of the three visitors. She was cold, stiff.

The visitors handled her things, asking, "How much? how much?"

"Non! Non!"

She clutched her treasures, replaced her brasses on the mantel-shelf, her irons on the hearth.

They saw the pile of cakes. The clergyman made long jumbled demands that they be allowed to taste.

"The English ladies want to try Breton cakes."

"Non, non, non!"

The woman took her cakes and put them away in a cupboard.

At last the visitors went. The woman's graciousness came back. Going to the cupboard, she heaped a plate with cakes and, pouring syrup over them, brought and set them on the table before me.

"Pour mademoiselle!"

Such a smile! Such a nod! I must eat at once! Shaking her fist at the door, the woman went outside, shutting the door behind her—burst it open—clattered in.

"Ahh!" she scolded. "Ahh!"

Again going out she knocked politely, waited. She was delighted with her play-acting, we laughed together.

Some five miles from St. Efflamme was a quaint village in which I wanted to sketch. I was told a butcher went that way every morning early, coming back at dusk. I dickered with the butcher and drove forth perched up in the cart in front of the meat, hating the smell of it. I sketched the old church standing knee deep in graves. I sketched the village and a roadside calvary. Dusk came but not the butcher. Dark fell, still no butcher. There was nothing for it but I must walk the five miles back. The road was twisty and very dark. I decided it would be best to follow along the sea-shore where there was more light. My sketch-pack weighed about fifty pounds. The sand was soft and sinky.

I was always stopping to empty it out of my shoes. I dragged into the hotel at long last, tired and very cross. Madame Pishoudo beckoned me from her little wine shop in the corner, beyond the parlour.

"That butcher! Ah! Yes, he drunk ver' often! His forget was bad; but Madame she does not forget her little one, her Mademoiselle starving in a strange village."

Madame had remembered—she had kept a little "piece" in the cupboard. Its littleness was so enormous a serving of dessert that it disgusted my tiredness. Madame Pishoudo forgot that she had supplied "her starved Mademoiselle" with a basket containing six hard-boiled eggs, a loaf split in half and furnished with great chunks of cold veal, called by Madame a sandwich, half a lobster, cheese, a bottle of wine, and sundry cookies and cakes. If one did not eat off a table, under Madame's personal supervision, one starved!

One day I shared a carriage with two ladies from Paris and we went sightseeing. I have half-forgotten what we saw of historical interest but I well remember the merry time we had. The ladies had no English, I no French words. We drank "cidre" in wayside booths, out of gay cups of Breton ware that had no saucers. I persuaded the woman to sell me two cups. I knew they sold in the market for four pennies. I offered her eight pennies apiece. She accepted and with a shrug handed them over saying the equivalent of "Mademoiselle is most peculiar!" We went into a very old church and my companions bowed to a great many saints. They dabbled in a trough of holy-water, crossing themselves and murmuring, "Merci, St. Pierre, merci." One of the ladies took my hand, dipped it into the trough, crossed my forehead and breast with it, murmuring, Merci, St. Pierre, merci!" It would be good for me, she said.

"Mr. Gibb, I have gone stale!"

The admission shamed me.

Mr. Gibb replied, "I am not surprised. Did I not warn you?—rest!"

"I dare not rest; in a month, two at most, I must return to Canada."

I heard there was a fine water colourist (Australian) teaching at Concarneau, a place much frequented by artists. I went to Concarneau—studied under her. Change of medium, change of teacher, change of environment, refreshed me. I put in six weeks' good work under her.

Concarneau was a coast fishing town. I sketched the people, their houses, boats, wine shops, sail makers in their lofts. Then I went up to Paris, crossed the English Channel, and from Liverpool set sail for Canada.

Rejected

I CAME home from France stronger in body, in thinking, and in work than I had returned from England. My seeing had broadened. I was better equipped both for teaching and study because of my year and a half in France, but still mystified, baffled as to how to tackle our big West.

I visited in Victoria, saw that it was an impossible field for work; then I went to Vancouver and opened a studio, first giving an exhibition of the work I had done in France.

People came, lifted their eyes to the walls—laughed!

"You always were one for joking—this is small children's work! Where is your own?" they said.

"This is my own work—the new way."

Perplexed, angry, they turned away, missing the old detail by which they had been able to find their way in painting. They couldn't see the forest for looking at the trees.

"The good old camera cannot lie. That's what we like, it shows everything," said the critics. This bigger, freer seeing now seemed so ordinary and sensible to me, so entirely sane! It could not have hurt me more had they thrown stones. My painting was not outlandish. It was not even ultra.

The Vancouver schools in which I had taught refused to employ me again. A few of my old pupils came to my classes out of pity,—their money burnt me. Friends I had thought sincere floated into my studio for idle chatter; they did not mention painting, kept their eyes averted from the walls, while talking to me.

In spite of all the insult and scorn shown to my new work I was not ashamed of it. It was neither monstrous, disgusting nor indecent; it had brighter, cleaner colour, simpler form, more intensity. What would Westerners have said of some of the things exhibited in Paris—nudes, monstrosities, a striving after the extraordinary, the bizarre, to arrest attention. Why should simplification to express depth, breadth and volume appear to the West as indecent, as nakedness? People did not want to see beneath surfaces. The West was ultraconservative. They had transported their ideas at the time of their migration, a generation or two back. They forgot that England, even conservative England, had crept forward since then; but these Western settlers had firmly adhered to their old, old, outworn methods and, seeing beloved England as it had been, they held to their old ideals.

That rootless organization, the Vancouver Ladies' Art Club, withered, died. It was succeeded by The Fine Arts Society, an organization holding yearly exhibitions in which I was invited to show.

My pictures were hung either on the ceiling or on the floor and were jeered at, insulted; members of the "Fine Arts" joked at my work, laughing with reporters. Press notices were humiliating. Nevertheless, I was glad I had been to France. More than ever was I convinced that the old way of seeing was inadequate to express this big country of ours, her depth, her height, her unbounded wideness, silences too strong to be broken—nor could ten million cameras, through their mechanical boxes, ever show real Canada. It had to be sensed, passed through live minds, sensed and loved.

I went to the Indian Village on the North Shore of Burrard Inlet often. Here was dawdling calm; no totem poles were in this village. The people were basket-weavers, beautiful, simple-shaped baskets, woven from split cedar roots, very strong, Indian designs veneered over the cedar-root base in brown and black cherry bark.

Indian Sophie was my friend. We sat long whiles upon

the wide church steps, talking little, watching the ferry ply between the city and the North Shore, Indian canoes fishing the waters of the Inlet, papooses playing on the beach.

The Village was centred by the Catholic Church—its doors were always wide. Wind entered to whisper among the rafters. The wooden footstools creaked beneath our knees. A giant clam-shell held holy water in the vestibule. The bell-rope dangled idly. When Sophie and I entered the church she bowed and crossed herself with holy water; so did I because it grieved Sophie so that I was not Catholic. She talked to the priest about it. The good man told her not to worry, I was the same and it was all right. Sophie and I were glad for this.

Behind the Indian Village, way up in the clouds stood "The Lions", twin mountain peaks, their crowns gleaming white against blue distance, supporting the sky on their heads.

In Spring the Village shimmered with millions of exquisite, tongueless bells of cherry-blossom (every Indian had his cherry-tree). Springtime flooded the village with new life, human, animal, vegetable. The dirt streets swarmed with papooses, puppies and kittens; old hens strutted broods, and squawked warnings against hawks and rats. Indian mothers had new papoose-cradles strapped on their backs or resting close beside them as they squatted on the floors of their houses, weaving baskets. Indian babies were temporary creatures: behaviour half-white, half-Indian, was perplexing to them. Their dull, brown eyes grew vague, vaguer—gave up—a cradle was empty—there was one more shaggy little grave in the cemetery.

When I visited Sophie her entertainment for me was the showing off of her graves. She had a huge family of tiny tombstones. She had woven, woven, woven baskets in exchange for each tombstone.

We took the twisty dirt road to the point of land on which the cemetery lay. Passing under a big wood cross spanning the gateway, we were in a rough, grassed field bristling with tipping crosses, stone, iron, wood crosses. In the centre stood a big, straight, steady cross raised on a platform, a calm, reassuring cross. Here Sophie knelt one moment before parting brambles to search for her own twenty-one crosses—babies dated barely one year apart.

"Mine, mine," Sophie stooped to pat a cold little stone, "this my Rosie, this Martine, this Jacob, this Em'ly." Twenty-one she counted, saying of each, "Mine, all me—all my baby."

The blue waters of the Inlet separated the hurry and hurt of striving Vancouver from all this peace—stagnant heathenism, the city called it.

Having so few pupils, I had much time for study. When I got out my Northern sketches and worked on them I found that I had grown. Many of these old Indian sketches I made into large canvases. Nobody bought my pictures; I had no pupils; therefore I could not afford to keep on the studio. I decided to give it up and to go back to Victoria. My sisters disliked my new work intensely. One was noisy in her condemnation, one sulkily silent, one indifferent to every kind of Art.

The noisy sister said, "It is crazy to persist in this way, —no pupils, no sales, you'll starve! Go back to the old painting."

"I'd rather starve! I could not paint in the old way—it is dead—meaningless—empty."

One sister painted china. Beyond mention of that, Art was taboo in the family. My kind was considered a family disgrace.

Victoria had boomed, now she slumped. We had not sold during the boom, now we were compelled to because of increased taxation. My father's acreage was divided into city lots and sold at a loss—each sister kept one lot for herself. Borrowing money, I built a four-suite apartment on mine. One suite had a fine studio. Here I intended to paint, subsisting on the rentals of the other three suites. No sooner was the house finished than the First World War came. Rentals sank, living rose. I could not afford help.

I must be owner, agent, landlady and janitor. I loathed landladying. Ne'er-do-wells swarmed into cities to grab jobs vacated by those gone to war. They took advantage of "green" landladies. No matter how I pinched, the rentals would not stretch over mortgage, taxes and living.

I tried in every way to augment my income. Small fruit, hens, rabbits, dogs—pottery. With the help of a chimney sweep I built a brick kiln in my back yard, firing my own pots. The kiln was a crude thing, no drafts, no dampers, no thermometer—one door for all purposes. Stacking, stoking, watching, testing, I made hundreds and hundreds of stupid objects, the kind that tourists pick up—I could bake as many as five hundred small pieces at one firing.

Firing my kiln was an ordeal. I stoked overnight, lighting my fire well before day-break so that nosy neighbours would not rush an alarm to the fire department when the black smoke of the first heavy fire belched from the chimney. The fire had to be built up gradually. The flames ran direct among the pots, sudden heat cracked the clay. First I put in a mere handful of light sticks, the clay blackened with smoke. As the heat became stronger the flames licked the black off. Slowly, slowly the clay reddened passing from red hot to white of an awful transparency, clear as liquid. The objects stood up holding their shapes with terrifying, illuminated ferocity. A firing took from twelve to fourteen hours; every moment of it was agony, suspense, sweat. The small kiln room grew stifling, my bones shook, anticipating a visit from police, fire chief, or insurance man. The roof caught fire. The floor caught fire. I kept the hose attached to the garden tap and the roof of the kiln-shed soaked. The kiln had to cool for twenty-four hours before I could handle the new-fired clay.

I ornamented my pottery with Indian designs—that was why the tourists bought it. I hated myself for prostituting Indian Art; our Indians did not "pot", their designs were not intended to ornament clay—but I did keep the Indian design pure.

Because my stuff sold, other potters followed my lead and, knowing nothing of Indian Art, falsified it. This made me very angry. I loved handling the smooth cool clay. I loved the beautiful Indian designs, but I was not happy about using Indian design on material for which it was not intended and I hated seeing them distorted, cheapened by those who did not understand or care as long as their pots sold.

I never painted now—had neither time nor wanting. For about fifteen years I did not paint.

Before I struck bottom it seemed there was one lower sink into which I must plunge. Taking over the entire upper storey of my house I turned it into a Ladies' Boarding House. Womanhood at its worst is the idle woman of small means, too lazy to housekeep, demanding the maximum, paying the minimum, quarrelling with other guests and demanding entertainment as well as keep and all for the smallest possible price.

Under the calm north light of the big studio window ten women satisfied their greed for all the things of which they had been deprived during the war. Limitation was over, but price still high. They were greedy over those foods which had been scarce. It was hard to satisfy them. I hated sitting at the head of my table forcing a smile—these creatures were my bread-and-butter, so I had to.

They jeered at my pictures on the wall, jeered before my very nose. (Could not the creatures see a burning red ear stuck onto either side of my head?)

Mrs. Smith would say to Mrs. Jones, "I am changing my place at table. Those totems turn the food on my stomach!"

"Mine too! I am positively afraid to come into this room after dark. The stare of those grotesque monsters! Do you suppose the things will ever have money value, Mrs. Smith?"

"Value? Possibly historical, not artistic," Mrs. Smith suggested.

"Daubs, bah! An honest camera—that is what records history."

There was no place other than the walls to store my pictures. I had to head my table and endure.

The ladies liked my food. When I started the boarding house people had said, "Artist cookery! Artist housekeeping!" and rolled their eyes. I proved that an artist could cook and could housekeep; but that an artist could paint honestly and keep boarders simultaneously I did not prove.

Clay and Bobtails saved me. I established a kennel of Old English Bobtail Sheep-dogs in the yards behind my garden. My property was bounded on three sides by vacant lots, treed and grassed. Here my "Bobbies" played; here I rushed to them for solace when the boarders got beyond bearing.

There was good demand for working dogs in those days. The war done, soldiers were settling on the land, raw land in lonely districts. There was not much sheep or cattle work for dogs but there were men to be guarded from themselves, from solitude after army life. No dog is more companionable than a Bobby.

I raised some three hundred and fifty Bobtail puppies. A large percentage of the pups went to soldiers. Clay and Bobtails paid my taxes—clay and Bobtails freed me from the torture of landladying.

"Eric Brown, Canadian National Gallery, speaking ... I should like to call upon Miss Emily Carr to see her Indian pictures."

I had never heard of Eric Brown nor of the Canadian National Gallery. To be reminded that I had once been an Artist hurt. I replied tartly through the phone, "My pictures, with the exception of a very few on my walls, are stored away."

"May I see those few on the walls?"

I gave grudging consent.

Mr. and Mrs. Brown came; looking, talking together while I stood indifferently apart, my eyes on a lump of clay upon the table, losing its malleability.

"Marius Barbeau, Government Anthropologist, told me of your work," said Mr. Brown. "He heard about it from the Coast Indians. We are having an exhibition of West Coast Indian Art in the Gallery this autumn. Will you lend us fifty canvases? We pay all expenses of transportation. Come over for the show. I can get you a pass on the railway."

"Fifty of my pictures! Me go East! Who did you say you were?" I frowned at Mr. Brown, dazed.

Mr. Brown laughed—A Canadian artist who did not even know that Canada *had* a National Gallery!

"Artists this side of the Rockies don't keep up with art movements, do they? Where did you study?"

"London, Paris, but I am not an Artist any more." A boarder passed through the room. I turned sullen.

"Obviously you have done some study along the line of the modern way. There is a book just out, *A Canadian Art Movement*—read it—all about the Group of Seven and their work—by F. B. Housser."

"Who are the Group of Seven?"

"Seven men who have revolutionized painting in Eastern Canada. Come East, I will see that you meet the Group."

"Oh, but I could not! I could not get away."

Mr. Brown said, "Think that over."

He had seen interest wake in me when he mentioned "New Art". No sooner was he out of the house than I ran to town and bought a copy of *A Canadian Art Movement*, and read it from cover to cover, and was crazy to start that very moment. To my great astonishment when I told my sisters about it they said, "Why not?" and offered to tend the house during my absence.

"I can come," I wrote Mr. Brown, then shipped my pictures east, and off I went, breaking my journey at Toronto. All the Group of Seven men lived there.

The Exhibition of West Coast Art was at Ottawa but I was not going East to see the Exhibition. I wanted to meet the Group of Seven and see their work. I did not know how it was going to be arranged, but I stopped off at Toronto, hoping something might happen, or possibly I should see some of their work around the city.

I had been only a few hours in Toronto when I received a telephone message through the Women's Art Association, inviting me to go to the various studios of the Group members. The women of the Art Association were to conduct me. My eagerness turned suddenly to quakes. These men were workers, I a quitter.

On the steps of the Association I was introduced to Mrs. Housser.

"Wife of the book!" I exclaimed, thrilled.

"Come to tea with us tomorrow and meet 'Mr. Book'."

Mrs. Housser was an artist too. I marvelled how they all accepted me.

First my escorts took me to the studio of A. Y. Jackson. Then we went to Mr. Lismer's, then to J. E. H. Mac-Donald's. Varley was away, Carmichael and Casson lived further out of town. They were more recent members of the Group. I met them later. Last of all we went to the studio of Lawren Harris.

"This is an honour," my conductress said. "Mr. Harris is a serious worker, he does not open his studio to every passerby."

I am glad Mr. Harris's studio came last. I could not so fully have enjoyed the others after having seen his work.

I had been deeply impressed by his two pictures reproduced in Mr. Housser's book. The originals impressed me yet more deeply. As Mr. Harris showed us canvas after canvas I got dumber and dumber. My escort was talkative. Mr. Harris left me alone to look and look and look. When it was time to go a million questions rushed to my mind. I wanted to talk then, but it was too late. As he shook hands Mr. Harris said, "Come again." Eager questions must have been boiling out of my eyes and he saw.

I went to Ottawa but all the while I was there I was saying to myself, "I must see those pictures of Mr. Harris's again before I go West." They had torn me.

The Ottawa show was a success. All the familiar things of my West—totem poles, canoes, baskets, pictures (a large percentage of the pictures were mine). It embarrassed me to see so much of myself exhibited. The only big show I had been in before was the Salon d'Automne in Paris. Out West I found it very painful and unpleasant to hang in an exhibition. They hated my things so! Here everyone was so kind that I wanted to run away and hide, yet I did want, too, to hear what they said of my work. I had not heard anything nice about it since I was in France.

In Ottawa all the time I was longing to be back in Toronto to see again Mr. Harris's pictures. I was saying to myself, "I must see those pictures again before I go West." They had torn me; they had waked something in me that I had thought quite killed, the passionate desire to express some attribute of Canada.

I arranged to spend two days in Toronto on my way home. I went straight to the telephone, then scarcely had the courage to ring. I had wasted one whole afternoon of Mr. Harris's work time, had I the right to ask for another? Urgency made me bold.

"I go West the day after tomorrow, Mr. Harris. West is a long way. May I see your pictures again before I go?"

"Sure! Tomorrow. Stay—come and have supper with us tonight; there are pictures at home, too. I will pick you up."

Oh, what an evening! Music, pictures, talk—at last "goodnight" and Mr. Harris said, "What time at the studio tomorrow?"

"You mean *this* is not instead of *that*," I gasped.

"Sure, we have not half talked yet."

So I went to Mr. Harris's big, quiet studio again.

"What was it you particularly wanted to see?"

"Everything!"

Starvation made me greedy—he understood and showed and showed while I asked and asked. No one could be afraid of Mr. Harris. He was so generous, so patient when talking to green students.

"I understand you have not painted for some time?"

"No."

"Are you going to now?"

"Yes."

"Here is a list of books that may help. You are isolated out there. Keep in touch with us. The West Coast Show is coming on to our Gallery after Ottawa. I shall write you when I have seen it."

"Please criticize my things hard, Mr. Harris."

"I sure will."

Three days after my return from the East I was at my painting. Mr. Harris wrote, "The exhibition of West Coast Art is at the Gallery. As interesting a show as we have had in the Gallery. Your work is impressive, more so than Lismer had led me to believe, though he was genuinely moved by it in Ottawa. I really have, nor can have, nothing to say by way of criticism. . . . I feel you have found a way of your own wonderfully suited to the Indian spirit, Indian feeling for life and nature. The pictures are works of art in their own right . . . have creative life in them . . . they breathe."

This generous praise made my world whizz. Not ordinary technical criticism, such as others had given my work. Mr. Harris linked it with the Indian and with Canada.

Sketch-sack on shoulder, dog at heel, I went into the woods singing. Not far and only for short whiles (there was still that pesky living to be earned), but household tasks shrivelled as the importance of my painting swelled.

By violent manœuvring I contrived to go North that summer, visiting my old sketching grounds, the Indian villages, going to some, too, that I had not visited before. Everywhere I saw miserable change creeping, creeping over villages, over people. The Indians had sold most of their best poles. Museums were gobbling them. The recent carvings were superficial, meaningless; the Indian had lost faith in his totem. Now he was carving to please the tourist and to make money for himself, not to express the glory of his tribe.

I sent two canvases east that year, thrilled that "The Group" included me among their list of invited contributors. Eastern Artists expressed amazement at the improvement, the greater freedom of my work. A. Y. Jackson wrote, "I am astonished." Like Mr. Gibb, Jackson patronized feminine painting. "Too bad, that West of yours is so overgrown, lush—unpaintable," he said, "too bad!"

I always felt that A.Y.J. resented our West. He had spent a summer out at the coast sketching. He did not feel the West as he felt the East.

Mr. Harris's letters were a constant source of inspiration to me. He scolded, praised, expounded, clarified. He too had tasted our West, having sketched in the Rocky Mountains. He understood many of my despairs and perplexities. Sometimes my letters were bubbling with hope, sometimes they dripped woe. I wrote him of the change taking place in the Indian villages—in Indian workmanship. His advice was, "For a while at least, give up Indian motifs. Perhaps you have become too dependent on them; create forms for yourself, direct from nature."

I went no more then to the far villages, but to the deep, quiet woods near home where I sat staring, staring, staring—half lost, learning a new language or rather the same language in a different dialect. So still were the big woods where I sat, sound might not yet have been born. Slowly, slowly I began to put feeble scratchings and smudges of paint onto my paper, returning home disheartened, wondering, waiting for the woods to say something to me personally. Until they did, what could I say?

"Wondering?" wrote Mr. Harris, "Why I can almost see your next step. In wondering we dedicate ourselves to find a new approach, fresh vision. . . . Wondering is a process of questioning. Why has the thing I am trying to express not a deep fulness of life? Why is it not clearly and exactly what I am trying to convey? . . . Deeper problem than most of us realize . . . has to do with the highest in us. . . . A talent or aptitude should be developed," he wrote. "Should be worked hard, if we are so placed that we can work (as far as I know you are so placed). Your peculiar contribution is unique. . . . In some ways if a body is removed from the fuss as you are, and, providing the creative urge is strong to keep him working, he is fortunate. . . . Good zest to your work, you can contribute something new and different in the Art of this country. The more joy in the work the better. No one feels what you feel. It will surely develop far reaching results."

These letters cheered and stimulated me. Of course I got into great snarls of despondency. Bitterly in my letters I would cry out, "When I hear of you Eastern Artists going off in bunches, working, sharing each other's enthusiasms and perplexities, I am jealous, furiously jealous!"

"Solitude is swell!" replied Mr. Harris. "Altogether too much chatter goes on."

I knew he was right—stupid me—hadn't I always chosen solitude, squeezing into tight corners in class, always trying to arrange that no one could stand behind and watch me work?

"You old silly!" I said to myself, and took myself in hand.

Two things I found of great help. First, there was the companionship of creatures while working (particularly that of a dog). I have taken birds, a monkey, even a little white rat into the woods with me while studying. The creatures seemed somehow to bridge that gap between vegetable and human. Perhaps it was their mindless comprehension of unthinking life linking humanity and vegetation. The other help was a little note book I carried in my sketch-sack and wrote in while intent upon my subject. I tried to word in the little book what it was I wanted to say. This gave double approach for thoughts regarding what you were after.

I stopped grieving about the isolation of the West. I believe now I was glad we were cut off. What I had learned in other countries now began to filter back to me transposed through British Columbia seeing. Ways suitable to express other countries, countries tamed for generations, could not expect to fit big new Canada.

At long last I learned, too, to surmount the housekeeping humdrum which I had allowed to drift between me and the painting which I now saw was the real worth of my existence.

An American Artist came to visit at my house.

"Come, let us go to Beacon Hill or the sea, while morning is still young," he said.

"The beds! the dishes! the meals!" I moaned.

"Will wait—young morning on Beacon Hill won't. Don't tether yourself to a dishpan, woman! Beds, vegetables! They are not the essentials!"

Suddenly I realized brag and stubborness had goaded me into proving to my family that an artist could cook, could housekeep. Silly, rebellious me! Hadn't I for fifteen years bruised body and soul, nearly killed my Art by allowing these to take first place in my life?

I corresponded with several Artists in the East and I made three trips to Eastern Canada during Exhibitions of the original Group of Seven, shows to which I was an invited contributor. These visits were a great refreshment and stimulus. The first time I came back a little disgruntled that I must always work alone, while they worked in companies and groups; after awhile I came West again from these visits happy. It was good to go when opportunity opened, good to see what others were doing, but the lonely West was my place. On one of my Eastern trips I slipped across the line. This is how it came about that I saw New York.

New York

"WHY NOT?" Mr. Harris said and closed the book of New York's splendours he had been showing me, photographs of the gigantic wonders, her skyscrapers, bridges, stations, elevated railways.

"Why not see New York now, while you are on this side of the continent? It is only a step across the line. New York is well worth the effort."

I protested, "I hate enormous cities cram-jam with humanity. I hate them!"

Mr. Harris said no more about New York. I had been much interested in his telling of his reactions to New York. He was just back from there, had gone to see a big picture exhibition. In spite of myself my curiosity had been aroused. Instead of sleeping that night as I ought to have done, I lay awake thinking, planning a trip to New York. Next day I acted; curiosity had won over fright. As I bought my ticket my heart sank to somewhere around my knees, which shook with its weight; but common sense came along, took a hand, whispering, "Hasn't it been your policy all through life to see whenever seeing was good?"

"I'm going," I said to Mr. Harris. "Can you give me a list of New York's Art Galleries, the most modern ones?"

"Good," he said and also gave me introduction to a very modern artist, the President of the "Société Anonyme" (New York's Modern Art Society).

This lady, Miss Katherine Dreier, was a painter, a lecturer and a writer. Her theme throughout was Modern

Art. She had just published *Western Art and the New Era*, quite a big volume.

A couple of warm friends of mine who used to farm out west had written me when they knew I was coming to Toronto inviting, "Cross the line and visit us." They now lived on Long Island where the husband had been for some years manager of a millionaire's estate. I wired my friend asking, "Could you meet me at the station in New York? I'm scared stiff of New York!"

Arrangements made, myself committed, I sat down to quake. I do not know why I dreaded New York. I had faced London and Paris unafraid. Perhaps *this* fear was because of what they had done to me and the warnings I had been given to "keep away from great cities". I said to myself, "This is only just a little visit, seeing things, not settling in to hard work."

Before ever the train started I had an argument with the porter. He insisted that my berth be made up so that I rode head first. I insisted that I would ride facing the engine, in other words feet first.

"If there is a axiden yous sho a dead woman ridin' dat-a-way."

"Well, perhaps there won't be an accident. If I ride head first, I shall be a seasick woman sure, certain, accident or not!"

He grumbled so much that I let him have his way, then remade my bed while he was at the other end of the coach.

I had no sooner fallen asleep than a flashlight, playing across my face, woke me. It was the quota and immigration official. "We are about to cross the line." He proceeded to ask all sorts of impertinent questions about me and my antecedents. I heard other angry passengers in other berths being put through the same foolish indignity. The dark coach hushed to quiet again except for the steady grind of the train-wheels a few feet below the passengers' prone bodies and ragged-out tempers. That was not the end. I was just conscious again when a tobacco-smelling coat sleeve dragged across my face and turned my berth light on. Bump, bump! the porter and the customs were under my berth grappling for my bags. First they rummaged, then they poured everything, shoes, letters, brushes, tooth paste, hairnets, over me.

"Anything to declare?"

"Only that you are a disgusting nuisance!" I snapped, collecting my things back into their bags.

"If folks will cross the line!" he shrugged.

"Drat your old line!" I shouted. "It is as snarly as long hair that has not been brushed for a year!"

No good to try and sleep again! I knew by the feel inside me that we were nearing a great city. The approach to them is always the same.

"New York! New York!" The porter and his ladder bumped into the people, uncomfortably dressing in their berths.

I raised my blind—tall, belching factory chimneys, rows and rows of workmen's brick houses, square, ugly factories, with millions of windows. Day was only half here, and it was raining.

Noises changed, we were slithering into a great covered station. There on the platform, having paddled through rain at that hour, was my friend, Nell. I nearly broke the window rapping on it. She waved her umbrella and both hands.

The station was about to wake and have its face washed. Sleepy boys were coming with pails and brooms. The breathless hither and thither rush common to all stations had not started as yet. Nell skirted the cleaners amiably. I never remember to have seen her ruffled or provoked. Once out west I went with her to feed the sow. Nell lodged her pail of swill in the crotch of the snake fence while she climbed over. Evangeline the sow stood up and snouted the entire pailful over Nell. There Nell stood, potato peeling in her hair, dripping with swill and all she said was, "Oh, Evangeline!"

Well, I suppose if one's disposition could take that it could take New York.

The distance from station to station seemed no way at all, we were talking so hard. Suddenly I remembered and said, "Why, Nell, is this New York?" Soon our train began skimming over beautiful green fields. The very up-to-datest farm buildings and fences were here and there, and such beautiful horses were in the pastures.

"Nell, where are we?"

"On Long Island. This is where the millionaires and the multi-millionaires come to recuperate when Society ructions have worn them threadbare. These sumptuous estates are what the millionaires are pleased to call their 'country cottages'."

My friends lived on the home farm of their own particular millionaire's estate, in a large, comfortable farm house.

During my week's stay on Long Island I never saw or heard a millionaire but I saw the extravagances on which they poured their millions and it amazed me. They had tennis courts glassed over the top so that they could play in all weathers. They had private golf courses, private lakes for fishing, they had stables full of magnificent race horses and every style and shape of motor cars. They had gardens and conservatories and, of course, they had armies of servants to keep the places in order and have them in readiness any moment the owners took the whim—"I'm sick of Society, it is such hard work. We will run down to our cottage on Long Island." Then a string of motor cars as long as a funeral would tear over the Island roads, endangering dogs and every one else's life, motors stuffed with the fancy equipment millionaires consider indispensable.

It was nothing, my friends told me, for a New York florist to send in a bill of seventy-five dollars just for providing cut flowers to decorate the house for a single weekend, and there were the rest of us mortals thinking twice before spending one dollar on a plant! The extravagance fairly popped my eyes.

The week of my stay on Long Island happened to be Easter. Our millionaires were giving a week-end party.

They kept the manager hopping. My friend's husband was the very finest type of Englishman. Life had given him some pretty hard knocks and left him strong, fine, honourable. The same applied to his wife. The millionaires thought the world of the pair and gave them complete trust, respect and love.

The beginning of Easter week the manager was bidden to search the Island nursery-gardens catering to the wealthy, till he could locate half a dozen blossoming trees. They must be in full bloom. It seemed that there were to be fishing parties on their private lake. Their stables were close to the lake side. The trees must be as high as the stables and hide the buildings from the fisher's eyes. But trees would not hurry growth for any old millionaire. They clamped their buds tight as a good parson's lips clamp on an occasion when only one well-rounded word could express his feelings.

At the last nursery we found six forsythia trees in full bloom. They were as gold as butter and as high as the stables. It took a separate lorry to move each tree. About an acre of dirt had to accompany each tree's roots. It took a battalion of men to do the job. They did it well. The forsythias did not wilt and the reflection in the lake was lovely. The millionaires were pleased. I have no idea what the performance must have cost!

The manager was also instructed to see that the tennis court was in good shape for play. An expert was called in to inspect.

"Carn't do nothin' by Easter," he said. Court needs makin' over from foundation. Best I can do is to patch her so she'll play 'em over the week-end. Patch'll cost three hundred dollars."

The owners said, "Certainly, go ahead." But the expensive patch was never used once during the Easter holiday.

Our millionaires were childless. Besides this place they had a mansion in New York. Also the wife, who was a millionaire in her own right, had a magnificent estate in

Belgium. It was their favourite of the three estates. They frequently visited there.

I heard that the Martha Washington Hotel in New York was a nice place for a lady alone so I went there. It was not as tall or as high priced as many of the newer hotels but it was very comfortable and conveniently situated for everything.

I quaked up to Martha's desk and asked the clerk, "Have you such a thing as a ground-floor room or at least one on second or third floor that can be reached by the stairway?"

The clerk's look was scornful and plainly commented "hayseed". He said, "We have such rooms, Madam; there is little demand for them. Higher the floor, better the light and air."

"I dislike elevators."

The clerk led the way to a room half a storey higher than Martha's lounge. He turned on the light. It was never more than twilight in that room, but I liked it in spite of its dimness. It had a private bath and I thought the price most moderate. My window opened into a well and I was at the very bottom; about a thousand other windows, tier upon tier, opened into my well.

Martha homed many girlish grandmothers, derelicts who had buried their husbands, or divorced them, married off their children and did not quite know what to do with life. They were be-curled, be-powdered and tremendously interested in their food. Martha had glass doors leading from the lounge to the restaurant. These grandmother-girls were always the first to be at the glass doors when the maids unlocked them at meal times. Martha's food was excellent. There was a door leading direct from the street into the dining room. Men were permitted to lunch at Martha's and a tremendous lot of business men came there for lunch. Martha's food was good and very reasonable.

My Long Island friend came up and took sightseeing tours with me. We went in big buses with bigger megaphones which deafened us when they told us about all the marvels we were passing. First we did the "High-Town" and then we did the "Low-Town" and by that time we were supposed to know New York by heart.

My dread of going around New York alone had completely vanished. I have often wondered what caused that fear, almost terror, of New York before I saw her. I had been raised on this continent and was much more in sympathy with the New than with the Old World. New York was clean, the traffic wonderfully managed and the people courteous.

I hunted up the Art Galleries. Alas, I found them mostly located on top storeys. My heart sank to a corresponding depth under the earth. I kept putting off the visiting of Art Galleries. I did do one on the fifteenth floor (with the exception of Roerich Gallery this was about the lowest). Shooting up was fearful but the thought of sinking down again appalled me. It spoiled the pleasure of the pictures.

On the fifteenth floor I stood aside, waiting for the other passengers to enter the elevator. Half in and half out, I paused. The operator got restive. Suddenly I backed out of the cage.

"Where's the stairs?" I started to run in the direction of his pointing thumb. His scorn followed me.

"Yer won't get to the bottom within a week!"

I knew I ought to be ashamed, and I was. I was sure the cable would break, or that the sink would stop my heart-beat entirely.

The Roerich Museum was on the banks of the river. The building was only half a dozen storeys high. The picture galleries occupied the three lower floors. Everything in the building was Mr. Roerich. . . . His pictures covered the walls of all the galleries. There was one room stacked to the ceiling with parchment rolls, whether by or about him I do not remember. He was for sale in book form and by photograph at the desk on the ground floor. The attendant lowered her voice to whispering every time she uttered his name. I am afraid I do not yet know just who Roerich was; his museum did not greatly interest me. He

seemed to have a large following and everybody knew all
about him.

I was not alone while I visited the Roerich Gallery. As
I went in the door I met Arthur Lismer of the Toronto
Group of Seven and a lady Art Teacher of Toronto. They
turned and went back with me. They were up in New York
to study the method of Art Teaching in the schools there
and also to see the spring Exhibitions. The Art Teaching
Lady immediately became a devotee of Roerich. She was
voluble as we went through the galleries, Mr. Lismer rather
silent. Presently the lady left us to run back to the desk
below and secure a few more books and photographs.

I said to Mr. Lismer, "These pictures don't make me
'quake', do they you? They are spectacular enough but. . ."

Mr. Lismer nodded, laid his finger across his lips and
rolled his eyes in the direction of the lady from Toronto.

"Don't spoil her delight: she is such an ardent adorer!"
He pulled his watch out. "Time!" he shouted over the
stair rail to the lady, and to me he said, "Old Toronto
student of mine meeting us here to conduct us to the new
spring shows, come along."

"I'd love to, only . . ." He laughed, knowing my pet
horror.

"Elevators? I'll fix that with the operators, come on."

Each time we were about to drop like a pail filled with
rocks Mr. Lismer whispered in the elevator man's ear
and we slid down slowly and gently. I have always felt gratitude towards Arthur Lismer for that.

Those modern exhibitions were a wonderment beyond
my comprehension, but they were certainly not beyond
my interest. In some of them I found great beauty which
stirred me, others left me completely cold; in fact some
seemed silly, as though someone was trying to force himself to do something out of the ordinary.

We saw Kandinsky, Bracque, Ducamp, Dove, Archi-
penko, Picasso and many others. Some had gripping power.
The large canvas, *Nude Descending a Staircase,* hung in
one gallery. I had seen reproductions of this painting be-

fore. Mr. Lismer stood looking at it intently. His student, the lady from Toronto and I were arranged beside him looking too, but with less understanding. The four of us were dumb, till Lismer said, "One thing certain, the thing is very, very feminine."

Not until my last day in New York did I meet Mr. Harris's artist friend, the President of the "Société Anonyme". I had tried to communicate with her by 'phone from Martha but without success—she lived in such swell Mansions. Ordinary people were not permitted to communicate with the mansion-dwellers except by some special telephonic gymnastics far too occult for me to grasp, so I wrote her a note. She immediately called at my hotel, which was most gracious of her. I happened to be out, so she left a message at the desk. Martha neglected to deliver it till within two hours of the departure of my train for Toronto. I was annoyed with Martha. I wanted to meet Miss Dreier. Martha atoned the best she could by sticking me into a cab and heading me for the Mansions. They faced on a beautiful park and were of over-powering magnificence. There were as many guards, door-attendants, bellboys, elevatresses and enquiry clerks as if it had been a legation (spies expected). All of them looked down their noses. I was such a very ordinary person to be asking for one of their tenants! Half a dozen attendants consulted. It was decided that one of the elevatresses, who, by the way, was costumed in black velvet, should take a bellboy and ascend. The boy would take my message and see if it was Miss Dreier's wish to receive me.

It *was* Miss Dreier's wish to receive me, but, the black-velveted lady informed me, "She is about to go out, so the visit must be brief!"

Such rigmarole! I began to wish I had not come, but, as soon as I saw Miss Dreier I was glad I had. She was friendly and kind. I explained about Martha's negligence in delivering her message. She asked about Mr. Harris and his work and a little about me and my work out West. I got up to go saying, "I believe, Miss Dreier, you were just about to go out."

"Only to my bank," she replied. "That can wait till another day. I do not meet artists from Canada every day."

She bade me sit down again. Her house was sumptuous. On the walls were fine paintings, all were canvases by Moderns, all "abstract". Then she brought out many canvases of her own painting. She talked about abstraction and abstractionists. She was particularly proud of a Franz Marc which had just come into her possession.

Among her own canvases was one called *Portrait of a Man.* I would never have suspected it. From the midst of squirming lines and half circles was something which rather resembled the outer shape of a human eye, but through its centre was thrust a reddish form that was really a very healthy carrot.

I looked a long time. I had to say something so I asked, "Please, Miss Dreier, why is that carrot stuck through the eye?"

"Carrot!" Miss Dreier gasped. "Carrot! I did think I had so plainly shown the man's benevolence! He was the most benevolent person I ever knew!"

I felt dreadfully wilted, dreadfully ignorant. To put me at ease Miss Dreier told me about her new book just published, *Western Art and the New Era.*

"I shall get it," I said. "Maybe it will teach me something about abstract art."

We discussed Georgia O'Keefe's work. I told of how I had met her in the gallery of Mr. Steiglitz.

I said, "Some of her things I think beautiful, but she herself does not seem happy when she speaks of her work."

Miss Dreier made an impatient gesture.

"Georgia O'Keefe wants to be the greatest painter. Everyone can't be that, but all can contribute. Does the bird in the woods care if he is the best singer? He sings because he is happy. It is the altogether-happiness which makes one grand, great chorus."

I have often thought of that statement of Miss Dreier's, also of how extremely nice she was to me.

"Thank Mr. Harris for sending you. I am so glad I had not already left for my bank," were her good-bye words.

Lawren Harris

MY FIRST impression of Lawren Harris, his work, his studio has never changed, never faltered. His work and example did more to influence my outlook upon Art than any school or any master. They had given me mechanical foundation. Lawren Harris looked higher, dug deeper. He did not seek to persuade others to climb his ladder. He steadied their own, while they got foot-hold.

The day that I picked my way over that Toronto slush pile outside the Studio Building, under a bleak, wintry sky, against which the trees of Rosedale Park stood bare and stark ... the day I entered the dreary building, climbed the cold stair, was met by Mr. Harris and led into his tranquil studio,— that day my idea of Art wholly changed. I was done with the boil and ferment of restless, resentful artists, cudgelling their brains as to how to make Art pay, how to "please the public". Mr. Harris did not paint to please the public, he did not have to, but he would not have done so anyway.

Just once was I angry with him; that was over a canvas, painted by myself, entitled *The Indian Church*.

I had felt the subject deeply, painting it from a close-to-shore lighthouse at Friendly Cove Indian Village out West. Immediately on completion I sent the canvas to an Eastern Exhibition. I had a red-hot hustle to get it to the show in time. *The Indian Church* had three would-be purchasers. To my unqualified joy and pride it was bought by Mr. Harris.

A few months later I went East for a "Group" Show.

252

After the preview, Mr. Harris entertained the Artists at his home.

Taking me by the arm, "Come and look!" he said.

Above the supper-table, beautifully framed and lighted, hung my *Indian Church*.

Surely Mr. Harris's house must have bewitched the thing! It was better than I had thought. I had hurried it into its crate, having hardly given a second glance at it.

I had scarcely the courage to look now. There were people all round the picture saying kind things about it. I was embarrassed, being unused to criticism of that sort. Out West, why, only a week before, I had attended an exhibition of the Island Arts and Crafts Society. My sisters invited me to take tea with them at the social function connected with the affair. I draggled behind them hating it. We had tea and gossip with friends. No one mentioned my two canvases, so I hoped that perhaps they had been rejected, for I shrank from facing them with my sisters present and with people I knew standing about, people who, I was aware, hated my work.

They were hanging in the last room, right in front of the door. With an angry snort my most antagonistic sister saw and turned sharply back.

"We will go again to the flower paintings. I like them," she said pointedly and we wheeled. My other sister gave one backward glance.

"Millie," she said, "I do like—" My breath stopped! She had never expressed liking of anything of mine.— "your frames," she finished.

Many times Mr. Harris wrote me enthusiastically of *The Indian Church*. He sent it to an exhibition in the United States and wrote, "I went to the U.S. Show. Your Church was the best thing there, a swell canvas. I do not think you will do anything better."

At that I flew into a rage. Mr. Harris thought I had reached the limit of my capabilities, did he! Well, my limit was not going to congeal round that Indian Church! I sent other work east. He compared it unfavourably with the Indian Church—I had thought this work just as good, perhaps better. Mr. Harris did not. He still praised the Indian Church.

"You limit me! I am sick of that old Church. I do not want to hear any more about it!" I wrote angrily.

His answer was, "Good! Still, that Indian Church is a grand thing, whatever and despite what you think of it."

We dropped the subject, but he went on writing helpful, encouraging letters. A lesser man might have huffed at my petulance, even stopped writing. If he had I would have broken.

I had now become independent of Indian material. It was Lawren Harris who first suggested I make this change.

I had become more deeply interested in woods than in villages. In them I was finding something that was peculiarly my own. While working on the Indian stuff I felt a little that I was but copying the Indian idiom instead of expressing my own findings.

To gain freedom I saw I must use broad surfaces, not stint material nor space. Material in the West was expensive, space cheap enough. I bought cheap paper by the quire. Carrying a light, folding cedar-wood drawing board, a bottle of gasoline, large bristle brushes and oil paints, I spent all the time I could in the woods. Once or twice each summer I rented some tumble-down shack in too lonesome a part to be wanted by summer campers. Here, with three or four dogs and my monkey, all my troubles left at home, I was very happy and felt my work gain power.

I sent a bundle of these paper sketches East. Mrs. Housser showed them to a group of artists in her house and wrote their comments to me. The criticism did not help much. However, they did all seem to feel that I was after something and this cheered me.

Lawren Harris wrote, "I saw the sketches. They are vigorous, alive, creative. . . . Personally I do not feel that your sketches are subject to criticism, they represent vital intentions. One can only say, 'I like this one or I do not like that.' They are unusually individual and soaked with what you are after, more than you realize, perhaps. . . . Don't let anything put you off . . . even if you come through with but one out of three or four endeavours, hitting the mark, the thing woven into vital song . . . keep at it."

"When, in my last letter," wrote Mr. Harris, "I said there is no evolution in Art . . . that I think is true, but not with each individual artist. Each artist does unfold, come to his or her particular fulness. But in Art as a whole, there is not evolution; there is change of idiom, approach and expression—development of means, media, and paraphernalia. . . . The old Masters have not been surpassed. Modern artists do different things in terms of their day, place and attitude. Great works of Art are the same yesterday, today and forever. We but endeavour to be ourselves, deeply ourselves; then we approach the precincts of Great Art—timeless—the Soul throughout eternity in essence."

Lawren Harris did not separate Art from life. You could chatter to him freely about what to most people seemed trivialities; observations on woodsey things and about animals as well as about work, honest observations interested him. I wrote him of my friendship with Sophie, the Indian woman.

"It goes to prove," he replied, "that race, colour, class and caste mean nothing in reality; quality of soul alone counts. Deep love transcends even quality of soul. . . . It is unusual, so deep a relationship between folks of different races."

Sometimes my letters were all bubble—loveliness of the woods and creatures—again, they dripped with despairs and perplexities. Then he would try to set my crookedness straight. He would write, "In despair again? Now that is too bad. Let us be as philosophical as we can about it. Despair is part and parcel of every creative individual. Some succumb to it and are swamped for this life. It can't be conquered, one rises out of it. Creative rhythm plunges us into it, then lifts us till we are driven to extricate. None of it is bad. We cannot stop the rhythm but we can detach ourselves from it—we need not be completely immersed ... we have to learn not to be! How? By not resisting. Resistance is only an aggravation!—one I think that we should escape from if we learned that all things must be faced, then they lose their potency. It is no good to tell you that your work does not warrant despair. Every creative individual despairs, always has since the beginning of time. No matter how fine the things are, there are always finer things to be done and still finer *ad infinitum*. ... We have to be intense about what we are doing but think what intensity does, what it draws into itself—then, do you wonder that, if things do not go as well as we anticipate, the reaction from intensity is despair? Keep on working, change your approach, perhaps, but don't change your attitude."

Arthur Lismer, the lecturing member of the Group of Seven, came west. He visited my studio, went through my canvases. Lismer's comments were so mixed with joke either at his own or at your expense that you never quite knew where you stood. His criticism left me in a blur. On the lecture platform Lismer draped himself over the piano and worked modern Art enthusiastically, amusing as well as impressive.

Lawren Harris wrote, "Lismer is back from the West, full of his trip. He had great things to say of your present work, could see it emerging into fruition. ... If I could convey to you his look when he talked about your work, discouragement would never enter your mind again. ... I suppose we are only content when all our sails are up and full of the winds of heaven—certainly the doldrums are trying. ... I hope all your sails are up and full of the winds of heaven under high great skies."

Mr. Harris wrote me of making a selection of pictures for an All Canadian Show in the United States, "The choice was left to Jackson and me. Yours were all damned good things. I feel there is nothing being done like them in Canada ... their spirit, feeling, design, handling, is different and tremendously expressive of the British Columbia Coast —its spirit—perhaps far more than you realize. We who are close to certain things hardly realize the intensity and authenticity of what we do to others who are less close. Your work is a joy to us here, a real vital contribution."

Thus he cheered, gave me heart.

In answer to a perplexed letter of mine he wrote, "The lady you speak of who was moved by your work was right; you may not think so, but, perhaps you are not seeing what you do entirely clearly. You get immersed in problems, the reaction from creative activity, dissatisfaction from the feeling that you have not realized what you desired. We all are in such matters, and it is all as it should be, there is no finality, no absolute standard, no infallible judge. . . . Life is creative and Art, creative Art is Life."

Every letter he wrote stimulated me to search deeper. Lawren Harris made things worthwhile for their own sake.

Again he wrote, "Everything you say describes the true Artist . . . there is no realization, only momentum towards realization. The *becoming of all*, satisfying, completion, fulfilment, something indeed that we cannot attain individually, separately, only as the complete spiritual solidarity, mankind. . . . Strive we must. . . ."

Again, "Your canvases hang in the O.S.A. show. The consensus of opinion, best opinion, is that they are a very great advance on your previous work. It is as if your ideas, vision, feelings, were coming to precise expression; yet nowhere is the work mechanical, laboured or obvious. For goodness sake, don't let temporary depression, isolation, or any other feeling interfere with your work. . . . Keep on . . . do what you feel like doing most. Remember, when discouraged, that there is a rhythm of elation and dejection; and that we stimulate it by creative endeavour. . . . Gracious, what we stir up when we really come to live! When we enter the stream of creative life, then we are on our own and have to find self-reliance, active conviction, learn to see logic behind the inner struggle. Do, please, keep on and know, if it will help you, that your work has tremendously improved; know, too, that the greater it becomes the less you will be aware of it, perhaps be almost incapable of being convinced; what does that matter? There is only one way—keep on.—How can greatness be true greatness unless it transcend any personal estimate? How can it live in great searchings, in the true spirit, in the informing unity behind the phenomena, if it knows itself as great? ... Creative imagination is only creative when it transcends the personal.... Personality is merely the locale of the endless struggle, the scene of the wax and wane of forces far greater than itself."

So Lawren Harris urged, encouraged, explained. I was often grumbly and not nice. On one occasion when I was cross I wrote a mean old letter to a fellow artist in the East who had annoyed me in some trivial matter. Lawren saw the letter. He scolded me and I felt very much shamed. He wrote me, "Tell you what to do, when you have need of 'ripping things up a bit' get it off your chest by writing to me. The party you tore up was a sensitive soul. Write me when you are rebellious, angry—Bless you and your work."

Once when I was in perplexity he wrote, " I don't suppose you do know precisely what you are after. I don't think in the creative process anyone quite knows. They have a vague idea—a beckoning, an inkling of some truth—it is only in the process that it comes to any clarity. Sometimes, indeed often, we work on a theme with an unformed idea and, when it has passed through the process, its final result is something we could never have predicted when we commenced. ... Of course there must be the urge, the indefinable longing to get something through into terms of plastic presentation, but results are nearly always unpredictable."

"Sold my apartment house! Moved into a cottage in a dowdy district, old fashioned high windows—think I can paint here," I wrote to Lawren Harris.

He replied, "Sounds good to me. Occasionally uprooting

is good for work, stirs up a new outlook, or refreshes the old one."

When later I reported, "Bought a hideous but darling old caravan trailer, am now independent of cabins for sketching trips," "Swell!" was Lawren Harris's hearty comment. "Swell!"

"Yes, I too have been working. My present approach is by way of abstraction. I have done quite a number and with each one learn a little more, or increase that particular way of perceiving. Feeling can be as deep, as human, spiritual and resonant in abstract as in representational work: but, because one has less to rely on by way of association, it requires a greater precision. . . . A struggle all right. . . . There is no doubt in my mind that abstraction enlarges the scope of painting enormously. It replaces nothing, it adds to the realm of painting, makes possible an incalculable range of ideas that representational painting is closed to, increases the field of experience—enlarges it— that is surely all to the good, but abstraction definitely cannot displace or replace representational painting. . . . If one has not zest, conviction and feeling, one is no better off in abstract, indeed less so.

"Our limitations may make abstraction seem remote, but then once we extend those limitations, which is the purpose of Art, the remoteness disappears. . . . Abstraction can have all the virtue of representational painting plus a more crystallized conviction. I feel that it will become more and more the language of painting in the future and no man can say what it may yet disclose. Some day I may return to representational painting—I do not know. At present I am engrossed in the abstract way.—Ideas flow, it looks as though it would take the rest of my life to catch up with them. . . . When, in your letter, you refer to 'movement in space', that is abstract, try it. . . . Take an idea, abstract its essence. Rather, get the essence from Nature herself, give it new form and intensity. You have the 'innards' of the experience of nature to go by and have done things which are so close to abstraction that you should move into the adventure much more easily than you perhaps think."

I was not ready for abstraction. I clung to earth and her dear shapes, her density, her herbage, her juice. I wanted her volume, and I wanted to hear her throb. I was tremendously interested in Lawren Harris's abstraction ideas, but I was not yet willing to accept them for myself. They seemed the right and natural development for his work. Now that I have seen his beautiful abstractions I think I would be sorry to see him return to representational painting. I do not pretend to understand, to be able entirely to follow the principle of abstract truth, but I do feel unwordable depths in it that move me very much. In Lawren Harris's abstractions I am as aware of truth as I was aware of the calm deep sincerity which uplifted the onlooker in his earlier representational work and in them too I am aware of great beauty and power. I cannot explain why Lawren Harris's abstracts move me so, I feel power there whereas in some abstractions I feel emptiness.

Green

woods you are very sly, picking those moments when you are quiet and off guard to reveal yourselves to us, folding us into your calm, accepting us to the sway, the rhythm of your spaces, space interwoven with the calm that rests forever in you.

For all that you stand so firmly rooted, so still, you quiver, there is movement in every leaf.

Woods you are not only a group of trees. Rather you are low space intertwined with growth.

Bless John Whiteley! Bless Algernon Talmage! the two painting masters who first pointed out to me (raw young pupil that I was) that there was coming and going among trees, that there was sunlight in shadows.

In the roof-peak of the apartment house I built was a little attic room, my favourite of all the rooms in that house.

A crooked stair led to it. The stair was in the corner of the studio. I chose this room with its wide view for my bedroom. It had low-drooped walls but the centre of the room was high. Its end walls were peaked. The naked ridge pole and studding showed, because the room was unlined. Rain pattered on the cedar shingles only a few feet above my face.

In its west-end wall the room had two large windows which appeared to be narrow because they were so high, beginning at the floor and ending right in the point of the gable. These windows let in an extensive view, a view of housetops, trees, sea, purple mountains and sky. The view seemed to come companionably into the room rather than to draw me out; and it had an additional glory, but for this glory you must look *out*, look *down*. Then you saw right into the heart of a great Western maple tree. Its huge bole culminated in wide-spread, stout branches. There was room for immense life in this bole.

The maple tree was always beautiful, always gracious. In spring it had a sunlit, pale-yellow glory, in summer it was deep, restful green, in autumn it was gold and bronze, in winter it was a gnarled network of branches. It was in winter you saw best the tree's reality, its build-up and strength.

On the whitewashed underside of the roof shingles of my attic room I painted two immense totemic Indian Eagles. Their outstretched wings covered the entire ceiling. They were brave birds, powerful of beak and talon. Their plumage was indicated in the Indian way—a few carefully studied feathers painted on wing, breast, and tail gave the impression that the bird was fully plumed.

Sleeping beneath these two strong birds, the stout Western maple tree beneath my window, is it wonder that I should have strong dreams, dreams that folded me very close!

One night I had a dream of greenery. I never attacked the painting of growing foliage quite the same after that dream I think; growing green had become something different to me.

In my dream I saw a wooded hillside, an ordinary slope such as one might see along any Western roadside, tree-covered, normal, no particular pattern or design to catch an artist's eye were he seeking subject-matter. But, in my dream that hillside suddenly lived—weighted with sap, burning green in every leaf, every scrap of it vital!

Woods, that had always meant so much to me, from that moment meant just so much more.

Alternative

"LADIES approaching seventy must not expect to work like girls of seventeen—it is unreasonable."

The doctor's voice was reproving but kindly.

"Overdoing has enraged your heart. To begin with we will see what a good long rest in hospital will do."

"How long?"

The doctor resorted to a professional shrug and the spreading of his palms.

"Another thing . . ." he paused. . . . His eyes roved round my studio, finally resting contemplatively on a small monkey and a mother dog and her four pups on the hearth rug. "I notice you have an aviary of birds on the veranda," he mused. "Livestock entails work. You must limit yourself now to a minimum of exertion, throw everything not imperatively necessary overboard. Goodness, you have done a lot of work!"

His eyes roved from my menagerie to my full canvas racks.

My breath caught, "Not half what I want to, Doctor. You don't mean—you are not telling me my painting days are done! Oh, lovely, all-alone caravan-days in the quiet, woodsey camps with my creatures! Seventy isn't so frightfully old!"

"We will talk of that after we see what rest does for that heart; meantime, take things very, very easy. I will engage a room in the hospital for you. One thing certain! Trips alone must be given up."

"Ugh, my stupid heart needs a chaperon! No thank you,

I will stay at home. I never could work with danglers hanging round."

The weeks in hospital sauntered slowly by till Eric Newton, noted Art Critic for the *Manchester Guardian*, paid a visit to the West. Eric Brown, Director of the Ottawa National Gallery, had asked Mr. Newton while out west to select some fifteen pictures of mine and ship east. He had prospective buyers. Mr. Newton wired me from Vancouver. Finding I was in hospital he came there to see me.

He said, "As I drove over the Island Highway I saw *Emily Carr pictures* in the woods no matter in which direction I looked. You have caught the Western spirit." Folding his hand over my two sick ones he added, "Get better, these hands are too clever to lie idle."

I turned my face away. What good getting better if I was never to roam the woods again, paint-sack on shoulder, dog at heel?

"Wa! Wa! Wa!"

The maternity ward was across the court from my room. New-borns were taking the unknown life before them hard. Ah! The price of being was this adjusting ourselves to life at different angles.

I blinked hard a time or two and turned back to Mr. Newton.

"All right, I'll try to get well."

When Lawren Harris advised me, "Put aside the Indian motifs, strike out for yourself, Emily, inventing, creating, clothing ideas born of this West, ideas that you feel deep rooted in your heart", I sat before the woods and stared, lost, frustrated. I had let myself be bound. It was not handling of paint but handling of thoughts which overwhelmed me. Trying to get around this problem, I took always in my sketch-sack a little note book. When I had discovered my subject, I sat before it for some while before I touched a brush, feeling my way into it, asking myself these questions, "What attracted you to this particular subject? Why do you want to paint it? What is its core, the thing you are trying to express?"

Clearly, and in as few words as possible, I had answered these questions from myself to myself, wording them in my little note book, presenting essentials only, discarding everything of minor importance. I had found this method very helpful. This saying in words as well as in colour and form gave me double approach. I knew nothing about the rules of writing.

The only author I had ever met was Fred Housser, who wrote *A Canadian Art Movement*. When I stayed with the Houssers in the East, Fred had let me read two of his manuscripts. He talked with me about them afterwards. When I went home I wrote an Indian story and sent it to Fred, asking criticism. He liked my story and wrote me a wonderful letter, finding much fault in my construction, taking infinite pains to explain a story's build-up.

"You do not want 'eye-wash'," he wrote and struck hard. The letter made a great impression on me.

When I grinned back at Mr. Newton and said, "I'll try to get better", I had this idea in the back of my mind—"One approach is apparently cut off, I'll try the other. I'll 'word' those things which during my painting life have touched me deeply."

"Doctor, may I write?"

"Write? Write what?"

"Describe places I've seen on my sketching trips, woods, Indians and things—nice Canadian things of the West, things that will heal, not rile my heart."

"You can try, but don't get excited, don't overtire."

The nurse was told to watch. She kept bouncing in and grabbing my wrist—she did not approve of the doctor's permission, but had to admit that, instead of doing me harm, it soothed and calmed me.

I did not know book rules. I made two for myself. They were about the same as the principles I used in painting— Get to the point as directly as you can; never use a big word if a little one will do.

So I wrote the stories that were later to be known as *Klee Wyck*, reliving those beautiful, calm places among the dear Indians. Their quiet strength healed my heart. Of course it could not heal old age, but it healed me enough that I could go home and take up that easy, easy life the doctor prescribed. No more was I to go off in my old van alone—that was too strenuous. About that he was firm.

While I was still in hospital, Eric Brown wrote me. For a good many years he had taken interest in and been most helpful about my work. He said my isolation out West was making me think for myself and it showed in my canvases. (I was sending each year to Eastern Exhibitions.) He now wrote, "Will you collaborate with a biographer? We want the 'struggle story' of your work out West written. Better still, will you write it yourself?"

"I don't know how to write," I answered Mr. Brown. "My Indian stories (I had told him about writing them) are just fun and they're medicine. I go back so vividly on those sketching trips, that I forget being sick."

I was fond of Eric Brown; he had dug me out of that dreadful slough of despair at the time when I was too disheartened to paint. I wanted to please him.

I said, "Nobody could write my hodge-podge life but me. Biographers can only write up big, important people who have done great deeds to which the public can attach dates. I could not be bothered with collaborators, nor would they be bothered with the drab little nothings that have made up my life. However, to please you, Mr. Brown, I will have a try."

I had only a few chapters written, and was still in hospital, when I got word that Eric Brown was dead. Following close on the news of his death came the death of my Indian friend Sophie around whom many of my Indian stories were written. Writing as well as painting paused a little inside of me, but soon the "easy" life began to bore me and I continued the biography.

I had two faithful women friends who were very patient in listening to my script—Ruth Humphrey and Flora Burns.

It is a tremendous help to hear words with the ears as well as to see them with the eyes; so I read aloud to these friends and received helpful criticism from them.

When I had about three chapters of the biography written I read them to my only surviving relative—a sister. She was very, very angry. She accused me of being disloyal to my family and altogether abominable.

It had been absolutely necessary for truth's sake to include a short few pages on our home life which for me had not been happy after the death of our parents. I had to show what drove me to the woods and to the creatures for comfort, what caused the real starting point of my turn to Art. My family had never been in sympathy with my painting, nor entered into my life as an artist. My home life was always a thing entirely apart from my art life.

My Indian sketches lay in my bureau drawer. My two friends thought I should endeavour to seek a publisher for them. They suggested I send them to a publishing firm in Toronto. I did so. For months I received no word, good or bad. At last I wrote the publishers and was coolly informed that they had been unable to use the stories but unfortunately they had lost them. They regretted the fact, but there it was—they were lost!

I was furious at their indifference and their carelessness. I wrote and wrote, giving them no peace. I wrote to the head, and the tail, and all the other members of the firm that I could attach a name to. I said, "I have no other copy of the manuscript. It is up to you—it must be found."

The manuscript remained lost for one whole year. Then it was returned to me. They claimed it had slipped off a desk and fallen among a box of books being packed for Queen's College. If that was the case, why had not Queen's College returned it to the publishers when they unpacked their books, not held it for a year? I am convinced it never would have turned up but for the unpleasant nagging I gave the entire lot of them. They told me they never were so glad to return anything to anybody, I had tormented them so.

I too was weary of the nuisance by then. I did not try another publisher. I stuck the manuscript away in a drawer and forgot it.

One of the faithful "listening ladies" who had sat patiently while I read my stories aloud borrowed them, took them to Vancouver and showed them to Ira Dilworth, one-time principal of Victoria High School, later Professor of English at the University of British Columbia and now attached to the CBC at Vancouver.

He was interested and said he would like to have some of the stories read over the radio. He came to see me about it.

The first series of six readings was done by Dr. G. G. Sedgewick of the University of British Columbia, who had seen some of the work earlier. The second series was read by Mr. Dilworth himself. They pleased the air audience. Shortly after reading the second series, Mr. Dilworth went East, taking with him the manuscript which he showed to his friends, Mr. and Mrs. Clarke. On his return from the East he came to see me. He said, "Mr. Clarke wants to publish two volumes of your writings,—one of the Indian stories, the other stories of your childhood."

"Is it possible!" I gasped.

My one publishing try had been so disastrous. I supposed my stories not up to much as they were so indifferent when they were lost.

"What about my punctuation and spelling, Mr. Dilworth? They are awful, you know."

"We can get around that. If it is all right with you, I shall act as your honorary editor."

I can well imagine the relieved "Oh!" I gave then. Spelling and punctuation always were such a horrible trial to me, and now here was a genuine professor offering to stand behind me, ready to be appealed to! His kindness lifted a tremendous load from me, just as if he had kicked all the commas, full stops, quotes and capitals right to another planet.

Mr. and Mrs. Clarke came West that Autumn. Mr. Dilworth brought them to see me. We were to proceed with the work at once. They conferred as to which book should be published first. At first it seemed in order that it should be the childhood stories. On the other hand, my Indian pictures had been exhibited quite a bit in the East. That would, to some extent, lay a foundation for the Indian stories. It was, therefore, decided that these should have first place.

I cannot describe the terror-shakings that overtook me as the stories and I awaited our Editor. I felt so shamed, so terrifically ignorant. I wished I had been a better student, that I had not scuttled off to San Francisco Art School, skipping my last year of "High". I had heard of Mr. Dilworth as a scholar and a very fine teacher. I should die of shame.

We sat down at a table in my studio and alternately read to each other from the script. In two seconds I was not afraid any more.

"Two 'l's there, one 's' only," he corrected as we read, or, "New sentence here, new paragraph there," but he made me feel such things were subservient and of secondary importance to the spirit of the text. At once I knew he loved Indians and the West just as I did. My Editor never altered my wording arbitrarily. Occasionally he suggested re-phrasing a sentence, always explaining why. He never added or omitted anything without consulting me. Sometimes he made suggestions, but he made me re-word the thought myself. He was a million times younger, a million times cleverer than I but he never made me feel an old fool, or finished, or stupid, or ignorant. Long before the work on the manuscript was finished he was just plain "Eye" to me.

I shall never forget the editing of *Klee Wyck*—the joy of those hours—nor all it taught me. I was almost sorry to see her finished and shipped off to the publisher. After a while she came back—a book!

Seventieth Birthday and A Kiss For Canada

Klee Wyck made her first appearance a few days before I was seventy. Victoria was astonished at her. Victoria had never approved of my style in painting. When my painting was accepted in the East a few Westerners tolerated it, a smaller number found they actually liked it. *Klee Wyck* and, a year later, *The Book of Small* Victorians took straight to their hearts and loved even before the favourable Eastern reviews appeared.

Klee Wyck got wonderful press reviews right across Canada. Letters, phone calls came from everywhere. People were not only warm but enthusiastic. I was staggered. My Editor wrote a foreword for *Klee Wyck*. He was also asked by *Saturday Night* of Toronto to write two articles, one on my work, one on me. Following the publication of *Klee Wyck* these appeared in two consecutive issues. Eye showed the script of them to me before sending it east. I wriggled with embarrassment. Those things could not be about me and my work! It was so strange a hearing for my ears. Out west they had slanged, ridiculed my painting.

I had just finished reading the two articles when Lawren Harris came to see me. He too had written a beautiful review of *Klee Wyck* for *The Canadian Forum*. I showed him Ira Dilworth's articles and told him how I felt about the whole matter. This was his answer—"Keep your nose from where it does not belong. We painters and writers have our own work to do—good, let us do it. The critic has his work to do. That is his business, not ours."

I put the critics and their reviews clean out of my head.

When reviews came, praise after praise from all over Canada (some from England too; the Oxford University Press have their head office there), I was just very pleased, read them to my sister who wanted to hear, put them away and thought no more about them. I had letters from such different kinds of people, from University professors, very kind about the way I used English in my writing, from lumbermen and fishermen who said, "It is our West Coast, dense, rugged and lavishly watered with mist and rain", from children who said, "We just love *Klee Wyck!*" Even two Missionaries who had worked among the Indians on the West Coast wrote liking the book. She was accepted by libraries and reading clubs, and was the subject of book reviews over the radio.

The Victoria Branch of the University Women's Club did me the honour of inviting me to be an honorary member of their branch. I was so astonished I did not quite know how to act. I had always maintained that unearned honours were stupid shams. Look how hard real members worked to earn their membership—why should I, never having even squeaked through High School, be honoured by a University Club membership? Half of me said, "I can't!" The other half said "But, I would be very proud." So I took, thanked and am.

A few days before my seventieth birthday, a member of the University Women's Club telephoned me congratulations on *Klee Wyck*. She said, "Our Club would like to honour you and *Klee Wyck* by having a little tea-party for you. Are you well enough? We know how ill you have been—and, by the way, have you not a birthday coming pretty soon?"

I replied that I had not been out since my illness, but that I thought I could manage it, that it was very kind of them and that the following Saturday was my seventieth birthday.

"Then that is the day we will set for the party," she

said, "I am lending my home for it. Some of the Club ladies will call for you."

I imagined it would be a gathering of perhaps six or at most a dozen of the Club members.

On Saturday I was dressed and waiting when in walked Eye.

"Ready?" he asked. "I've come to take you to the party."

"The University Women's tea-party? I am expecting them to pick me up, they promised, so I can't go with you, but how did you know there was to be a party?"

"I am invited. Furthermore, I am going to read out of *Klee Wyck*. It's a big affair, men as well as women coming to honour you and *Klee Wyck*."

"Oh," I said, "I thought it was only half a dozen ladies and a cup of tea."

"It's going to be mammoth—your townspeople, as many as the house will hold—don't get scared."

"Will there be speeches?"

"I should say so!"

"Will I have to reply?"

"I do not think it will be expected of you. They know you have been ill."

"It would be very ungracious to say nothing at all. They have been so kind to me and to the book; I'll scribble a few words and if, as so often happens, my voice goes, will you read them for me, Eye? Oh, I am so glad you are going to be there, I'm frightened."

"Don't worry, you'll be all right."

I scratched a few words on an envelope and clapped it in my spectacle case; then the ladies came for my sister and me.

Our hostess, Mrs. Young, had a big house, large rooms. When I saw them packed with people I dropped into the first chair inside the front door and wilted. Mrs. Young came and stood beside me protectingly so that people would not know I had come. After a few moments I got up and took her arm.

"I'm ready."

She led me into the drawing room and sat me on a pink sofa under a stand lamp. It had commenced to blow and snow outside. Inside all was cosy. My sister was on another sofa across the room and Mrs. Young saw that she had people about her that she knew because my sister is shy and nearly blind; she looked happy and I made up my mind I was going to enjoy my party to the full.

"The Reverend T. Laundy," Mrs. Young said, "will open the occasion with a short invocation."

The Reverend offered a short prayer. I was glad Mrs. Young had invited God to my party.

Then the master of ceremonies came forward, a sheaf of open letters in his hand—letters of congratulation from Victoria's citizens and from the various organizations in the city, good wishes for my birthday and for *Klee Wyck*. A mail box had been placed beside my sofa and I had wondered why. Now I saw that many of the guests carried envelopes. The first letter read was from the Lieutenant-Governor regretting he was not able to be present but sending best wishes; then came letters from the Mayor and Aldermen, the University Women's Club, the Canadian Club, the Native Daughters. There was one from the head of Indian Affairs on behalf of himself and the Coast Indians. After the master of ceremonies had read that many aloud, men and women representatives from many other organizations in Victoria stepped up to my mail box, dropped in their societies' letters and shook hands with me.

Eye stood close beside my sofa. If I did not quite know how to act or what to say, he told me. He was strength and comfort as he had been over editing *Klee Wyck*. Dear Eye! He knew the right way and it made me feel safe.

There were flowers, such beautiful flowers! Bouquets, boxes, corsages heaped round my sofa—someone was always coming up with more. It was like having a beautiful funeral only being very much alive to enjoy it. Such an easy, comfortable party! I found myself having a very good time.

After my right hand had nearly been shaken off there were speeches. Lovely things were said about *Klee Wyck*. When everybody had said everything there was to say, came a tiny pause. I whispered to Eye, "Is it my turn now?" I was shaking with fright. He nodded but, when I went to rise, he put his hand on my shoulder and kept me sat.

"Sure you can make it?"

"Yes," I replied.

My voice rang out strong as a bull's and I was not scared. This is what I said—the envelope is still in my spectacle case—"Thank you everybody for giving me such a splendid, happy birthday party and for being so kind to *Klee Wyck*. I would rather have the good-will and kind wishes of my home town, the people I have lived among all my life, than the praise of the whole world; but I did not write *Klee Wyck*, as the reviewers said, long ago when I went to the West Coast Villages painting. I was too busy then painting from dawn till dark. I wrote *Klee Wyck* one year ago in hospital. They said I would not be able to go about painting here and there any more, lugging and tramping. I was sore about it, so, as I lay there, I relived the villages of *Klee Wyck*. It was easy for my mind to go back to the lovely places. After fifty years they were as fresh in my mind as they were then because while I painted I had lived them deep. I could sail out of hospital and forget about everything. It was *Klee Wyck* gave my sick heart courage enough to get better and go home to the easy life the doctor had told me I had to expect now."

"Bravo! You'll be a public speaker yet!" whispered Eye in my ear. Then he took *Klee Wyck* in his hands and stood in a central spot to read. When the chairs and sofas were full, people sat round on the floor.

Eye is a beautiful reader. He read *Canoe* and *Juice*.

Then he talked about several of the longer stories. He commented on *Klee Wyck's* place in Canadian literature and how privileged I had been to see the Indian people in their own homes and villages. He said by writing *Klee Wyck* and by painting our woods I had made a contribution to Canada's art and literature.

Eye stopped speaking and the room was very still, so still I was scared—"Perhaps everyone does not like Indians!"

Then everybody began to chatter at once. Praise, praise, praise for *Klee Wyck*. I ducked my face into a box of beautiful chrysanthemums and red carnations that the Canadian Press had sent me.

I did not see or hear Eye cross the room, but suddenly I was aware of a great kindness there before me and the kindness stooped and kissed my cheek!

It was the proudest moment of *Klee Wyck's* success when, before them all, Eye stooped and gave me that kiss for Canada, prouder far than when *Klee Wyck* won the Governor-General's medal for best non-fiction for Canada in 1941. The medal looked to me to be made of the same metal as our old cow-bell. "It is the honour," everyone said, "and remember it is war time!" But the kiss for Canada was made of the pure, real stuff, unadulterable.

We had refreshments and a huge lighted birthday cake and grapefruit punch for healths and "God Save the King". Again I went to stand, again Eye's hand kept me down. "You are tired enough," he said. "Come", and took my sister and me home to begin my seventy-first year.

The Book of Small

ONE YEAR after the publication of *Klee Wyck, The Book of Small* appeared. I had wintered in a Nursing Home. Domestic help and fuel problems were difficult owing to war. I was quite eligible for a Nursing Home because I was really ill.

There I lay waiting and waiting for Small to come from the publisher. The publishing houses were under a heavy war strain—men, presses, material; but at last the book came in a smart green jacket with a medallion of the little old Small in the centre.

The Book of Small was entirely different from *Klee Wyck*. She was bigger. Some people liked her more, some less. The first half of Small was a collection of childhood (our childhood) stories, the life we lived in the far West where Father and Mother pioneered and raised their large family.

The other half of Small was called *A Little Town and a Little Girl*. It told of little old Victoria before she was even a town. Nearly all the people who lived there were English and they had a good many difficulties to cope with. They had only small Chinaboys as helps, no plumbing, only pumps and wells, no electric light and no telephone. Indians went round the streets selling their beautiful cedar-bark baskets or trading them for old clothes, or peddling clams or pitch wood tied in bundles for the lighting of fires. *The Book of Small* told of the slow, conservative development of Canada's most Western city.

My Editor was up north on a business trip. He had

waited impatiently for the appearance of Small. She came the day he left. He wrote me, "I suppose you are being swamped with fan mail."

No, Small lay shut in a drawer. I could not bear to look at her. She lay there for three or more weeks. No reviews, no letters came about *The Book of Small*. They had followed the appearance of *Klee Wyck* immediately or within a few days. In bitterness and disappointment I turned to the wall. My Editor came back from the North and, coming to Victoria, dashed into my room.

"The reviews? The letters?"

"There aren't any. Oh, Ira, she's flopped, Small has flopped dead, I'm so shamed!" and I cried till I nearly drowned him. He looked perplexed.

"I can't understand it. Clarke and I both thought she was the equal, if not better than *Klee Wyck*. She can't have flopped!"

I hid my shamed face in the pillow.

"I don't care so much about Small and me, but I've disappointed you and Bill Clarke."

I howled quarts of tears that had been strangled back for three weeks.

"The Press too, Small will be a dead loss to them. I wrote Bill last night and told him how dreadful I felt."

"Cheer up, remember it's war time and everything is higgledy-piggledy. There has been a hold-up somewhere. It's a marvel to get a book published at all these days! All dates are uncertain. Reviewers can't review till they have got the stuff, nor the booksellers sell till they have the books."

He left me cheered, but not convinced. I could only wail, "She's flopped, she's flopped! Small's flopped!"

"Silly!" said my Editor, "you'll see. Small's all right. Look at the reception *Klee Wyck* got; Small will too—give her time."

Letters came from both Mr. and Mrs. Clarke. Kind letters they were, very upset that I should have thought Small had flopped. There had been delays, just as Eye had said, owing to war conditions. The date of publication had had to be postponed several times, the reviews could not come out till the critics got the books and read them. Shipments of books had been late going to the bookstores and libraries. The reviews were just as good, just as complimentary, as those of *Klee Wyck*.

Eye wrote from Vancouver, "What did I tell you? All who read Small (and everyone is reading her now) love her. Book stores are sold out of copies!"

Mr. Clarke made his autumn trip to the West—dear Bill and his kind little wife felt so sorry about all the doldrums I had been through because of Small. Bill's first question was, "Is the next book ready? I plan to publish one each year." The script was ready, but we were deeper than ever in war. Hitler is a nuisance from every possible angle!

Wild Geese

SPRING was young, I over seventy. With Spring all about me I sat sketching in the clearing that was now given over to second growth—baby pines, spruce, hemlock, cedar and creeping vines, fireweed, bracken.

The clearing was off the Happy Valley Road at Metchosen, not far from Victoria. Seventy years had maimed me, loggers had maimed the clearing. I could no longer scramble over great logs nor break my way through networks of brambles, creep under bushes and drown myself crown-high in lush, young growth. I had to be taken out, set down and called for, which was a nuisance, but I got immense delight in just being there, in the quiet wood, nobody for company but Spring.

Though everything was so still, you were aware of tremendous forces of growth pounding through the clearing, aware of sap gushing in every leaf, of push, push, push, the bursting of buds, the creeping of vines. Everything expanding every minute but doing it so subtly you did not actually see anything happen.

In spite of the doctor I went into the woods to paint a few times more. The longing was too terrific to subdue and I felt better. I did not go in my old van (it was deteriorating with unuse so I had sold it). I rented a cabin and took a maid along to cook and carry for me.

The maid was too busy attending to her own work to bother about me; she carried my things out into the woods and came back for them and me later. I was very happy but the last expedition I over-did and came smash.

For a year painting lay dormant but I did some writing. One day a friend took my sister driving. On the way they planted me in a thick lonely place just off the high road while they took a long ride. It was here that I painted *The Clearing* and here the wild geese flew over.

Hark! Hark! High up in the blue, above the clearing, wild geese migrating. Honk, honk, ya honk! A triangle of noisy black dots.

Every Canadian thrills at the sound—the downpour of cackling honks broken, irregular, scattering with the sharp monotony of hailstones while the geese sail smooth and high, untroubled by fear of men, for migrating geese fly far, far above man's highest shooting.

On the ground the wild goose is a shy, quiet fellow. In the sky he is noisy and bold.

I lifted my face to watch the honking triangle pass across the sky. The day was clear, not dazzle-bright. I could look into the face of the sky without blinking. There was just one cloud. The geese caught up with the cloud. The leader dove into it, his flock followed. For a few seconds the cloud nestled the geese to her breast, emptying the sky, muffling the honkings, but the company pierced through the cloud. The leader and those few birds that fly in close formation behind him appeared, then the two long wavering side lines of singly-spaced birds emerged, to continue their way sailing, sailing into the north, one glad rush of going, one flock unswervingly following one leader. At that height each bird appeared no bigger than a small black bead, evenly strung one goose behind the other, a live necklace flung across the throat of heaven.

The racket passed over the clearing, the sky was again still, my eyes came back to the greying stumps amongst which I sat. Young growth had already hidden some. Even the echoes had forgotten how they had shrieked sympathy when the axes bit into the great original forest giants, forgotten the awful crash, the groan, the tremble of the ground as each tree fell.

Today the clearing was not sun-dazzled, rather it was illumined with Spring, every leaf was as yet only half unfurled and held light and spilled some.

Today at seventy I marvelled more at the migration of the geese than I had at the age of seven when, standing in our cow-pasture holding Father's hand and looking up into the sky, I heard Father tell the story of bird-migration and only half believed. Today a new wondering came to me as I watched the flight. What of the old or maimed goose who could not rise and go with the flock? Of course there *was* the old, the maimed goose. What of him when the flock, young and vigorous, rose leaving him grounded? Did despair tear his heart? No, old goose would fill the bitter moment, pouring out proud, exultant honks that would weave among the clatter of the migrating flock. When the flock were away, animal-wise he would nibble here and nibble there, quietly accepting.

Old age has me grounded too. Am I accepting? God give me the brave unquestioning trust of the wild goose! No, being humans, we need more trust, our hopes are stronger than creatures' hopes. Walt Whitman's words come ringing, —*We but level this lift to pass and continue beyond.*